May 68 in French Fiction and Film

OXFORD STUDIES IN MODERN EUROPEAN CULTURE

GENERAL EDITORS

Elizabeth Fallaize, Robin Fiddian and Katrin Kohl

Oxford Studies in Modern European Culture is a new series conceived as a response to the changing modes of study of European literature and culture in many universities. Designed to combine focus with breadth, each title in the series will present a range of texts or films in dialogue with their historical and cultural contexts—not simply as a reflection of history but engaged in a mediation with history, conceived in broad terms as cultural, social and political history. Flexible, interdisciplinary approaches are encouraged together with the use of texts outside the traditional canon alongside more familiar works. In order to make the volumes accessible not only to students of modern languages but also to those studying the history or politics of modern Europe, all quotations are offered in both the original language and in English.

May 68

in French Fiction and Film

Rethinking Society, Rethinking Representation

Margaret Atack

OXFORD
UNIVERSITY PRESS

OXFORD
UNIVERSITY PRESS

Great Clarendon Street, Oxford OX2 6DP
Oxford University Press is a department of the University of Oxford.
It furthers the University's objective of excellence in research, scholarship,
and education by publishing worldwide in

Oxford New York

Athens Auckland Bangkok Bogotá Buenos Aires Calcutta
Cape Town Chennai Dar es Salaam Delhi Florence Hong Kong Istanbul
Karachi Kuala Lumpur Madrid Melbourne Mexico City Mumbai
Nairobi Paris São Paulo Singapore Taipei Tokyo Toronto Warsaw
and associated companies in Berlin Ibadan

Oxford is a registered trade mark of Oxford University Press
in the UK and certain other countries

Published in the United States
by Oxford University Press Inc., New York

British Library Cataloguing in Publication Data
Data available

Library of Congress Cataloging in Publication Data
ISBN 0-19-871514-5
ISBN 0-19-871515-3 (Pbk.)

10 9 8 7 6 5 4 3 2 1

Typeset by Graphicraft Limited, Hong Kong
Printed in Great Britain
on acid-free paper by
Biddles Ltd., Guildford and King's Lynn

To Monique Deneuville

To the memory of Frédéric Deneuville (1954–1993)

Acknowledgements

In 1996–7 I was awarded a Leverhulme Research Fellowship which enabled me to devote myself to this project. I cannot imagine how the book would have been written without this and I acknowledge most gratefully the help of the Leverhulme Trust, as well as that of the Department of French at the University of Leeds which has helped financially with research trips, and sabbatical leave covered by my colleagues.

I am also very grateful for all the help I have received from the staff of the following: the Brotherton Library at Leeds, the Bibliothèque d'Information Contemporaine at the Université de Nanterre, the Bibliothèque Publique d'Information at the Centre Pompidou, the Vidéothèque de Paris.

I owe special thanks first to Elizabeth Fallaize who has been a tower of strength throughout, encouraging me from the very beginning, offering meticulous and extremely helpful criticism on early drafts, showing great patience with my various lapses and transgressions, and being unfailingly positive and supportive. Secondly to David Macey who has somehow found time to read it all, despite his own massive commitments, giving me invaluable advice and producing relevant contemporary material from his voluminous personal archives in the process, as well as supporting our whole household virtually single-handed during the weeks when the writing took over.

Many friends and colleagues have contributed with invitations to write or speak, loans of material, information, support for the project, as have my children, our very own *mouvement du 22 mars* in more ways than one, by their friendly support and inspirational energy. It is therefore a great pleasure to be able to thank the following: Aaron Macey, Paul Brooke, Malcolm Bowie, Terence Cave, Chantelle Macey, Colin Davis, David Coward, Jill Forbes, Claire Gorrara, Marie-Anne Hintze, Jim House, John Macey, Diana Knight, Mike Kelly, Rachel Killick, Annette Lavers, David Looseley, Ed Lovatt, Joëlle Pénochet, David Platten, David Roe, Richard Sacker, Michael Scriven, Anne-Marie Smith, Philip Thody, Christopher Todd, David Whitton.

This book is dedicated to my dear friend Monique Deneuville, who has been welcoming me into her home for over thirty years (including in June/July 1968), from my first arrival as a 17-year-old *jeune fille au pair* to help with her five children. My knowledge of contemporary France just would not have been the same without her generosity and friendship. With her son Frédéric too I enjoyed an extraordinary dialogue about literature, politics, culture, family, friends, until his sadly early death. It is a great shame he never knew about this project, and I have really missed being able to discuss it with him.

I should just add that all translations are my own.

Contents

Introduction **L'imaginaire de mai**

Etincelle, catalyseur, fête, révolte de la jeunesse, tourbillon, happening et puis encore révolte libératrice, autodéfense enjouée, irresponsabil-ité exemplaire, humour corrosif, naïveté grave, impatience raisonnée, désordre constructif, certes, ce fut tout cela le printemps des enragés.[1]

Quand l'extraordinaire devient quotidien, c'est qu'il y a la Révolution.[2]

May was an unprecedented event in French history. The violence of the street battles with the police, the level of popular support for the pro-testors, the size of the demonstrations, the millions out on strike, the festival atmosphere, the challenge to institutions and knowledge, and the endless discussions everywhere, particularly in the occupied campuses and workplaces, created an extraordinary, unforgettable experience. It felt like a revolution. The old order was being torn apart, and anything was possible, a theme of so many of the famous slogans: 'Fermez la barricade: ouvrez la voie.' 'Il est interdit d'interdire.' 'Prenez vos désirs pour la réalité.' 'Soyez réalistes, demandez l'impossible.' 'L'imagination au pouvoir.'[3]

Spontaneity and immediacy are two of the most important notions connoted by May, which was the very antithesis of a slow, studied, well-prepared, well-rehearsed, gradual development; it was an explosion, a breach in society's walls and defence, a cry of rage, a scrawled graffiti, an improvised battle of street stones and burning cars. 'On spontane'[4] was the improvised verb of one slogan, for words were as much part of this violent political earthquake as were the actions. 'On a pris la parole comme on a pris la Bastille', wrote both Barthes and Michel de Certeau:

---

[1] 'Spark, catalyst, fête, revolt of youth, whirlwind, happening and then again liberational revolt, cheerful self-defence, exemplary irresponsibility, corrosive humour, solemn naivety, reasoned impatience, constructive disorder, certainly the spring of the *enragés* was all of that.' *Après mai 1968: Les Plans de la bourgeoisie et le mouvement révolutionnaire*, 19: drawn up by the activists of the action committees of the Sorbonne, Vincennes, Nanterre (Maspero, 1969).

[2] 'When the extraordinary has become everyday, it means there is a revolution.' Frequently quoted in May, usually attributed to Che Guevara.

[3] 'Close the barricade, open the path.' 'It is forbidden to forbid.' 'Take your desires for reality.' 'Be realistic, ask for the impossible.' 'Let imagination take power.'

[4] 'One spontaneates'. Julien Besançon (ed.), *Les Murs ont la parole* (Tchou, 1968), 13.

the citadel of language is stormed and liberated. New forms of speech are deemed a political act.[5]

But the constitution of 'la parole' is a very complex process, and all the imaginative literature and films on May will show how complex it is. May is mediated by other texts, although constantly helping to rewrite them; May is shadowed by itself as text; as utopian discourse, May is at one and the same time a text of now and of the future; from whichever angle one approaches it, the vision of May is a double vision. As in the shot of the young women in the advert for Dim tights in Godard's film *Tout va bien*, which simultaneously shows them dancing on a kind of stage, and in the little screen in a camera which is filming them, the frame of May as text, and its framing texts, within which it is seen and without which it would be invisible, are always implicitly or explicitly present. Edgar Morin wrote of this structure in his analysis of 'l'esprit du temps'. At any moment there are the conventions, the views, beliefs, and ideas, the imaginary projections and intellectual formations, which together make up a constantly shifting but ever present text. The relationship between the real and the imaginary is that of the mobius strip, or recursive loop, of seamless join and self-inflecting movement.[6]

From the very beginning, May is founded in the images and discourses of May, as 'l'esprit de mai' is forged in the convoluted interplay between real and imaginary. During the first night of the barricades, participants clustered round radio sets trying to get an overview. In the central court-yard of the occupied Sorbonne were large screens covered in photographs of the night battles. The streets of Paris and the occupied sites were turned into great sets for May, with their draped banners and graffiti everywhere. Writers groups met to discuss and create appropriate slogans: Marguerite Duras is credited with 'Sous les pavés, la plage', Jean Duvignaud with 'Soyez réalistes, demandez l'impossible'. Maurice Clavel wrote of his joy on first seeing 'Sous les pavés, la plage' as an anonymous graffiti by an unknown hand, but another of his May articles for the newspaper *Combat* was turned into a tract and pinned on trees.[7] 'Tables rondes' on the events, preceded by a historical overview, were being held before the month was out, May was an object of historical knowledge before it even began to be over. As well as the tracts and subversive journals, large amounts of newsprint were being devoted to the events. Alfred Willener

---

[5] Barthes, 'Écriture de l'événement', *Communications*, 12 (1968), 109; Michel de Certeau, *La Prise de parole et autres essais* (Seuil, 1994), 40; Denis Hollier, 'Actions, No! Words, Yes! 1968 May', in Hollier (ed.), *A New History of French Literature* (Cambridge, Mass.: Harvard University Press, 1989), 1034–40.

[6] Edgar Morin, *L'Esprit du temps*, i (Grasset, livre de poche, 1962), 13–14.

[7] *Combat de franc-tireur pour une libération* (Jean-Jacques Pauvert, 1968), 131.

points out that one of the few sources for journalists writing about the early disturbances at Nanterre was Godard's *La Chinoise* (the film of a group of Maoist students which had been filmed there). A few years later, the song the workers sing in *Tout va bien* will be chanted on the streets of Paris during a demonstration.[8]

Contemporary newsreels shadowed the story of May from university crisis to national crisis as the May riots and strikes gained progressively in prominence. Early in May, for Gaumont, the student revolt was only the third of five items, with pride of patriotic place being given to the first French heart transplant in April 1968, followed by a lengthy item on Julie 'Jools' Driscoll's visit to Paris, showing the fascination with contemporary English music which has become one of the connotations of the rather dismissive term 'les sixties'.[9] Gaumont's scenes of the early May street battles stressed their violence, through the use of dramatic music and the script of the voice-over: 'les pavés volèrent, les boucliers se levèrent, et les matraques aussi'.[10] Even though Che Guevara, Rudi Dutschke (the German student leader), and Peking (China had been in the throes of its Cultural Revolution from 1966–7) are mentioned as examples the French student leaders invoke to send off their troops to do battle with the university structures, it is suggested that these events are not political: 'Le souci majeur des étudiants est d'avoir un diplôme qui leur serve de laisser passer pour l'avenir. Est-ce une raison de transformer un quartier de Paris en champ de bataille? Nous ne le croyons pas.'[11] But by 29 May all cinema newsreel producers were showing a common documentary report: 'La France face à son drame.'[12]

There is therefore a 'hall of mirrors' aspect to the lived experience of May. The event is lived as completely outside normal experience. It is unique, other, and immediate. It is therefore, by definition, ephemeral, a fact registered in the numbers of books gathering and preserving documents, the collections of photographs, the special issues with photographs and quotations. The inscriptions would be effaced, the actions would not be repeated. To be authentic, representations of May must partake of the discourse of immediacy and difference, and some narratives underline this through the fragmentary nature of the experiences and the absence of an overview for any individual.

---

[8] Willener, *L'Image-action de la société* (Seuil, 1970), 292, Calvet, *La Production révolutionnaire*, 85–7.

[9] Those too young to have caught her first time round will probably best know her as the singer on the signature tune, 'Wheels on Fire', for the television programme *Absolutely Fabulous*.

[10] 'Paving stones flew, shields were raised, and truncheons too.'

[11] 'The students' prime concern is to have a diploma which will be a pass to the future for them. Is that a reason to transform a district of Paris into a battlefield? We do not think so.'

[12] 'France faces crisis.'

May is a grand spectacle for its participants, a fact compounded by the historical self-consciousness inseparable from building barricades in central Paris. May is grounded in repetition, of images of revolt from 1871 or 1944, and of discourses of history, of anti-fascism, of the German Occupation, of the Algerian War. The French Revolution had engineered the political as public spectacle, and one political activist, Roumain Goupil, spoke seriously of missing May. As a leading organizer, in over 100 meetings a week, he saw nothing of the graffiti and the spectacle—although he was involved in helping to organize some of the rehearsals of chants for demonstrations . . .

While the theatricality of its scenes and actions were frequently dismissed as a simulacrum, an empty imitation of *real* revolution, others saw a distinctive feature in the aesthetics of the street scenes. The theatricality of the riot police's extraordinary appearance features in many of the close-ups of the *Cinétracts*, the short films composed of stills and photographs made during the events. The images of May combine singularity and multiplicity in very striking ways: the individual throwing a *pavé*, a solitary figure set against a backdrop of ranks of riot police; the crowds at meetings, on demonstrations; the piles of *pavés*, or of rubbish; images of May give a particular stress to patterns, repetitions, variations, to a profusion of objects, or people, producing a harmonious symmetry. It shows how, within the iconography of May, the collective and the individual are mutually reinforcing: the former is the multiplicity of the latter. The very scale of May is shown in the number of individual fragments it sweeps together. May is often shown in aerial shots, combining the city and the politics, placing, as in the Revolution, the political spectacle on public display. But unlike the aerial shots of the impressionists, for example, who embraced the city as a blurred mass, these shots are razor sharp in order precisely to render the pattern of multiplicity. Just as any autobiography can only be articulated within collective codes of subjectivity—and May is, from many points of view, one of the major autobiographical moments of the century, when the value of individuality and self-expression was immense[13]—so the one exists as one in so far as it is one of many. It is the collective text of May which is shadowing and articulating the possibility of the text of the individual.

---

[13] It is truly striking how many different people committed their accounts of May to paper, including politicians, policemen of high rank and low, and even an army general. Yve-Alain Bois argued that *La Vie tu parles: 160 lettres de courrier des lecteurs de 'Libération'* (Seuil, 1984), was emblematic of a period which saw the autobiographical and personal witness gain a new dominance. In Denis Hollier (ed.), *A New History of French Literature* (Cambridge, Mass.: Harvard University Press, 1989), 1040–5.

The new politics, with their stress on culture, ideas, beliefs, indoc-trination, and repressive tolerance, was also blurring boundaries be-tween public and private. The configuration of themes associated with *gauchisme* is at the heart of May, its motivations and its projects. As Viansson-Ponté noted, the participatory study groups and general meet-ings in the occupied universities were enacting their utopian vision of a different society in practice as well as in theory.[14] Some of the major ele-ments of the politics of *gauchisme*, particularly the importance of culture and the theorizations of class associated with Althusser, will be important in the structuralist ´take-over' as the dominant intellectual analysis of the post-May years. But at the time, these were part of a different set of concepts indebted to readings in marxism and sociology, particularly Marcuse and Lefebvre, the situationist movement, and Sartre. All the various *groupuscules* (that is, the proliferation of left-wing groups outside the organized socialist and communist parties) were committed to the destruction of capitalism, to revolution as the means to achieve this. Central to this, and to understanding the nature of action during May, was the argument that behind repressive tolerance lay state violence. Mao, Marx, Lenin, and Engels all taught that power came out of the barrel of a gun.[15] The *gauchistes*' analysis was an international one: capitalism was a global economic order, spearheaded by the United States, and was seek-ing to maintain itself as such. Vietnam, China, and the Third World were eloquent proof of the impoverishment and exploitation of capitalism, of its hegemonic ambitions, and its untrammelled use of violence against any opposition. Gilles Bousquet points out how important Cuba was too in the political imaginary of the time.[16]

The analysis of France followed a similar logic: the State was directed to maintaining the power of the dominant class, the bourgeoisie, and a system which ensured its privileges and riches, and the impoverished status of the exploited working classes. Parliamentary politics, the press, education, the mass production of consumer goods, were all governed by the interests of the dominant social order, in order to produce satis-faction and acquiescence. Marcuse's analysis of the elimination of real opposition, of the ways in which politics and ideology led people to desire the satisfactions provided by consumer society, was very influential. The leading May activist Daniel Cohn-Bendit cites him as an important point of reference for his criticism and rejection of both capitalism and so-called socialism: '[Marcuse] montre l'unidimensionalité de l'homme,

---

[14] *Histoire de la république gaullienne*, ii. 492.
[15] Étienne Rambert, 'Les Nouveaux Idéologues', *Magazine littéraire* (May 1968).
[16] *Apogée et déclin de la modernité* (L'Harmattan, 1993), 116–25.

c'est-à-dire, en fait, que notre société forme exactement son type d'homme. (. . .) Il démontre que la critique et la destruction sont un début de la construction. Quand on critique radicalement une chose, on construit.'[17] *L'Homme uni-dimensionnel* was published at the end of May 1968 (with 1,000 copies a day being sold, it was the bestseller of the year[18]), but his work was known to Lefebvre and other sociologists, he had taught at the École Pratique des Hautes Études in 1958–9, and written articles and introductions to his own work for *Arguments* for example.[19]

Vietnam, the relationship between power and violence, the explanatory power of the new marxism, blending Trotsky, Mao, the Frankfurt School, and Marcuse, the all-pervading nature of politics: these were the themes which were giving a new impetus to social critiques, and a new willingness to translate political commitments into direct, public action. Reactions to the student demonstrations had confirmed much of this: the violence of the police response to the protestors had shocked many. Newspapers, radio, and newsreels gave detailed coverage of demonstrators being clubbed on the ground. The night of 10 May was described as an 'affrontement sanglant' where the students, 'secourus par la population, résistèrent plus de quatre heures de façon surprenante'.[20] The judgement on the riot police of *Miroir de l'histoire*, 'Par leur calme ils ont évité une révolution sanglante',[21] is not shared, and indeed, Chris Marker's famous retrospective *Le Fond de l'air est rouge* suggests that, in the repeated and unnecessary charges against the barricades with tear gas on the night of 10 May, the riot police created May 68: 'c'est la naissance d'une légende' ('a legend is born').

Cohn-Bendit articulates brilliantly the connections made between the international and national dimensions on the one hand, and between the different kinds of battles being waged.[22] Recognizing the importance of 'les tiermondistes', and their fight against imperialism and exploitation in the Third World, he seeks to connect it to France: 'La lutte du tiers monde doit être soutenue par des actions visant à détruire (. . .) les centres

---

[17] 'Marcuse shows the one-dimensionality of man, that is to say that our society forms precisely its own kind of man. He demonstrates that criticism and destruction are the beginnings of construction. When one criticizes something radically, one is constructing.' Interview with Pierre Hahn before the events, published in the *Magazine littéraire* (May 1968), reprinted Labro *et al.*, *Ce n'est qu'un début*, 29.

[18] Ed. de minuit, trans. by Monique Wittig and the author. See *Les Idées en France*, A. Simonin and H. Clastres (eds.), (Gallimard, 1989), 249. *One-Dimensional Man* had first been published in 1964.

[19] 'De l'ontologie à la technologie', *Arguments*, 18 (1960); L'Amour et la mort', *Arguments*, 21 (1961).

[20] A 'bloody confrontation'; 'helped by local people, they surprisingly resisted for more than 4 hours'. Gaumont actualités: 'La grande colère des étudiants'.

[21] 'By their calm they avoided a bloody revolution', *Miroir de l'histoire* (June–July 1973), 49–50.

[22] As P. Vidal-Naquet noted, 'Le Sens du mouvement', *Esprit* (June–July 1968), 1049.

de son exploitation qui sont à notre portée, en France même.'[23] That all are exploited and oppressed was the vision on the basis on which the students' condition could function as a paradigm of oppression. That there was a totality of separate but comparable oppressions, embracing students, workers, unemployed, the Katangais,[24] the marginal and the excluded, and the Third World, was essential to May's political imaginary.

La révolution est une immense bibliothèque[25]

Finally, May is a monstrous library. There were 120 books published on the events by the end of October 1968, and it has never stopped. A year later, Certeau saw the proliferation of titles as proof of an inability to think.[26] By 1988, the term 'le mystère 68' was in use. May is an unsolvable puzzle, a text which can never be deciphered, or so it seems. Virtually every serious publication, conference, or special issue on May bemoans the volume of writing on May, and also the fact that it has not dealt with the (variously defined) essential issue. 'Much remains to be done' is the complement of 'too much has been done'. Experimental writer Jean Thibaudeau said something similar in his radio play, *Mai 68 en France*: by 5 May, everything had been written, all the elements which would constitute May were in print, but everything was still to write, because History is always 'to be written'. The individual 'parole', or text, is necessarily situated within a problematics of writing, simultaneously free and unfree.

As well as the immense library on May 68, there are also libraries to be had on French feminism, intellectuals, Situationism, memory and history in the postwar period, French cinema, and *le roman policier*. Treading the line between generality and detail in the name of succinct exposition of context and intertext across these varied fields has not been easy; my aim throughout has been to communicate a sense of the creative richness and real complexity of the many works and systems of thought engaged with May 68, and to resituate it at the heart of modern cultural history. It was the crossroads through which history, social change, social and political theorizations of the individual and society, have all passed.

---

[23] 'The struggle of the Third World must be supported by actions seeking to destroy the centres of its exploitation which are within our reach, here in France.' Interview in the *Nouvel Observateur* (8 mai), quoted L. Rioux and R. Backmann, *L'Explosion de mai* (Robert Laffont, 1968), 160.

[24] Designation of the members of the criminal underworld who joined the occupation of the Sorbonne.

[25] J.-A. Bernard, 'Une "pensée 68" ', in P. Ory, *Nouvelle histoire des idées politiques* (Hachette, coll. Pluriel, 1987), 699.

[26] 'Une société devenue incapable de se penser', *La Prise de parole*, 106.

It has not been my intention to try and offer an exhaustive account of May 68 and narrative, even if that were possible, but rather to explain a group of texts in function of some of the 'moments forts' of May: the student revolt, the social revolt, the intellectuals' moment, feminism, the history and memory of the past, the *polar*, and the reflection on textuality and representation.[27] The first chapter, devoted to the 'avant-mai', examines the social and cultural context on which May drew, and narratives which are widely seen as anticipating May, but in part to convey May's difference: themes of alienation, oppression, and violence, for example, are just not the same when there are barricades, pitched battles, and a sense of revolution and mass celebration in the streets, and when there are not.

I have not sought to propose, or to trace the effects of, a unitary definition of May, but to read the stories of these narrative texts against that which is at stake in their elaboration. Or to put it more technically, to read the *énoncé(s)* against the *énonciation(s)* on the basis of the judgement that the latter are not readable without May,[28] as well as following thematic strands such as anti-Gaullism, and the intellectual configurations of *gauchisme*, which have in my view often been neglected. It seems to me that focusing upon May 68 forces a reconsideration of the theoretical paradigms governing the existing maps of postwar history of ideas and culture, particularly in relation to the well-established oppositions between structuralism and existentialism, between political fiction and textual fiction, and between the *mode rétro* and the Resistance myth.

May problematizes the speaking subject, it problematizes the production of text and discourse, and their relationship to 'the event', whose immediacy depends on being rendered visible through these mediations, and it problematizes history. There is no text of May which does not bear the mark of one or all of these aspects.

---

[27] Availability of material has been a significant consideration in the choice of the key texts, excluding for example such well-known works as Lainé's *L'Irrévolution* or Douillon's film *L'An 01*.

[28] By *énoncé*, I am referring to that which is narrated; by *énonciation*, to the act and process of narration.

1 L'avant-mai: la France s'ennuie

It is one of the great ironies of cultural history that Godard's *La Chinoise*, the film that seems in so many ways to be the May 68 film *par excellence*, came out in August 1967. It was shot partly at Nanterre and focused on a group of maoist students who, totally committed to a cultural and political revolution in France, excoriated the Communist Party, the university system, bourgeois culture, bourgeois ideology, and bourgeois art. But the inflexibility of dates does at least have the virtue of demonstrating in a very concrete fashion that history has many different, interlocking chronologies. In the period preceding May 1968, debates about society, politics, and culture in the arts and social sciences, in creative and critical writings, and in the media, were formed by an amalgam of many strands and themes, including the university, Vietnam, consumer society, the modernization of France, capitalism and imperialism, class, memories of the Algerian War, as well as theoretical and philosophical work on culture and society.

By common consent 1966 is the *annus mirabilis* of structuralism, with the publication of Lacan's *Écrits*, Foucault's *Les Mots et les choses*, Lévi-Strauss's *La Pensée sauvage* (and the special issue of *Les Temps modernes* on 'Problèmes du structuralisme'). It was also the date that Simone de Beauvoir's novel, *Les Belles Images*, appeared, a novel which attacks structuralism in passing (the public debate between the existentialists and the structuralists, particularly on the terrain of history and politics, had been going for some time by 1966). *Les Belles Images* also attacked contemporary France in terms which have much in common with Godard, Christiane Rochefort, Georges Perec, and with the sociological and philosophical reflection on France associated with *Arguments*, with Georges Friedmann, Jean Fourastié, and situationism.[1] Their common focus is consumer society, class, and representation, not in itself, but in the context of social change and the condition of modernity.

---

[1] *Arguments* was a journal of marxist and sociological theory founded by Edgar Morin. Sociologists Georges Friedmann and Jean Fourastié wrote influential studies of work and of contemporary France respectively. The 'Situationist International' was an important group which developed out of surrealist and other art groups in the 1950s. It elaborated influential theories of culture, art, literature, and society, and the works of Guy Debord have become key texts in the theorizations of political art and everyday life.

In the months preceding May 68, there was much public debate on the university crises: student unrest, antagonism to university structures, selection, and examination. Journals carried special issues on the topic— *Esprit* published the soon-to-be famous essay of Cohn-Bendit and others, 'Pourquoi des sociologues?', in its May issue, prepared before the events. The Vietnam War was another dominant theme, polarizing opinion, providing a political focus for the critique of consumerism and the economic logic of capitalism. The argument for the overthrow of imperialism and colonialism in the name of independence and freedom, the lesson that the bourgeois state imposes its interests through violence, these were significant elements of the *gauchiste* world-view. Talks on the war between the North Vietnamese and the Americans opened in Paris on 3 May 1968. *Les Temps modernes* was gradually adopting a more and more *gauchiste* line, and Sartre and Beauvoir were members of the International Tribunal set up by Bertrand Russell in 1966 to investigate the basis of the war and war crimes. The support in *La Chinoise* for the heroic peasant fighters taking on the might of the American Army reflects the broad left view of the rights and wrongs of the war. *Loin du Vietnam*, a collective film on the Vietnam War involving seven different directors including Godard, came out in 1967, as did his *Made in USA*, accentuating the vision of France as a consumerist and moral jungle.

In a long interview devoted to *La Chinoise*[2] Godard cited a range of political and cultural references: to working-class revolt in the Rhodacieta strike, to the lessons learnt from Algeria, to Sollers and *Tel Quel*, Barthes, Foucault, and Sartre, demonstrating his *gauchiste* politics were combined with a keen awareness of cultural criticism, although he marks his distance from both Barthes and Foucault. The reference to Algeria lay behind the use of Francis Jeanson in the film. He appears in one sequence, holding a political and philosophical discussion with Véronique (Anna Karina) on the train to Nanterre. Jeanson, already well-known as Sartre's secretary in the 1950s, and a member of the *Temps modernes* board, author of works on Beauvoir and a truly remarkable study of Sartre, was arrested and tried *in absentia* at the height of the Algerian War for helping to organize support networks supplying money (carried in suitcases) to the rebel Front de Libération Nationale (FLN).[3] He had also happened to be Karina's philosophy teacher at university.

Godard's denunciation of bourgeois culture and of capitalism did not begin with the very obviously political films which came thick and fast in

---

[2] 'Lutter sur deux fronts', *Cahiers du cinéma*, 194 (Oct. 1967).
[3] See Hervé Hamon and Patrick Rotman, *Les Porteurs de valise: La Résistance française à la guerre d'Algérie* (Albin Michel, 1979).

1967 and 1968, but had also informed earlier work on contemporary France such as *Une femme mariée* (1964) and *Alphaville* (1962), combining an analysis of oppression in contemporary society with a dissection of its images and knowledge. Simone de Beauvoir's novel *Les Belles Images* brings together many contemporary strands of political, social, and philosophical reflection on contemporary France and its consumer society, from a position that can only be described as one of despair. Unlike Christiane Rochefort, whose *Une rose pour Morrison* has many similarities with *Alphaville* in its exploitation of science fiction as dystopian discourse, Beauvoir has not to my knowledge explicitly related *Les Belles Images* to 68, and in fact, her comments on 68 are curiously neutral, especially given her high-profile involvement in support for the banned maoist paper *La Cause du peuple* after 68. The context for her comments is at best elliptical. She is talking about her sense of personal development in culture and knowledge over the previous ten to twenty years:

> Mais quel prix possède aujourd'hui à mes yeux la culture que je détiens? J'avoue ne pas être de ces intellectuels que Mai 68 a profondément ébranlés. La contradiction que Sartre a dénoncée entre les visées universelles de l'intellectuel et le particularisme où il est enfermé, j'en étais déjà consciente en 1962 quand j'achevais *La Force des choses*. De nouveau elle m'a gênée lorsque j'ai commencé ce livre.[4]

Although she gives later a sympathetic account of the great fête which was the occupied Sorbonne and her visits to the Writers' Centre,[5] this rather disjointed passage both recognizes and denies May's claim of 'cultural revolution', implicitly acknowledging the post-May marginalization of the existentialist intellectual, but on the grounds that the 'death of the intellectual' had already taken place. The historical knowledge of the *énonciation*, of the structuralist tide sweeping all before it, proclaiming the end of the Sartrean intellectual as universal figure (although the dilemmas and contradictions of precisely that figure were indeed the subject of the lectures by Sartre to which Beauvoir is referring[6]), shadows these short, dense, and convoluted comments. None the less, it is true that there was no change of philosophical or intellectual direction for her, but one has only to compare the rather depressed isolation in which she found herself, politically, in the early years of the Fifth Republic, with her

---

[4] *Tout compte fait* (Gallimard, 1972), 286: 'But what value does my culture hold for me today? I confess I am not one of those intellectuals profoundly shaken by May 68. I was already well aware of the contradiction which Sartre denounced between the universal aims of the intellectual and the particularity he is confined to, when I was finishing *The Prime of Life*. It affected me again when I began this book.'

[5] Ibid. 580–8.   [6] *Plaidoyer pour les intellectuels* (Gallimard, 1972).

enthusiastic and lively involvement with the women's movement from the early 1970s onwards, to see what a difference a new form of politics had made.

Quand la France s'ennuie

In May 68 *Le Bulletin du Club Jean Moulin* was extremely proud of its pre-science in the way it had discussed the situation of young people in its June 1966 issue, when it had underlined the power of youth both to denounce injustice and to reveal, by violent opposition, society's con-tinuing evolution.[7] Similarly, Christiane Rochefort considered that the themes and ideas of *Une rose pour Morrison*, published in 1966, had been vindicated by the events of May. According to her introduction to the rather tardy paperback edition, it had been less well greeted than her other works, yet for her it was a special text, written in an intensive session of twenty-four days and nights, the source of which remained obscure until the events of 68 when she finally understood her 'crise de prémoni-tion'.[8] Pierre Viansson-Ponté had less luck. He branded France with the word which had in fact been a constant theme across literary, sociolog-ical, and philosophical interrogations of the state of things, and which was about to be spectacularly disavowed.

'Ce qui caractérise actuellement notre vie publique, c'est l'ennui. Les Français s'ennuient'[9] are the opening words of his article published in *Le Monde* of 15 March 1968, entitled 'Quand la France s'ennuie', which has come to symbolize the short-sightedness of many who could not see what was happening under their nose, as well as the completely unexpected nature of the explosion of social disorder. [10] Yet Viansson-Ponté's views were shared by many, that in the France of modernization, affluence, and comfort, people's heads, and especially young heads, were filled with the trivia of popular culture rather than social or political problems, 'une jeunesse (. . .) désintéressée de tout, émasculée par le confort et la vie facile', as Jean Bertolino puts it.[11] Viansson-Ponté argued that the great

---

[7] *Bulletin du Club Jean Moulin*, 70 (14 May 1968), 1.

[8] 'Lettre d'introduction pour un petit canard', *Une rose pour Morrison* (livre de poche, 1983), 9–10. First published Grasset, 1966.

[9] 'Public life is today characterized by boredom. The French are bored.'

[10] Philippe Labro and the team of the special edition, *Ce n'est qu'un début* (Editions et Publications Premières, 1968) 5–6. Viansson-Ponté's own analysis of his article is very clearly indebted—at times word for word—to Labro's book. *Histoire de la république gaullienne* (Fayard, 1971), ii. 388–92.

[11] *Les Trublions* (Stock, 1968), 10: 'young people not interested in anything, enfeebled by comfort and good living.'

convulsions in the world, Vietnam, Middle East, Cuba, Latin America, were arousing only fleeting interest. Students were in uproar elsewhere, whereas French students were only interested in getting permission for the girls to go into the boys' bedrooms at Nanterre . . . It is easy to address the mockery of hindsight to this, and many have, but as Labro perceptively points out, Viansson-Ponté is pointing the finger particularly at television and its representation of the world, the divorce between popular and intellectuals' awareness of these issues, linked directly to the loss of France's imperial status as a Great Power: 'Heureusement la télévision est là pour détourner l'attention vers les vrais problèmes: l'état du compte en banque de Killy, l'encombrement des autoroutes, le tiercé, qui continue d'avoir le dimanche soir priorité sur toutes les antennes de France.' He concludes: 'Dans une petite France presque réduite à l'héxagone, qui n'est pas vraiment malheureuse ni vraiment prospère, en paix avec tout le monde, sans grande prise sur les événements mondiaux, l'ardeur et l'imagination sont aussi nécessaires que le bien-être et l'expansion.'[12]

As an article bemoaning the trivial nature of the national, popular culture, smothering awareness of real problems under the comfortable affluence of a modernized France, it would no doubt have gone unremarked were it not for its timing and the delicious juxtaposition of ennui and the imminent conflagrations of May, for such sentiments had been aired time and time again in various forms for many years. Study of 'le bien-être' and 'l'expansion', the industrialization and modernization of France, the growth of consumer society, the nature of work and leisure, had been a dominant sociological theme since the 1940s, in narratives of enrichment and happiness which were consistently presented as problematic. *Difficultés du bien-être* was the title of a special issue of *Arguments* for example. In her critical view of bourgeois ideology and behaviour in the affluent middle class, Beauvoir's is not a lone voice.

Ennui is a metaphysical as well as a psychological term: synonym of 'dégoût de la vie', mal du siècle, conveying the anguish caused by the human condition. It is the dark cloud of existential agony that life is not worth living. One of the most complete expositions of the dynamics of the anguish is to be found in Baudelaire; human awareness of and aspiration to the infinite is contrasted to the finite nature of existence, a constant

---

[12] 'Luckily, television is there to focus attention on real problems such as the state of Killy's [a skiing star] bank account, overcrowded motorways, the *tiercé* [Tote] which still has first place on all channels on Sunday evening. In this little France which has almost been reduced to the hexagon, which is neither really unhappy nor really prosperous, at peace with everyone, without any great influence over world events, enthusiasm and imagination are as necessary as physical well-being and economic growth.'

degradation and fall into the realities of mortality, the repetitions of chronology. *Les Fleurs du mal* captures the conflicts of the human condition: the sinister ennui of everyday life, the quest for escape, for intoxication, to realize the unrealizable aspirations of the human spirit. Poetry both celebrates and laments the impossible quest for spirituality. Flaubert's Emma Bovary displays a kindred spirit, albeit in a degraded, tawdry form; her aspirations are fed by romantic and religious cliché. This dynamic of the material and the spiritual, so characteristic of Baudelaire and Flaubert, is a knowing reference in the 1960s. Sylvie et Jérôme, the hapless protagonists of *Les Choses*, Perec's masterly dissection of *le vécu consumériste*, are Emma Bovary's spiritual heirs, as critics were not slow to point out: 'Le leitmotiv est alors la France qui s'ennuie, qui a écouté Guizot, s'est enrichie, et bovarysé sur son magot.'[13] Beauvoir's heroine Laurence is prey to an anguish she cannot name or define, a dissatisfaction, a yearning for things to be different. Finding only on her father's face a 'reflet d'infini', it still does not save her from the emptiness of existence: 'Elle a connu quelques aigres déchirements, une certaine irritation, une certaine désolation, du désarroi, du vide, de l'ennui: surtout de l'ennui. On ne chante pas l'ennui . . .'[14] Sociologists, novelists, and philosophers of the years of abundance agree: in the widest sense of the word, France is a spiritual wasteland.

After the massive devastation of the war, the 1940s and 1950s saw the bases of the economic structures and planning which were to produce a spectacular growth in the 1970s. Describing the modalities of this, the nationalizations of key sectors, the state planning and intervention, the control of energy, transport, and finance, Serge Berstein makes the telling point that there was more change between 1945 and 1970 than there had been between the end of the nineteenth century and 1945.[15] Rapid industrialization led to the population working the land to fall from seven million to three million. Expenditure on health, housing, transport, and leisure increased very substantially as incomes grew. Institutional sectors also were transformed, with the shift from primary to tertiary sectors, the expansion of education, and the exodus from the countryside; these were

---

[13] 'Its leitmotiv is therefore that France is bored, has listened to Guizot [19th-cent. historian and politician, responsible as prime minister for the expulsion of Marx from France to London, and with whom is associated the phrase "Enrichissez-vous"], has got rich, and "bovarysed" [dreamt meaningless/impossible dreams] over its pot of gold.' Leenhardt, postface to Perec, *Les Choses* (1966), 151.

[14] *Les Belles Images* (Gallimard, 1966), 36: 'She has known some bitter rifts, a certain irritation, grief, bewilderment, emptiness, and boredom. Above all, boredom. There are no songs to boredom . . .

[15] For this and the following details, see S. Berstein, *La France de l'expansion*, i. *La République gaullienne* (Seuil, 1989), esp. Chs. 4 and 5. Jean Fourastié makes the same point in relation to his two villages Cessac and Madère, *Les Trente Glorieuses: Ou la révolution invisible de 1946 à 1975* (Fayard, 1979: edn. cited, Hachette/Pluriel, 1988), 72.

sweeping changes which provoked hostility.[16] But although the law of economic merger led to the creation of large conglomerates in industry and agriculture, although there was rapid growth in the tertiary sector, in contrast to this it was also true that small businesses, small agricultural holdings, were still very significant, and in some cases dominant. The change in mentalities was therefore very uneven across France, giving one reason for the May explosion: tensions between modernization and the consumer mentality faced with an authoritarian political mentality (de Gaulle treating citizens like children) and also with the strong affirmation of values unchanged since the nineteenth century in some sectors. A dominant theme of May interpretations is, therefore, that in the cultural and ideological and political spheres, May ushered in the modern world.

Jean Fourastié, in his famous text *Les Trente Glorieuses*, described these years as 'la Révolution invisible', such is the contrast between the France of 1945–50 and the France of 1970–5. His analysis, which is a mine of information about the economic and social transformation of France, is also typical of sociological comment on the postwar years, in its concomitant preoccupation with what one can only call metaphysical issues of the nature and meaning of the human condition. Already in 1950, a sense of anxiety and anguish associated with modern society had been noted: 'La "crise du progrès" dont les signes étaient déjà manifestes et multiples à la fin de l'entre-deux-guerres, est désormais un courant torrentueux qui, débordant les milieux intellectuels, pénètre (. . .) la sensibilité de l'homme de la rue.'[17] (Although for Fourastié as for others, it was the sensibility of the 'femme de la rue' which would be crucial in its representation.) Sociological work on the years of the expansion and growth in prosperity is at one and the same time a comment on the quest for human happiness, and the conclusion is rarely totally positive: 'En vérité, ces trente années sont glorieuses. Elles ont résolu des problèmes tragiques et millénaires —quoiqu'elles soient loin d'avoir résolu tous les problèmes tragiques et millénaires de l'humanité; quoique même elles en aient fait naître de nouveaux, qui ne se posaient pas dans un monde où les hommes étaient pauvres et impuissants.'[18]

---

[16] Fourastié, *Le Grand Espoir du XX siècle*, definitive edn. (Gallimard, 1963), 239.

[17] 'The "crisis of progress" of which there were already many clear signs at the end of the interwar period, is now in full flood. In this pivotal year of the 20th century, it has flowed out beyond academic circles, and entered the feelings of the man in the street.' Georges Friedmann, *Où va le travail humain?*, 3rd edn. (Gallimard, 1963), 9.

[18] 'In truth, these thirty years are glorious. They have resolved tragic, age-old problems—although they are far from having solved all the tragic, age-old problems of humanity; and although they have even created new problems which did not arise in a world where men were poor and powerless.' Fourastié, *Les Trente Glorieuses*, 28–9.

Les Trente Glorieuses, this history of industrialization and modernization, opens interestingly enough with a discussion of two villages, followed by the story of two girls divided by five generations—'Séverine est la
petite fille de la petite fille de Marie'[19]—illustrating in terms of daily life,
experience, mentality, and attitude, the lived historical gap between pre-
industrial and industrial France. Contrasting sharply with Marie's life
of childbearing, early widowhood, and early death, rendered more difficult by dependency on the vagaries of weather and harvest, is Séverine's
pampered existence, presumably put together as some statistical iden-
tikit portrait, consisting of student life, marriage, children, and possibly
divorce. Her story is governed by the connotation 'frivolous': she is not
a student, but a 'student', studies unspecified ('elle est "étudiante", du
moins cela est son statut officiel'); as a 'student' she travels abroad, not to
learn but to 'do' Rome, Tunis, London, and Madrid. She has sexual partners
before marriage, but neither a job nor a career. At 45, when poor Marie
was trembling with exhaustion and facing her early death, 'Séverine a
encore devant elle 34 années de vie avec retraite, Sécurité sociale et peut-
être institut de beauté.'[20] It is difficult not to wonder whether she might
not be another Laurence, heroine of *Les Belles Images*, suffering as a result
of her apparently easy life. Certainly, Fourastié later argues that this is the
case, and although the message is rendered ambiguous by his stereotypical presentation of her—it is difficult to imagine the discourse of luxury,
idleness, and intellectual confusion being allied with masculinity to
symbolize the 'trouble' of contemporary society—the configuration once
again links modernity and 'ennui'. Séverine's mind is bombarded with
information from the four corners of the earth, pouring out from the media,
friends, travel,[21] but this is not progress: 'Enormément d'informations
sur le monde, mais plus de conception du monde, plus d'explication du
monde. Dans les mauvais jours, Séverine ne sait plus pourquoi elle souffre;
elle ne sait plus pourquoi elle vit.'[22] Plotting the discourses of hygiene,
domesticity, and modernization in the 1950s and early 1960s, Kristin Ross
has argued that women were the enthusiastic conduits of modernity,[23]
but one has to wonder how typical this is, for it is also true that from
Madame Bovary onwards, women are the ciphers of the suffering, the

---

[19] 'Séverine is the grand-daughter of Marie's grand-daughter': Bousquet, *Apogée et déclin*, 70.
(Bousquet also discusses this section of *Les Trente Glorieuses*.)
[20] Ibid. 71: 'Séverine still has 34 years of life ahead of her, including retirement, social security, and perhaps beauty parlour.'
[21] Ibid. 174.
[22] Ibid.: 'Copious information on the world, but no world-view, no understanding of the universe. On
her bad days, Séverine does not know why she is suffering, nor what she is living for.'
[23] *Fast Cars, Clean Bodies* (Cambridge, Mass.: MIT Press, 1994), 92.

anguish, and the dissatisfaction inherent in the modern condition. 'Pourquoi est-ce que j'existe?' ('Why do I exist?') is the question from the 10-year-old Catherine which haunts her mother Laurence. She is indeed a sister in confusion to Séverine.[24]

Fourastié's text, published in 1979, could not form part of the *sottisier* Beauvoir compiled for her new novel, but some of his more congratulatory statements might have found a home there, celebrating 'les 30 glorieuses' as the years when France and the West freed great numbers of people from hunger and poverty, and extended intellectual and spiritual culture beyond the tiny minority that had traditionally enjoyed it.[25] And what about Auschwitz, Algeria, the Third World, any reader of *Les Belles Images* must find themselves asking. If they espouse Laurence's rather than Jean-Charles's point of view, that is.

Simone de Beauvoir describes the motivation behind her novel in the following terms:

J'ai repris un autre projet: évoquer cette société technocratique dont je me tiens le plus possible à distance mais dans laquelle je vis; à travers les journaux, les magazines, la publicité, la radio, elle m'investit. Mon intention n'était pas de décrire l'expérience vécue et singulière de certains de ses membres: je voulais faire entendre ce qu'on appelle aujourd'hui son 'discours'. (. . .) La difficulté c'était, sans intervenir moi-même, de faire transparaître du fond de sa nuit la laideur du monde où elle étouffait. (. . .) Il s'agissait de faire parler le silence.[26]

The subject is society, and the technical problem is to enable the society to talk 'against itself', in spite of itself. There are several things to note about this description of her project: first, the interdependence of the personal and the non-personal. It is not possible, for Beauvoir, to choose to absent oneself from society, for society is indubitably part of one's own identity. Secondly, the extent to which she shares the views of Viansson-Ponté, Fourastié, and others, that it is the media which are the vehicles of transmission and prime articulators of the new society.

Les Belles Images opens with a caustic presentation of the lack of individuality inherent in consumer society, as Laurence sits in her mother's

---

[24] Cf. *Les Belles Images*, 99: 'C'est comme la psychanalyse, le Marché commun, la force de frappe, elle ne sait pas qu'en penser, elle n'en pense rien.' ('It's like psychoanalysis, the Common Market, the nuclear deterrent, she does not know what to think about it, she has no views on it.')

[25] *Les Trente Glorieuses*, 170.

[26] 'I took up another project: to write about this technocratic society from which I try as best I can to distance myself but in which I live; through newspapers, magazines, advertising, and radio, it forms part of my life. My intention was not to describe the individual, lived experience of some of its members, but to make what is now called its "discourse" heard. The difficulty was to bring out from the depths of its darkness the ugliness of the world where she was suffocating, without directly intervening myself. It was a case of making silence talk.' *Tout compte fait*, 172.

garden, and reflects on the multiplicity of identical pictures to be found at that moment across France—what she is experiencing, the same exchanges, the same surroundings, is being experienced 'dans un autre jardin tout à fait différent, exactement pareil'.[27] Just as the farmhouse, choice of flowers, and garden furniture bear the mark of the contemporary women's magazines, so all their actions are reproductions too. Catherine looks like all the other happy little girls stretched out reading on the carpet. The message of the uniformity and conformism promoted by technological consumer society is shown to be a virtual tyranny. Daily life is inescapably saturated with its images and aspirations. Both Laurence and Jean-Charles work in sectors which were particularly affected by consumerism: advertising and architecture (housing) respectively, and Laurence attempts to dream up slogans that also apply to home improvement. Fourastié exempts leisure from conformity, although Dumazedier, the famous sociologist of leisure, does not, and for Friedmann also, leisure is the domain of the individual. In contrast, Beauvoir and Perec show the commodification of leisure, equally subordinated to the demands of economics; the two novelists are offering serious reflection on the nature of individuality, on the question of what might be described as specific to the individual in such a context.

The images of the advertisements, and the way they symbolize the extent to which everyone needs to live the images, live the social messages, are one alienating factor in contemporary society. Stereotypes, clichés, and received ideas inflect personal identity too. Existentialist philosophy never considered the self to be an autonomous entity, and always theorized the self–other relationship as being constitutive of the self. Without the other, there is no self. Otherness is not just another individual confronting me; otherness is all that is not self, and the social discourses of individuality and being are part of that otherness which is constituting my sense of personal identity. But to invest myself totally in living that image is to know yet another alienation, in abandoning my own responsibility and in attempting to elude the contingent nature of existence by giving myself an illusory sense of purpose through the other. Laurence and Catherine are the means of questioning the myths and ideologies of French consumer society, at every level, up to and including a questioning of humanist philosophy, and the nature of signification.

The beautiful images in a society whose central purpose is dedicated to the idea of technology, scientific progress, and greater material benefits producing ever greater happiness, are contested first by that which is not beautiful, 'la laideur du monde'. The discourse to be spoken in the silence

[27] *Les Belles Images*, 7, 9: 'in another garden, completely different, but exactly the same'.

of the beautiful images is a discourse of ugliness. Bourgeois beauty is morally repulsive. 'Les horreurs du monde, on est forcé de s'y habituer, il y en a trop: le gavage des oies, l'excision, les lynchages, les avortements, les suicides, les enfants martyrs, les maisons de la mort, les massacres d'otage, les répressions, on voit ça au cinéma, à la télé, on passe.'[28] It is governed by the order of habit, routine, repetition, the stasis and proliferation of the present; nothing is stable, nothing is, in the final instance, meaningful. For Catherine, then, this applies to her own existence too. What is the purpose of any existence: none except that which it invents for itself, is the existentialists' right answer, yet that does not take away the anguish at the realization that no one is individually *needed*. Jérôme and Sylvie in *Les Choses* exemplify the way objects can fill this metaphysical void, producing them as necessary, as they return from another session of window shopping:

> **De station en station, antiquaires, libraires, marchands de disques, cartes des restaurants, agences de voyages, chemisiers, tailleurs, fromagers, chausseurs, confiseurs, charcuteries de luxe, papetiers, leurs itinéraires composaient leur véritable univers: là reposaient leurs ambitions, leurs espoirs. Là était la vraie vie, la vie qu'ils voulaient connaître, qu'ils voulaient mener: c'était pour ces saumons, pour ces tapis, pour ces cristaux, que, vingt-cinq ans plus tôt, une employée et une coiffeuse les avaient mis au monde.[29]**

The technological society, ruled by technocrats, governed by possessions, is an anti-humanism, with its ideological counterparts in structuralism and the Nouveau Roman. Jean-Charles's annoyance, that Laurence avoided running over a cyclist but damaged the car, is typical of the absence of the human as value.[30]

Guy Debord argued that even our dreams are produced by consumerism: 'A mesure que la nécessité se trouve socialement rêvée, le rêve devient nécessaire. Le spectacle est le mauvais rêve de la société moderne

[28] p. 30: 'One is forced to get used to the horrors in the world, since there are too many of them: force-fed geese, cliterodectomy, lynchings, abortions, suicides, martyred children, the houses of death, the massacres of hostages, and repression. We see all that, and more, at the cinema, on the TV.'

[29] p. 85: 'From stop to stop, antique shops, bookshops, record shops, restaurant menus, travel agencies, shirt-makers, tailors, cheese-shops, shoe shops, sweet shops, luxury delicatessen, stationers, their itineraries composed their true universe: there they found their ambitions and hopes. True life was there, the life they wanted to know, the life they wanted to live: it was for these salmon, these rugs, these crystals, that, twenty-five years earlier, an office worker and a hairdresser had given birth to them.'

[30] Cf. '"Apprenez le geste qui sauve" ou l'humanisme occidental en quatre leçons', a short item listing four events where individuals were victims of car accidents or murder, and no one came to their aid. In the final one, the execution of children in a war zone in Africa was delayed while the Italian cameraman dealt with a technical problem. It was then carried out; and filmed. *Socialisme ou barbarie*, 39 (Mar.–Apr. 1965), 86–7.

enchaînée, qui n'exprime finalement que son désir de dormir. Le spectacle est le gardien de ce sommeil.'[31] Material possessions are not meaningful in themselves; systems of signification invest goods with meaning. To live in consumer society is, it appears, to live in ideology unmasked. When the bourgeois concepts of 'taste' and 'refinement' suggest the 'things-in-themselves' are superior or inferior (as if the aesthetic superiority and value of the antique desk over the formica-topped table came from the objects themselves), there is a sense of confusion, both moral and existential, engendered in those who try to take them literally, not unlike Emma Bovary's quest to translate Walter Scott and the sensuality of mystical sentimentality into her own life. And they find themselves in a spiritual desert, a hall of mirrors with no sense of meaning and purpose of existence; unease or bad faith at all the 'messiness' which does not fit, as Jérôme and Sylvie learn: 'Ils vivaient dans un monde étrange et chatoyant, l'univers miroitant de la civilisation mercantile, les prisons de l'abondance, les pièges fascinants du bonheur.'[32] 'Leur vie n'était pas conquête, elle était effritement, dispersion. Ils se rendaient compte, alors, à quel point ils étaient condamnés à l'habitude, à l'inertie. Ils s'ennuyaient ensemble, comme si, entre eux, il n'y avait jamais eu que le vide.'[33]

Les Belles Images explores the nature of living in contemporary France from a variety of angles. Culture and signification are the terrain of personal, political, social, and philosophical investigation, as much as anything through the character of Laurence. Beauvoir wrote that she wished her novel to be read as a detective story, and certainly learning to hear the silent quotation marks placed around the ideas, aspirations, and feelings as the social and cultural scenarios of ideology are acted out, is a kind of quest; the only secret identified as such and which Laurence is keen to unearth is the secret of her father's difference, of his superiority. The revelation, during their trip to Greece, that there is no secret or difference, that the bourgeois humanism he subscribes to is yet another variant of bourgeois mythology, with images of fine ruins and picturesque peasants masking yet again poverty, exploitation, and ugliness, knocks away the one area in which she still believed (as opposed to watching herself willing herself to believe) that appearance and being authentically and

---

[31] 'As necessity is now dreamt, socially, so dreams become necessary. The spectacle is the bad dream of modern chained society, which finally is expressing only its desire to sleep. The spectacle is the guardian of that sleep.' *La Société du spectacle* (Gallimard Folio, 1992), 24–5.

[32] p. 80: 'They were living in a strange, shimmering world, the glittering universe of mercantile civilization, the prisons of affluence, the fascinating traps of happiness.'

[33] p. 81: 'Their life was not a conquest, it was a frittering away, a dispersal. They realized then the extent to which they were condemned to habit and inertia. They were bored together, as if, between them, there had never been anything but emptiness.'

meaningfully reflected each other. For Laurence is the Outsider, the one who cannot participate in the rites and rituals, but who suffers because she does not understand why,[34] for whom the behaviour, wishes, and desires of others appear as cultural processes without a subject, quite depersonalized; hence the side swipes at the Nouveau Roman and Foucault's work on the death of man, as respectively reflecting and justifying the apersonal processes of cultural signification governed by economics and power. Laurence's hope, that the humanism represented by her father is different, crumbles, for this is bourgeois humanism, the humanism which Sartre dissected in the images of the good bourgeois of Bouville in *La Nausée*, naturalizing an exploitative social and economic order. Laurence is the outsider, as she acknowledges at the end ('je me sens étrangère') because she can no longer see any of it as natural, she can only see processes of signification. Her daughter sees a poster of a starving child, and sees a starving child. But Laurence had seen a sign, not a child, a sign of something else (the fight against poverty), eliminating the picture itself. She is a mythologist who can no longer get back to the material of the myth; she inhabits the metaphysical wasteland, the cruel knowledge of mortality and contingency, which the society of abundance, in the bad faith of its alienation, refuses to acknowledge. *Les Belles Images* dramatizes a place outside it, in the person of Laurence, but it is a place of madness and alienation.

Beauvoir herself stresses primarily the social and psychological aspects of the novel, but it is undoubtedly a political text also. There is no simple positive message about any political organization or political commitment to changing society, and in that sense it is not a 'roman à thèse'. It is a novel bearing the traces of the political despair Beauvoir described in relation to Gaullist France. It was the Algerian War which particularly alienated Beauvoir from her compatriots. She and Sartre had supported the cause of Algerian independence, and Sartre had become the target for right-wing attacks—a bomb exploded outside his flat. Beauvoir co-authored a book about Djamala Boupacha, who had been tortured in Algeria, and the references in the novel to a woman being tortured are very significant: the torture carried out in the name of France in Algeria proved to be an acute crisis for many French people, recalling very uncomfortably the Nazi Occupation of France, with the French now in the role of hated occupiers. The murder of Jewish children during the Occupation haunts Laurence as a child; the torture of an Algerian woman provokes her first breakdown; Beauvoir shares the political critique of consumerism,

---

[34] Cf. the opening section, with its many judgements and questions: 'Pourquoi est-ce je pense cela?' (p. 8). 'Mais qu'ont-ils que je n'ai pas non plus?' (p. 14).

that its affluence is based on the exploitation of others, its abundance is reflected by their want, its life by their deaths. Laurence reacts very badly to Jean-Charles's dismissive comment: 'Ah! ne recommence pas à me faire une crise de mauvaise conscience comme en 62',[35] and its revelation that, while pretending to take it seriously, the bourgeoisie will always accommodate protest, and recuperate it.

The complexity of the theories of ideology and culture, with their use of imagination, desire, and representation, must in part explain the complexity of the writing of *Les Belles Images* and the other texts mentioned here. Godard's *La Chinoise* and Rochefort's *Une rose pour Morrison* are texts of denunciation, attacking the culture and social order of the bourgeoisie, its institutions, what it constitutes as knowledge, its ideological and sexual repressions. Both involve elaborate use of wordplay, puns, ironies, to fragment, to render strange, to display as ideological the dominant culture. But the knowing awareness of irony, in order to work, does demand similar knowledge from its audience. In his discussion of *La Chinoise*, Godard comments upon the comrades of the *Cahiers marxistes-leninistes* being upset by his group of fanatical maoists, wondering if calling them Red Guards would have made things clearer.[36] Admittedly the 'groupuscules' were not exactly famed for their sense of political humour, but presumably the most literal-minded of them would have coped with the ironic textualities involved in the depiction of *Weekend*'s hippie commando, the *Front de Libération de Seine-et-Oise*.

Perec's stylistic tour de force oscillates between sociological report and fiction, with all the instability about the status of the subject of enunciation and the mode of reading which that implies. One of Beauvoir's great gifts as a writer was her talent for irony, for writing the myth without quotation marks, but using a variety of techniques—lexical, semantic, syntactic, structural—to establish a critical distance from it. Like Flaubert, she is able to reproduce discourse and simultaneously hold it up for display. Godard, Rochefort, Beauvoir, and Perec are all writing texts governed by the double structures of denunciation, which, through irony, through mechanisms displaying the discourse as artifice, through exploiting the language of derision, establish a critical discourse in the course of their own narrative. Their target is the ideological nature of culture and knowledge, the contamination of all processes of meaning by the tyranny of the meaning-making machine that is consumer society, through advertising and the media. Baudrillard will argue in *La Société de consommation* that all contestation is already positioned within the discourses of consumer

---

[35] p. 133: 'Ah! don't start on your crisis of bad conscience again, like in 62.'
[36] 'Lutter sur deux fronts', 15.

society and is inexorably a part of it. This is not forgotten during May: is 'la contestation de la société du spectacle' a reality, or little more than 'le spectacle de la contestation'?

Talking about my generation

> Qu'au plus fort des 'Trente Glorieuses', alors que le PNB croît de 5% l'an, que le chômage est à peine 'frictionnel', que les menaces de guerre s'éloignent à l'horizon, que la société d'abondance, de loisirs, de communication adopte sa vitesse de croisière, que tous les plaisirs de la vie semblent s'offrir aux citoyens de pays développés, la jeunesse occidentale lève soudainement l'étendard rouge et noir de la révolte, voilà qui me paraît toujours inexpliqué, sinon inexplicable.[37]

Weber's view was widely shared, and depoliticization was the constant refrain of much literature of the left, yet at least one serious study[38] suggested that it was a more complicated phenomenon than was often realized, and that, in student circles particularly, disaffection with the established political parties should not be seen as depoliticization. Moreover, Fourastié complained that 'les jeunes' were the only ones to be churlish about consumer society, failing to recognize its benefits.[39] In *Les Belles Images* it is the young, Laurence's daughter Catherine and her own younger self, who are still able to see the raw materials of life and existence. It is a rare discourse which does not have its anchoring point; as with the languages of May, the novel presents the convergence of youth and the *prise de parole* of the socially marginalized as the voice of authenticity, confronted with the discourses which fill most of the novel, the deviousness and duplicities of bourgeois culture and ideology. In the words of François Mitterrand: 'Ils s'étaient abolis dans une communauté dont la moindre ambition était de tout refaire, à commencer par l'homme. Ils avaient senti que vivre c'était autre chose que les gestes, les fatigues, les renoncements de leurs aînés, autre chose que leur agitation d'écureuil

---

[37] 'That it was at the height of the "30 glorieuses", when the GNP was growing by 5% a year, when unemployment was hardly an issue, when all threat of war was disappearing over the horizon, when the society of affluence, leisure, and communication was getting onto cruising speed, when all the pleasures seemed to be available to the citizens of the developed world, that Western youth suddenly raises the black and red flag of revolt, this is something which has always been unexplained, if not inexplicable, to me.' Henri Weber, *Vingt ans après* (Seuil, 1988), 9–10.

[38] Georges Vedel (ed.), *La Dépolitisation: Mythe ou réalité?* (Fond. nationale des sciences politiques, 1962).

[39] *Les Trente Glorieuses*, 27.

dans la cage.'[40] And the marxist argument that change has to mean violent change had become common currency.

Étienne Rambert argued that the students had seen the older generation accept war, the arms race, inequality, unemployment, in the name of order, and 'ils constatent que l'Occident est gros d'une nouvelle génération de monstres dont il aime à peupler l'univers: racisme, chauvinisme, exploitation, crises, guerre, fascisme'.[41] This is the 'désordre établi' which they will not accept: 'Ils choisissent le remède des marxistes: la révolution.'[42] This is now. Before, came the world of 'les aînés', the rejection of whose ideas, attitudes, and way of life is understood as a major impetus behind May. The commonalties which can exist across the generations were therefore sometimes masked. The 'Sous Commission de Sociologie', one of the study groups in the occupied Sorbonne, argued against consumerism in terms which reproduce very closely the perceptions of Beauvoir and Perec: 'S'il y a toujours eu contestation, elle restait ces dernières années inconscientes, chez beaucoup (cf angoisses, pathologie mentale).' [43] Their list of alienations starts with the 'société de pure consommation': 'Ce qui est critiquable, ce n'est pas l'existence d'une société industrielle, mais son utilisation aliénante quant aux fins et aux moyens.'[44] As in the 1930s, critique of the socio-economic system goes hand in hand with a critique of the alienated, distorted conception of man, turned into a consumer of products with artificially stimulated needs. Capitalism itself is therefore identified as the immediate target of the protest movement.[45] The text goes on to tackle advertising, leisure, and depoliticization.

In one of the first special issues published on May, the June issue of *L'Événement*, its director Emmanuel d'Astier de la Vigerie, a former Resister who will reach a wide audience through his interview in *Le Chagrin et la pitié*, concludes his analysis of the month of May by saluting a renewal of society in the new forces unleashed by the young protesters. For him as for many others, the protest movement had broken through

---

[40] 'They had merged into a wider group, the least of whose ambitions was to redo everything, starting with man. They had felt that living amounted to more than the gestures, the weariness, and the renouncements of their elders, more than the frantic movements of a squirrel in a cage.' Quoted in Weber, *Vingt ans après*, 159.

[41] 'They see that the West is spawning a new generation of the monsters with which it like to fill the world: racism, chauvinism, exploitation, crises, war, fascism.' *Magazine littéraire* (May 1968), 10.

[42] Ibid. 'They choose the marxists' solution: revolution.'

[43] 'There has always been contestation, but in recent years it was unconscious (cf. anxieties, mental pathology)', *Université critique* (stencilled document put out by the Law and Economics Strike Committee, described in Ch. 4), 6.

[44] 'What is criticizable is not the existence of industrial society, but its alienating use in terms of ends and means.' Ibid. 7.

[45] Ibid.

the shackles of established political approaches, suggesting new ways of thinking the questions of happiness and well-being, separated from the pursuit of material goods encouraged by the consumer society. For d'Astier the young have given new life to the socialist ethic of participation, responsibility, and autogestion, pushing aside the consumerism of capitalism and communism alike with their authoritarian insistence on work, obedience, and structures of governance. There may not yet be a solution, but the right questions were being asked.

Or, as Epistémon put it: 'Je ne m'ennuie plus.'[46]

---

[46] Epistémon, *Ces idées qui ont ébranlé la France* (Fayard, 1968), 12: 'I'm not bored any more.'

2 Nanterre-la-Folie

Voir Nanterre et vivre.
Allez mourir à Naples avec le Club Mediterrannée[1]

Faculté des //Lettrés et des Sciences InHumaines[2]

On 2 April 1968, a meeting in the 'grand amphithéâtre B2' at the Nanterre campus brought together 1,500 students addressed by speakers representing the SDS (West German Socialist Students Federation), the situationists, communists, anarcho-syndicalists, and revolutionary communists.[3] Maoists, trotskyists, marxist-leninists, and various combinations of all the above, formed a bewildering proliferation of political groups: JCR, CLER, FER, VO, PCF, UNEF, UJCm.l., CVN, CVB, 'les prositus' (pro-situationists), 'les prochinois', UEC, SNESup, 'le mouvement du 22 Mars', and 'les enragés', the favoured term, adopted from a ministerial insult, for the 'communistes révolutionnaires, anarchistes, situationnistes, "antiautoritaires" comme on dit en Allemagne',[4] these are some but by no means all of the groups active at Nanterre and in May. The numbers were small, as the epithet 'groupuscules' implies: Jean-Pierre Duteuil estimates the militants to number at the very most 10 per cent of the

---

[1] 'See Nanterre and live. Go and die in Naples with the Club Mediterrannée.' Reproduced in Julien Besançon, (ed.), Les Murs out la parole mai 68 (Claude Tchou, 1968), 85.
[2] Altered inscription set over the entrance to a faculty building; university unidentified. Alfred Willener, L'Image-action de la société (Seuil, 1970), illustration no. 9 (inset 320 and 321, English trans.).
[3] Gilbert Tarrab, 'Qu'est-ce que le s.d.s.?', L'Homme et la société, 8 (Apr.–June 1968), 133.
[4] A. Schnapp and P. Vidal-Naquet, Journal de la Commune étudiante (Seuil, 1988), 123. SDS: Sozialistischer Deutscher Studentenbund (West German Socialist Students Federation); JCR: Jeunesse Communistes Révolutionnaires (Daniel Bensaïd, Henri Weber, Alain Krivine were national leaders); CLER: Comité de Liaison des Étudiants Révolutionnaires; out of it came FER: Fédération des Étudiants Révolutionnaires; PCF: Parti Communiste Français (Roland Leroy); VO: Voix Ouvrière; UNEF: Union Nationale des Étudiants Français (Jacques Sauvageot); UJCml: Union des Jeunesses Communistes marxistes-léninistes (Jean-Pierre Le Dantec, Robert Linhart); CVN: Comité du Vietnam National; CVB: Comité du Vietnam de Base; adherents/supporters of the Internationale Situationniste (see later in this chapter); prochinois: maoists; UEC: Union des Étudiants communistes; SNESup: Syndicat National de l'Enseignement Supérieur (Alain Geismar); Mouvement du 22 mars (Cohn-Bendit, Jean-Pierre Duteuil).

12,000 students at Nanterre.[5] UNEF (Union Nationale des Étudiants Français) had 45,000 registered in 1968, far below the 100,000 during the Algerian War,[6] but they were prodigiously energetic for their own revolutionary causes (cultural revolution, workers' revolution, student-worker alliance, Vietnam), against the university authorities, against right-wing groups and commandos, and against each other: splits and schisms are constantly adding to the acronyms. There were also groups of the right and the extreme right equally prepared to do battle for their views, Occident being the most notorious.

Nanterre is where it began, and there have been many accounts of the time leading up to May and beyond.[7] Extracts from the diary of events established by Duteuil[8] give a snapshot of campus life and the causes agitating Nanterre, which ends up in a state of permanent high tension, especially as this pattern is being replicated on the national stage, with strikes, demonstrations, political street battles, clashes with the police, involving *lycée* students, workers, students, and internationally too, in Germany, Japan, the United States. From February 1967 onwards, students were protesting, demonstrating, agitating, and occupying, over a range of issues such as the free access to female students' bedrooms, the 'listes noires', secret lists of politically active students allegedly held by the central administration, demands for better funding for universities (5,000 demonstrated in Paris in November 1967). Students in the Sociology Department went on strike in December 1967 for demands which included better resources and representation, and the following February 3,000 students voted for a continuation of the strike. In that same month the police were called onto the campus for the first time in postwar France, to disperse an anarchist demonstration against the 'listes noires'. The second-year sociology student Daniel Cohn-Bendit (later known as 'Dany le rouge' for his red hair and red politics, and even 'le sublime Rouquin') had been singled out as a trouble-maker, in part because of his heckling of Minister Missoffe during the official opening of the campus swimming pool in January 1968 (he challenged him on the contents of a government brochure on sexuality), and his threatened expulsion became a *cause célèbre*. In March a student was arrested for breaking the windows of the American Express office in Paris, and the administrative

[5] *Nanterre 1965–66–67–68* (Mauléon, Association Acratie, 1988), 11.
[6] A. Delale and G. Ragache, *La France de 68* (Seuil, 1978), 48–9.
[7] Duteuil, *Nanterre 65–66–67–68*, is very comprehensive. See also Christian Charrière, *Le Printemps des enragés* (Fayard, 1968), Rioux and Backmann, *L'Explosion de mai, 11 mai 1968* (Robert Laffont, 1968); Alain Touraine, *Le Communisme utopique* (Seuil, 1968, 1972); Jean Bertolino, *Les Trublions* (Stock, 1968); P. Labro *et al., Ce n'est qu'un début* (1968); Schnapp and Vidal-Naquet, *La Commune étudiante*.
[8] *Nanterre 65–66–67–68*, 7–10.

building was occupied for a day in protest. Late at night, a Manifesto of the 142 present was produced, and the movement which had in effect then begun was baptized the 'Mouvement du 22 mars'. Students renamed lecture theatres (to Che Guevara, Babeuf, Rosa Luxembourg). Incidents continued through March and April. Students, including Cohn-Bendit, were arrested and released. An issue of the *Bulletin du 22 mars* demonstrated how to make a Molotov cocktail.

On 2 May, a day when the campus was in a state of high alert over the possibility of an attack by extreme-right-wing commandos, the Dean decided to close the campus. And it all moved to Paris . . .

One inscription scrawled in the Sorbonne read: 'Dieu, je vous soupçonne d'être un intellectuel de gauche'. 'Dieu je vous soupçonne d'être un nouveau romancier' would have been appropriate for Nanterre, so perfect was the match between the spatial organization and the student protest, starting with the improbable fact that it was built in the district of Nanterre called 'La Folie'. Nanterre is a geopolitical microcosm of the thematics of May: class, knowledge, and power. It is a symbolic site in more ways than one, as transitional link between the student protest and the events of May, and as embodiment of the relation of the University as institution to other sites of state power and to the powerless.

The university was built on the site of an army barracks and a bidonville. A train ran from Saint-Lazare to the small ramshackle station where under the platform sign 'La Folie' was another sign: 'Complexe universitaire'. The university itself was a bleak site with its tower blocks of student halls, administrative and other buildings (but symptomatically, no library, at first) surrounding a vast empty space. The Résidence was as functional as the rest: 'mille cinq cents garçons et filles y vivent dans de petites chambres de 9m². (. . .) Et la fenêtre sur les bidonvilles ou les parkings.'[9] There was no infrastructure, virtually nothing in recreational facilities; the mere sight of it was a lesson on the politics of education in modern France. 'L'isolement de la Faculté est total, son intégration en milieu urbain, nulle. Et pour cause. Autour du complexe universitaire: des usines, des entrepôts, des voies de chemin de fer, des H.L.M. et l'un des bidonvilles les plus atroces de la région parisienne. (. . .) Un peu plus loin, les buttes de terres jaunâtres du chantier du métro express.'[10]

---

[9] 'One thousand five hundred young men and women live in small rooms 9 metres square. And with a view onto the shanty towns or the carparks': Rioux and Backmann, *L'Explosion de mai*, 40.

[10] 'The isolation of the Faculty was absolute, it was not integrated at all into the town. And for good reason. The university buildings were surrounded by factories, depots, railway lines, and one of the most appalling shanty towns in the Parisian region. A little further on, there were the heaps of yellow earth where they were building the new express metro line.' Ibid. 41.

Nanterre's history is a history of Paris and its limits: it is in Paris, yet not in Paris, part of the great belt of the *banlieue rouge*, and the story of May, with its intermingling of centre and periphery, of Paris and Nanterre, is a restaging of an old history, not least in the unleashing of the forces of disruption from the *banlieue*.[11] 'Ville-usine, ville-dortoir, ville-universitaire' is how the narrator of *Derrière la vitre* sums up Nanterre.[12] To which one could add *ville-bidonville*.[13] 10,000 people, mainly North African, lived in the *bidonvilles* around it, shanty towns which seemed forever bogged down in mud through which the inhabitants had to trudge to get water from the few stand pipes on the edge of each area.[14] The quagmire of the building site which greeted the first students as the rest of the campus was slowly built repeated this association of Nanterre and mud. The University and its surroundings offered a daunting image of modern society:

> N'était-ce pas là le symptôme le plus alarmant de cette société: encasernement, dépersonnalisation des uns, ségrégation à l'égard des autres, laissés au hasard de la rue. Pas besoin d'aller en Algérie, au Vietnam, en Inde, pour découvrir le tiers monde, il palpitait aux portes de la faculté de Nanterre, avec sa peau olivâtre, ses cheveux crépus, ses hardes, comme une évidence à échelle réduite de l'exploitation par les sociétés capitalistes de la misère universelle.[15]

The University was built to house the Faculté des Lettres (humanities, social sciences, law) which was moved from the Sorbonne where there were simply too many students. Students had to get to any lecture at least half an hour early to have any hope of finding a place in the gangways, let alone a seat. The same problem would quickly recur in the outpost. It opened in 1964 for 2,000 students; there were 12,000 in 1968. Moreover, many of the students were from the affluent districts of the west of Paris: 'Entre les jeunes filles de Neuilly en kilt et les Africains qui marchent dans la boue, les étudiants de la résidence reçoivent à toute heure un cours de sociologie appliquée sans égal.'[16] It has been argued that it was no accident

---

[11] See Annie Fourcaut (ed.), *Banlieue rouge 1920–1960* (Autrement, 1992), which includes a history of the relation of Paris to its dangerous 'zone', the periphery outside the walls where ramshackle settlements grew up, constituting a major feature of the imaginary of Paris with the classic oppositions of frontiers: inside/outside, safe/dangerous, licit/illicit, etc.

[12] R. Merle, *Derrière la vitre* (Gallimard, 1970), 25.

[13] The Nanterre *bidonvilles* and their history are also presented in some detail, ibid. 23–4.

[14] See Abdelmalek Sayad, *Un Nanterre algérien, terre de bidonvilles* (Autrement, 1995), 10–11, 41–64.

[15] 'Was not that the most alarming symptom of this society: confinement and depersonalization for some, segregation for others, left to take their chances on the street. No need to go to Algeria, to Vietnam, to India, to discover the Third World; olive-skinned, with frizzy hair, and in rags, the Third World was living at the gates of the Nanterre Faculty, a clear sign, on a reduced scale, of the exploitation by capitalist societies of universal poverty.' Bertolino, *Les Trublions*, 61.

[16] 'Between the young women of Neuilly in their smart kilts, and the Africans walking in the mud, the students living on campus are getting at all hours of the day and night an unparalleled lesson in

Nanterre was chosen for *La Chinoise*, since it was already developing a reputation: 'Nanterre, c'est Cuba', 'Nanterre, c'est un Viêt-nam de
banlieue.'[17]

'C'est à Nanterre, cauchemar en béton, dans un paysage de cauchemar
(le bidonville) dans le bâtiment C, celui des philosophes, psychologues et
sociologues, que "tout" a commencé. Pourquoi Nanterre, pourquoi des
psychologues et des sociologues?'[18] The answer of Cohn-Bendit, Duteuil,
and others who signed the manifesto/essay 'Pourquoi des sociologues?',
which had circulated at Nanterre from mid-March 1968 and which was
published in the May issue of the journal *Esprit*, was primarily the manner
in which sociology was seen to serve industry and the State, by studying
the worker so that he was better able to work, by understanding the rioter
or delinquents the better to deal with them. Its powers of political recuperation were also noted: 'la majorité de nos sociologues sont des marxistes'. The work of Michel Crozier and Alain Touraine was singled out for
attack in its final section, 'le cas de Nanterre'. They were just two of the
eminent intellectuals who taught at Nanterre, who included psychologist
Didier Anzieu, sociologists Jean Baudrillard, Michel Crozier, René Lourau,
Henri Lefebvre, anglicist Robert Merle, the arabist Jacques Berque, philosophers Mickael Dufrenne, Emmanuel Lévinas, Jean-François Lyotard,
Paul Ricoeur (who had a difficult stint as Dean in the post-May turbul-
ence), and the historian René Rémond (who succeeded Ricoeur as Dean).
It is striking how many of them committed their views on the events to
paper, *Le Communisme utopique*, *Ces idées qui ont ébranlé la France*,
L'Irruption: De Nanterre au sommet, being among the most famous.[19]
The Dean, Pierre Grappin, who bore the brunt of much student protest
and vilification, was a liberal man who thought Nanterre offered the
opportunity for creating better conditions for students, with greater

applied sociology.' L. Joffrin, *Mai 68* (Seuil, 1987). See also Bertolino, *Les Trublions*, 227–30, for
detailed discussion of the social distinctions between the rich students, the 'minets and minettes'
arriving in their cars, the petits-bourgeois from the provinces who lived on campus; the dress codes
of small groups of political activists, deliberately unkempt and as obviously different as possible
from designer chic.

[17] Rioux and Backmann, *L'Explosion de mai*, 41.
[18] 'It's at Nanterre, a nightmare built in concrete, in a nightmare landscape (the shanty town), in
C Building, home to the philosophers, psychologists, and sociologists, that "it" began. Why Nanterre,
why psychologists and sociologists?' Schnapp and Vidal-Naquet, *La Commune étudiante*, 102.
[19] Among the others, see the contributions of Jacques Berque in 'Table ronde: pourquoi les étudiants?', *L'homme et la société* (Apr.–May–June 1968), 3–43; Michel Crozier, *La Société bloquée* (Seuil,
1974); René Lourau, 'Sociology and Politics in 1968', in C. Posner (ed.) *Reflections on the Revolution in
France: 1968* (Pelican, 1970); Jean-François Lyotard, *Dérive à partir de Marx et Freud* (10/18, 1973); Paul
Ricoeur, 'Réforme et révolution dans l'université', *Esprit* (May 1968), 987–1002; Jean-Louis Lecercle,
'Le "Mouvement à Nanterre"', *La Pensée*, 140–1 (Aug.–Oct. 1968), 31–9.

communication between staff and students. As he had been an active *Résistant* he suffered particularly from the denunciations of 'fascist'.

Having had bruising encounters as a result of the techniques of 'la contestation permanente', including extreme verbal and occasional physical violence, established staff withdrew to their tents, as Pierre Vidal-Naquet put it,[20] after the closure of the campus. It was the teaching assistants, economically marginal and in vulnerable positions, yet highly politicized also because of the Algerian War which the students were on the whole too young to know about, who were directly involved and sometimes leading the campus discussions.[21] Posters and graffiti reveal the importance of the politics of anti-imperialism in relation to French history: 'Fascistes échappés de Dien Bien Phu, vous n'échapperez pas à Nanterre'; 'Paras! vous vous êtes fait étriper en Algérie, au Vietnam, ça va recommencer à Nanterre!'[22] But all the actions, all the diverse political targets, are anchored in the student protest: 'Mais le point de départ de la politisation qui fait que nous nous solidarisons avec les exploités, ce point de départ, tout comme en Allemagne, c'est la condition qui nous est faite à l'Université.'[23]

Debout les damnés de Nanterre[24]

'Nous pouvons affirmer, sans grand risque de nous tromper, que l'étudiant en France est, après le policier et le prêtre, l'être le plus universellement méprisé.'[25] Thus begins the pamphlet *De la misère en milieu étudiant*, distributed at Nanterre in May 1967. *De la misère* was produced at Strasbourg by students and members of the Internationale Situationniste, which has been recognized as playing a strongly influential role in the attitudes and ideas of students. The situationist 'bande dessinée', 'Le Retour de la colonne Durutti', with its delightful comic-strip images of, for example, cowboys discussing reification, was distributed at Nanterre in November 1966, and ends with an exhortation to obtain *De la misère*.[26]

[20] *Esprit* (June–July 1968), 1056.   [21] Ibid.
[22] 'Fascists who escaped from Dien Bien Phu [defeat of French Army in Vietnam in 1954] you will not escape from Nanterre'. 'Paratroopers! You were torn to pieces in Algeria and Vietnam, it'll happen again at Nanterre!' Duteuil, *Nanterre 65–66–67–68*, 211–12.
[23] 'The starting-point of the political process which leads to our solidarity with the exploited, this starting-point, as in Germany, is the condition imposed on us at the University.' Cohn-Bendit interview in *Nouvel Observateur* (8 May), quoted in Rioux and Backmann, *L'Explosion de mai*, 160.
[24] Cartoon by Siné, *Action*, 1. (It is a parody of the first line of the *Internationale*: 'Debout les damnés de la terre'/Arise the wretched of the earth.)
[25] 'We can say, without much risk of being wrong, that in France students are the most widely despised group, after the police and priests.'
[26] Reproduced Duteuil, *Nanterre 65–66–67–68*, 69–72.

De la misère is a fine exposition of the situationist political analysis of the contemporary world and the necessity to change it. With both marxist and Sartrean echoes, it also owes much to sociological thinking on the politics of everyday life, and the spectacle of consumer society. It dramatizes contemporary society as being in a state of struggle between the old and the new, but this is not an opposition marked old-negative/new-positive, for capitalism is itself locked into battles between new and old forms. This identification of the nature of modern capitalism as being all-encompassing, to the extent that even new ideas and forces are in fact advancing its power rather than breaking with it, is a major feature of situationist thinking. 'La puissance du spectacle actuel est qu'il gouverne non seulement le monde qu'il produit, mais aussi les rêves que ses victimes se fabriquent pour échapper à son règne.'[27] And so the pamphlet compares 'real' and 'illusory' protests, since there are ways of challenging capitalism which are fighting it on its own terrain, engaging in a battle of mirrors and shadows. Neither the unions, nor the Communist Party (singled out here as so often with particular venom), nor the spontaneous revolt of the 'blousons noirs' offers any threat to the totalitarian enemy which has their positions already staked out within itself, although, like the black looters of America, the latter are definitely admired.[28] The power of derision in such criminality, taking the edicts of consumer society literally, is subversively championed.

The pamphlet points to the student's peculiar position within modern society to explain his literal poverty and moral wretchedness. His income is lower than a low-paid worker, yet by birth and ambition he is a member of the richest classes. Ideologically, he considers himself an adult, yet in reality he is still in tutelage to his family and to the state, with all the infantilization that implies. His terrain is the terrain of knowledge, which explains both his marginalization and his power. Unlike the worker, who still constitutes a threat to the capitalist order, the student's substance is ideology. He lives and breathes false consciousness and alienation, yet this is also his salvation: given an understanding of his position, his protest and challenge is an immensely dangerous one, for he can rock directly the most important boat of all in the society of spectacle, the boat of its totalitarian control of its representations and knowledge which is crucial to its continuing reproduction. Spontaneity *per se* is always negative for the situationists, since it unthinkingly reproduces its own situation. It is

[27] 'The power of the spectacle today is that it governs not only the world it is producing, but also the dreams that its victims are making to escape from its rule.' 'Avant-propos', *De la misère* (Aix-en-Provence, Editions Sulliver, 1995), 5.

[28] 'Le Déclin et la chute de l'économie marchande et spectaculaire', *Internationale Situationniste*, 10 (Mar. 1966), 3 (repr. separately 1993 under Guy Debord's name).

the recognition of the tyranny of mythology, of spectacle that leads to the importance of political theory and a political *prise de conscience*.

To add to his unhappiness, it is argued that the student is living through a particularly acute moment of confrontation between the old and the new forms of knowledge. Modern society no longer needs an élite: the university masses are to be given just the knowledge necessary to perform their function as managers and agents of the technocratic. Most vociferous in their defence of the status quo are the 'feudal' teachers who are losing their power and their prestige, their individual control over knowledge and learning.[29] To challenge the archaic and authoritarian nature of some of the teaching practices is to help to hasten in capitalism's brave new world. It is an impossible contradiction, unless one accepts the revolution of permanent contestation, because the layers historically accreted to form the 'vieux monde' (described in terms strikingly similar to Sartre's *pratico-inerte*) inevitably give shape to the world and our views of the present and future: 'Les morts hantent encore les cerveaux des vivants.'[30]

La révolution n'est pas un spectacle pour anglicistes

One of the more enigmatic graffiti seen in Nanterre itself,[31] the above statement could be read as a rather ironic announcement of one of May 68's most famous novels, *Derrière la vitre*, written by the anglicist Robert Merle, lecturer at Nanterre and well-established novelist.[32] It is frequently quoted for its documentary value as a source on Nanterre. Since Merle states in his introduction that his project to write about student experience at Nanterre predates the events of May, and that from November 1967 onwards he had been talking to students about their life on campus, the slogan may well indeed have been an in-joke and direct reference to him.

The day of 22 March 1968 on the campus at Nanterre, the day which came to baptize a movement, is used as the framing device for the novel, from its first dated section starting at 6 a.m. as Abdelaziz gets up for work on the campus building site, until '23 heures 30', when the administrative

---

[29] Cf. *Révoltes logiques*, special issue on May, on the transition from the elitist system and professorial power to the production lines of mass education.

[30] *De la misère*, 44: 'The dead still haunt the minds of the living.'

[31] Hall C Rz Nanterre, quoted Besançon, *Les Murs*, 57. 'The revolution is not a spectacle for English specialists.'

[32] He won the Goncourt in 1949 for *Weekend à Zuydecote*, set during the evacuation of Dunkirk. *La Mort est mon métier*, a fictionalized study of the Auschwitz commander, and *Un animal doué de raison* were also well known. He was a 'more English than the English' specialist of English, often inviting students to his room for afternoon tea.

building top floors are occupied in protest at the arrest of Xavier Langlade of the Comité Vietnam National. The novel is composed of short chapters (eleven main chapters, the majority with several subchapters) covering a wide cast of characters: students, teaching staff, North African labourers, administrators.

There is a small group of characters at the centre of the novel about whom the reader, by the end of the narrative, has learnt a great deal. Lucien Ménestrel, interminably struggling with his financial problems, his medieval French translation, and his *explication de texte*. His father died during his 'philosophy year'[33] and his mother refuses to continue her support after the *bac*, even though she is in the financial position to do so. She writes him stilted letters explaining she cannot afford to send him money and at the same time detailing the work she has had done on the grounds of her estate. His attempt to secure work, via the patronage of his former lycée teacher Demiremont, looking after the children of a Mrs Russell, is a significant strand of the plot. Abdelaziz is an Algerian worker living on the bidonville, and working on the campus building site. Through interior monologue, and interaction with his friends, we hear a great deal about his life and aspirations, his past attempts to learn to write, his friendships, the racism he faces, and the relations between the workers, the tensions of their lives, the precariousness of their social situation. Through this character, the *banlieue* is created, not as an urban wasteland of criminality and violence, but as a place of desolation blighting social aspirations which are taken for granted as realities by the other characters: family, education, friendships, and money. David Schulz is very rich, Jewish, an anarchist who is politically active in the *groupuscules*, and the son of a liberal, supportive father. Merle has him composing with Cohn-Bendit and Ben Saïd the famous text resulting from the administration occupation, the first public statement from what will become *le mouvement du 22 mars*. Jaumet is a member of the French Communist Party with intransigent anti-*gauchiste* views; many of the received views of the Communist Party in May are reiterated here: it is acknowledged by the lecturers to be the only non-disruptive political group on campus, which is simultaneously praise from them, confirmation of the argument that the PCF was on the side of law and order, and therefore also confirmation of a discourse of condemnation. Denise Fargeot is also a politically active PCF member. Her plotting to develop a closer personal relationship with Jaumet is another important strand followed through the text; with the final words of the novel she finally plucks up the courage to invite him to go on holiday with her. Simon is one of the workerist students (whose

---

[33] The equivalent of the Upper Sixth, the final year leading to the *baccalauréat*.

politics is characterized by unconditional support for and celebration of
the working class), very impatient with the anarchists, who pronounces
his decision in the final scene to leave Nanterre and take a factory job; his
girlfriend Josette immediately decides to imitate him, though not for
political reasons. Jacqueline Cavaillon, Levasseur, and Delmont are
teaching assistants, and the latter particularly suffers very much from the
insecurities of his position. For many of these characters, the narration
switches back and forth between the first and third persons, a traditional
technique to heighten the individual psychological dramas, as both the
introspective and the interactional dimensions of characterization come
into play; they are also part of a much larger group of characters who occa-
sionally move centre stage. The consequence is that a sense of typicality is
conveyed, that the totality of Nanterre is being represented. The use of
historical figures such as Cohn-Bendit, Duteuil, Ben Saïd, Krivine, and
Dean Grappin, serves to reinforce this, as does the recognizable geography,
and historical reality of the events.

In his introduction to the novel, Merle draws attention to the technique
of 'simultaneity' he has used: 'Pour réaliser mon dessein, j'ai employé,
j'espère en le renouvelant, un procédé (. . .) qui avait cours dans les
années trente de ce siècle et qui s'appelait, je crois, le simultanéisme.'[34]
The return to this literary technique of the 1930s is revealing. A technique
which had a decisive influence on French literature, the most famous
example perhaps being Sartre's second volume of his *Chemins de la liberté*
trilogy, *Le Sursis*, it is associated most particularly with the work of John
Dos Passos in his monumental trilogy *USA*. Philippe Labro echoes the
same sentiments many years later: 'Dans ma vie multiple de journaliste-
romancier-témoin-un petit peu acteur (. . .) cette impression, donc, de
vivre un chapitre de Dos Passos. Oui, bizarrement, dans l'accumulation
quotidienne d'événements disparates et de paroles folles, dans ce climat
d'attente et d'imprévisible, c'était la musique des romans de Dos Passos
qui traversait le jugement littéraire que j'essayais de porter.'[35] For just
such a chaotic and uncontrollable accumulation of events, Nanterre-
la-Folie was dubbed Nanterre-la-folle in May, and the first conclusion to
draw from the exploitation of this well-known technique, governed by
the representation of 'lived experience', is its role in guaranteeing the

---

[34] 'To achieve my aims, I used and, I hope, renewed a technique current in the 1930s and which was called, I believe, simultaneism.' *Derrière la vitre*, 11.

[35] 'In my multifaceted existence as journalist, novelist, witness, and, to a small extent, protagonist, I had the impression of living a chapter from Dos Passos. Yes, strangely, in the daily accumulation of disparate events and insane words, in that climate of expectation and unpredictability, it was the music of the novels of Dos Passos which informed the literary judgement I tried to make.' François Armanet *et al.* (eds.), *Sous les pavés la plage: Mai 68 vu par Gilles Caron* et al. (La Sirène, 1993), 55.

authenticity of this representation of May, given that an important dimension of the collective imaginary of May associates it with immediacy and multiplicity. Moreover, Merle's narratives have their origin in student narratives and his own personal experience, so that a second major element of authenticity in narrative is therefore firmly in place, namely the autobiographical. Merle is also true to the historiography of Nanterre in the use of the well-known sequences of events: the Missoffe drama at the swimming pool, the réforme Fouchet, Grappin and the Nazi insult, the geopolitics of the site, the 'listes noires', the police on campus, the disruptions of lectures, all the famous events are either recalled or are part of the narrative development of the 22 March.

However, Merle adds another element to the question of simultaneity:

> Il s'agit de personnages, présentés sans liens entre eux et vivant isolément et parallèlement, dans un même lieu, dans un même temps, des existences séparées. C'est parce que le thème de la solitude et de l'incommunicabilité m'est apparu dès le début, à travers les confidences qui m'étaient faites, comme le thème majeur de la vie d'étudiant à Nanterre, que j'ai utilisé ce type de narration.[36]

A number of characters do register their sense of isolation, and difficulties of communication of all kinds fill out the warp and weft of the unfolding narrative, reinforced by the use of both *je* and *il/elle*: the narrator and reader share the insights of silent introspection not revealed to any other characters. The psychological juxtaposition of individuals echoes the spatial and social juxtapositions of class and Nanterre, particularly class and race. Robert Frye has drawn attention to the importance of closed worlds in Merle's fiction;[37] the student world behind the window—where again, Merle is being true to established representations, for Nanterre is frequently described in terms of a ghetto, living 'en vase clos'—is replicated in other more symbolic, thematic, psychological, partitions.

The novels of Dos Passos sought to create a collage effect, like a kind of narrative cubism, to render the immediacy of life as it is lived; they appealed to Sartre because of the effective rejection of the figure of the omniscient narrator. There is, he argued, no position outside the world, outside history, from which to have an overview of people's lives, and therefore in the name of historicity (the fact that our being cannot be

---

[36] 'These are characters, without links between them, who are living separate existences in isolation, next to each other, in the same place, at the same time. I used this kind of narration because the theme of solitude and lack of communication appeared to me from the beginning, in the secrets imparted to me, to be the major theme of student life at Nanterre.' *Derrière la vitre*, 11–12.

[37] Robert D. Frye, 'An Introduction to Robert Merle: A World Under Siege', *Stanford French Review*, 11/3 (Fall 1987), 345–57.

divorced from the moment of history we live in), Sartre sought to change the mode of narration which belonged to a time when there was more confidence in the notion of a sense of intelligible purpose to human endeavour. Simultaneity is therefore privileging horizontal time over vertical time: synchrony over diachrony, the experience of the everyday over history. This relationship is very important for *Derrière la vitre*, but interestingly enough Merle discusses it not in relation to simultaneity, but in relation to the choice of the day of 22 March:

> **Je sais bien que le 22 mars qui, sur le moment, fut vécu comme un simple épisode de la guérilla anti-autorité des gauchistes, fut magnifié par *ce qui se passa ensuite* et devint, dans l'esprit des participants, une journée importante, insigne, digne de donner son nom au mouvement qui prétendait incarner, mieux qu'aucun autre, 'l'esprit de la révolution'. Pour le romancier, pourtant, qui cherche à retrouver la vérité du moment sous les fastes de l'Histoire, le 22 mars appartient à la quotidienneté de Nanterre et ne doit pas en être détaché.[38]**

All history is retrospective. The anecdote of the civil servant effusively congratulating the father of Victor Hugo as he registered his son's birth ('c'est *vous* le père de Victor Hugo! mes félicitations!') gets the point across as a joke: Hugo's date of birth is only significant historiographically; the baby and the author belong to different narratives, as transposing the author into the baby's present shows. In his preface, Merle is seeking to make a distinction between fiction and History: the former renders the contingencies of the present, the latter casts a different coherence over it, as though the former mimics the formlessness of living while the latter imposes meaning. Yet narrative too is retrospective. In any narrative, the events are related because of their significance; the point of the story will be unknown to the listener, but it has to be known to the narrating subject.

What Merle is saying is that his narrative is a double one. It is because of the tension between history and the everyday that he has chosen 22 March, a date in history, in order to narrate it from the point of view of the everyday, the realm of one damn thing after another. That tension can be traced in the text, and there are points of slippage between the historical knowledge of the enunciation (that this is where May starts) and the ignorance of the *énoncé*, the lived experience of the characters. One example

[38] 'I am aware that although 22 March was lived at the time as a simple episode in the anti-authority guerrilla war of the *gauchistes*, it was magnified by *what happened later*, and became, in the minds of the participants, an important day, a day of note, worthy of giving its name to the movement which claimed, more than any other, to embody "the spirit of the revolution". For the novelist, however, who is trying to retrieve the truth of the moment from under the ceremonies of History, 22 March belongs to the everyday life of Nanterre and ought not be detached from it.' *Derrière la vitre*, 10–11.

would be the ironic denial of any importance to the events themselves from Jaumet at the end, offering his view that 'les groupusses ne réussiront jamais à mettre derrière eux assez d'étudiants pour devenir une force réelle de contestation, et (*petit rire*) ils réussiront encore moins à faire bouger les masses'.[39] Similarly the Vietnamese student Nunc, an informer with a long past of political activism against *gauchisme*, communism, and the FLN in Algeria, thinks that these *gauchiste* leaders were very sharp and would go far.[40] The stress on the everyday as the antithesis of history also has the effect of embodying another important element of the imaginary of May, its unpredictability. The more the characters comment on the political ineffectiveness of the experiences at Nanterre, the more they are confirming the historical narrative: May will take everyone by surprise.

Although one can in this way identify the subject of the enunciation as a historically situated subject, with knowledge of May 68, Merle's view is the novelist operates with a different knowledge, the knowledge of the everyday. But his other comments on narrative technique in his preface suggest that, while the everyday may be incompatible with history, its own coherence, and even the possibility of getting at the novelist's truth, is also in doubt here. Merle contrasts his approach with the pyrotechnics of the Nouveau Roman: 'une religion nouvelle, vieille déjà de quelques années, veut que le récit soit cassé, les situations annihilées, les personnages mis en pièces. En fin de quoi, l'auteur se met lui-même en question et se détruit.'[41] While unconvincingly protesting his lack of hostility to such techniques, Merle argues that to render everyday life, during an ordinary day rounded off by an extraordinary night, his needs are different: 'J'avais donc besoin de personnages crédibles, de situations réelles, de récit cohérent.'[42] He therefore needs the subjectivity of an author overseeing all that. But this is where things let him down: he finds it impossible to determine a view over events. While this is not supposed to be narration for narration's sake, but a coherent story, a story told for a purpose, with 'un point de vue défini', the narrative defeats the author's philosophy. Instead of a truth to see off the external imposed distortions of history,

---

[39] 'The *groupuscules* will never manage to get enough students behind them to become a real force of contestation, and (with a little laugh) even less will they manage to get the masses to move.' Ibid. 540. Professor Schwartz told the *groupuscules* exactly the same thing ('ce n'est pas en paralysant la faculté que vous ferez tomber de Gaulle'), and later considered the very fact that they nearly achieved their aims to indicate an unsuspected power in their strategy. (Bertolino, *Les Trublions*, 373.)

[40] *Derrière la vitre*, 531–2.

[41] Ibid. 12: 'a new religion, already a few years old, is demanding that the story be broken up, plots eliminated, and characters torn to pieces. After which, the author challenges and destroys himself.'

[42] Ibid. 13: 'I therefore needed credible characters, real situations, a coherent story.'

what he discovers are the uncertainties of fictionality. While he presents this as a judgemental rather than a theoretical problem—the contradictions of events were such that it was impossible to settle for *one* view of them—it is difficult not to see the incoherences of fiction aping the incoherences of history, given the structural homogeneity of historical and fictional narrative. Effectively he has ended up in spite of himself with the language of the Nouveau Roman, the indeterminacy of narrative, the death of the all-knowing narrator. Paradoxically, it is the present-absent knowledge of the fact of May 68 which emerges here as the degree zero of narrative truth: May will come next. But this gives no access to meaning. Like the historiographies of May, the fictions of May are the scene of self-conscious dramas of the failure of interpretation.

Patrick Combes argues that *Derrière la vitre* focuses on private events and psychological narratives, thus participating in the collective elaboration of a myth of May which, like all myth, is depoliticized by being naturalized, which is, in his view, a particular travesty, given May's stress on the ideological. It is certainly true that *Derrière la vitre* develops the psychological as a value in the narrative, both thematically and structurally. Yet it is at the same time faithful to the dominant themes and ideas of the student protest in its depiction of the student condition: the dependency of students who are not fully autonomous adults (*Derrière la vitre* gives a significant amount of space to the family, to the politics and psychology of this crucial institution); the hybrid, transient nature of their situation (students are said to be less concerned with what they are than with their futures); the hierarchical relationship between academic staff and students; the hierarchical relationship within the academic profession, with the 'maîtres-assistants' at the bottom of the heap; and the inadequate pedagogy. The details of the latter are beautifully accurate: the lack of liaison between lecturers and seminar tutors over the material taught, the lack of books, the old, old, curriculum, the unthinking humiliation of Danièle Toronto who manages to get through an exposé to a lecture-hall of students, very nervously, and receives congratulations, yet the lecturer then proceeds to expound the authoritative truth with no reference to anything she has said. Through its multiple stories, fictional and non-fictional, the major themes of politics, class, and sexuality are treated. *Gauchiste* themes are well represented too: the political nature of knowledge, knowledge serving the interests of the bourgeoisie; workerism; Vietnam; police-state; repressive sexualities; the need for provocation and contestation.

But the novel is not just reproducing this as the indexing of reality. It creates its own perspective which places these themes in a particular angle of vision. First, by the use of North African characters, the multiplicities of Nanterre are integrated into the plot. Merle contrasts the bedrooms in the *résidences* with the rooms, shared by several men, in the *bidonville*. Differences in education (from which the North Africans are excluded), work, and sexuality are underlined. We learn about Abdelaziz's various relations with white girls, his painful memories of dances in France, his friends' wives at home in Algeria. The importance of this juxtaposition is revealed in the fact that it is Abdelaziz who sees the students 'derrière les vitres' as he toils on the buildings which will house more of them, and David Schulz sees the North Africans 'de l'autre côté de la vitre'. Interestingly enough, these two characters meet, and cross the divide. David goes over to talk to the Algerians, and invites Abdelaziz into the Résidence. And while one might think that the effect of the *bidonville* would be to rob the student protest of significance (the students are not in exile, subject to discrimination, they are privileged within society), in fact these points are well registered within the novel by Ménestrel and David. The ideological critique of racism advanced by Abdelaziz, who argues that Camus's *L'Étranger* demonstrates the breathtaking ignorance and arrogance of much literary criticism that can completely ignore the novel's basic lack of verisimilitude in having a white man executed in the 1940s in Algeria for killing an Arab, confirms rather than invalidates the *gauchiste* view of the political nature of knowledge and culture.[43] Furthermore, the hostility of other Algerian workers to the French activates the memory of the Algerian War and racism.[44]

A second structuring theme is revealed in the amount of space devoted to women and sexuality. Combes argues that the importance of sexuality, the fantasies, aspirations, relationships of the male and female characters, undermines the politics of the students, suggesting the former is much more important that the latter. 'Pour Merle, c'est net: la jeunesse politique est plus hantée, à Nanterre, par des difficultés sexuelles que motivée politiquement. Le thème de l'éducation sentimentale, érotique, le dispute dans son récit aux péripéties militantes du 22 mars. Le militantisme est une hystérie.'[45] I would disagree, on two grounds. First, the writing of sexuality in the novel is immensely complex, involving history, geography, politics as well as psychology, and is not just subordinated to a discourse of trivialization; secondly, it is articulated with other related elements: sexual liberation, women, and femininity, which in themselves

[43] *Derrière la vitre*, 145.
[44] There are two references to Charonne, the deaths of nine people at the métro station on the occasion of a communist demonstration against the war. There are none to 17 Oct. 1961, when over 200 Algerian demonstrators died at the hands of the police. See Ch. 6.
[45] 'For Merle, it is clear, Nanterre's political youth is more haunted by sexual difficulties than politically motivated. The theme of their emotional, erotic education tries to dominate the story of the militants on 22 March. Militant politics is a hysteria.' Patrick Combes, *La Littérature et le mouvement de mai 68* (Seghers, 1984), 180.

are not only sociologically important, but also suggest that, in relation to the representation of 1968, *Derrière la vitre* is a political text in the sense that politics will come to be defined, that is, not just confined to political activism but embracing culture and society. The thematic importance of women and gender in the text is therefore well in keeping, whether the author liked it or not, with a feminist definition of politics.[46] There is also voluminous evidence of the importance of discussion of sexuality in *gauchisme* in general and to Nanterre in particular, in conferences on Reich, and in the stress on non-repressive, non-bourgeois sexuality. This is not to say that the representation is not male-centred: it tends to be typical of the kind of notions of sexual liberation that will be severely criticized by feminists; but in the prominence it gives to gender, relationships, and women students, it is actually developing a configuration that is becoming increasingly important, politically, rather than just recycling a stereotypical dichotomy sex/politics.

From the opening words of the novel, Merle places women at the centre of the relationship between Paris and Nanterre, and at the same time complicates the 'centre v. periphery' structure. 'A l'endroit même où s'élève aujourd'hui l'église de Nanterre, les jeunes filles, au Moyen Age, venaient de la capitale supplier l'ombre de Geneviève de dissiper les premiers symptômes des maternités imprudentes.' The patron saint of Paris was born in Nanterre. The pilgrimages in spiritual times were pilgrimages to seek forgiveness for illicit sex, although the transgressors came from Paris. As the secular age displaced the religious one, the pilgrimages ceased, and Nanterre's virtuous young girls take centre stage: 'Les filles étaient vertueuses, et plus que tout autre, la rosière, élue chaque année par le conseil municipal avec l'approbation du curé. (. . .) Sa présence choqua, chose curieuse, un préfet du second Empire. (. . .) L'année suivante, l'abbé resta dans son presbytère, et avant même l'avènement de la IIIe République, la première rosière laïque fut élue à Nanterre.'[47] The Third Republic introduced compulsory education for girls; the postwar boom years brought girls into higher education in unprecedented numbers. Merle uses history to say that for contemporary women students the journey from Paris to Nanterre is no longer a journey from transgression

---

[46] Merle's next novel *Les Hommes protégés*, was roundly berated on both sides of the Atlantic, for its views on masculinity.

[47] *Derrière la vitre*, 19–20. 'On the site of Nanterre's church today, girls came in the Middle Ages from Paris to implore Geneviève's shade to make the first symptoms of imprudent pregnancies disappear.' 'The girls were virtuous, and the most virtuous of all was the 'rosière', elected every year by the local council with the approval of the parish priest. Curiously enough, his involvement shocked a prefect of the Second Empire. The following year, the priest remained in his presbytery, and even before the commencement of the Third Republic, the first secular 'rosière' was elected in Nanterre.'

to salvation and innocence, as far as their bourgeois parents in the rich districts of Passy and Neuilly are concerned: 'Quoi, dirent les pères, nos filles, élevées avec le plus grand soin, seraient déportées dans des banlieues industrielles, contaminées par les communistes et violées par les bidonvilles.'[48] Yet they are wrong. Neither the *bidonvilles* of the families nor the new office blocks with their 'cellules monastiques [où] personne ne dort et personne n'a besoin d'intimité'[49] offer any corruption. But the university has been built on the very site of one of the *bidonvilles*, scattering families, and their student blocks of tiny cells are certainly not monastic.

The interplay of spaces, sexuality, and the history of modern times through the day of 22 March is shadowed by these other histories. Nanterre has burst out of the 'vieux murs' of the Sorbonne, which can no longer contain it, but the practices of medieval Paris still haunt the present: 'Comme le seigneur du Moyen Age avait droit à son pigeonnier, l'administration de la Fac de Nanterre, afin que nul n'ignore qu'administrer est plus important qu'enseigner, a reçu en partage une tour.'[50] Ménestrel grapples with his medieval translation, and the teaching practices are, to borrow from another commentary, 'des structures hiérarchisées d'une société figée dans un autoritarisme médiéval'.[51] The ultimate expression of industrial modernity, the glass and concrete of Nanterre contains the pre-industrial world of the medieval Sorbonne, and sits in the mud of Nanterre, surrounded by *bidonvilles*, 'taudis' of the industrial world replicating nineteenth-century conditions.[52] The symbolization of Nanterre as a juxtaposition of closed worlds with their glass frontiers is interwoven with other juxtapositions through time, through the archeology of superimposed sites. The migrations and passages are not only continually reversing the positions of centre and margin, but also have their own 'archeology'. Truly 'les morts hantent les cerveaux des vivants'. May 68 bursts out of Nanterre towards Paris, and for a time Nanterre is the symbolic heart of Paris. The relationship between the periphery and the centre is reconfigured by the dramas of modernity and sexuality at Nanterre.

[48] *Derrière la vitre*, 24. 'What', said the fathers, 'our daughters, raised with the greatest care, are apparently to be deported to the industrial suburbs, infected by communists and raped by the shanty towns?'
[49] Ibid. 51: 'monastic cells where no one sleeps and no one needs intimacy.'
[50] Ibid. 63. 'Just as the lord in the Middle Ages was entitled to his dovecote, so the administration of the Faculty of Nanterre was endowed with a tower block so that no one could remain ignorant of the fact administration is more important than teaching.'
[51] Rioux and Backmann, *L'Explosion de mai*, 57: 'hierarchical structures of a society stuck in medieval authoritarianism.'
[52] Charrière, *Le Printemps des enragés*, 17.

Bouillon de culture

'Quand j'entends le mot "culture" je sors mes CRS';[53] 'Touraine, ou le non-dépassement devenu invivable';[54] 'Professeurs vous êtes vieux . . . et votre culture aussi';[55] 'Vive la cité unie-vers cithère';[56] 'Je t'aime!!! Oh! dites-le avec des pavés!'[57] 'Ne vous emmerdez plus! Emmerdez les autres!'[58] From slogans on the wall to tracts such as that of the Tendance fédéraliste révolutionnaire on the 'misère de l'étudiant': 'Quand on ne lui chie pas dans la gueule on lui pisse au cul',[59] 'l'esprit de Nanterre' is synonymous with wit, irreverence, and the more brutally confrontational 'dérision', a prime method of attack against culture, knowledge, and pedagogy. 'Ne dites plus: Monsieur le pédagogue. Dites: crève, salope!'[60] The first meaning of 'bouillon de culture' is 'culture' in the scientific sense of the term, in which bacteria can be grown, and although one inscription suggests it can evoke something rather mechanical, 'La créativité n'est pas un bouillon de culture',[61] detached from this it rendered the sense of a profusion of new cultural forms associated with May, including the imaginative, joyous, and angry exploitation of language as the embodiment of the struggle between the old world and the new. Paul Thibaud accurately points to the premonitory qualities of cinema, especially *Weekend*, *La Chinoise*, and *Pierrot le fou*, in encapsulating the extraordinary maelstrom they were about to live through:

[53] 'When I hear the word "culture" I get out my CRS' (*Miroir de l'histoire* (June–July 1973), 28, a reference to the well-known phrase of the 1930s representing Nazi hostility to culture: 'When I hear the word culture I get out my revolver.' CRS, the Compagnie Républicaine de Sécurité, is a police organization primarily responsible for state security and public order. Although they had a prominent role in May, and featured strongly as enemy figures in the posters and slogans, many think they were more disciplined and less violent than the Paris police.

[54] 'Touraine, or non-transcendence having become unliveable.' Besançon, *Les Murs*, 64.

[55] 'You lecturers are old, and your culture is too.' Duteuil, *Nanterre 65–66–67–68*, 161.

[56] Ibid. In this slogan 'Long live the student residence' the word 'universitaire', is dismantled into a poetic-sounding homonym 'cité unie-vers cithère' (united-towards/verse cithère) which does not mean anything; but 'cithère' recalls 'cité', and the rather exotic musical instrument, the cithara, and the multiple ambiguities created recall both the situationists and the surrealists in the hi-jacking of the ordinary in order to destroy it. That this poeticization is applied to the usually hideous student residence blocks in itself raises a smile.

[57] 'I love you!!! Oh! say it with paving stones!' Ibid. 18; Hall A1 Nanterre.

[58] 'Don't be bored any more! Annoy others!' Ibid.; Hall C Rz Nanterre.

[59] 'When they are not shitting into his gob they are pissing up his arse.' (Taken from a footnote in the text of *De la misère*.) Duteuil, *Nanterre 65– 66– 67– 68*, 73.

[60] 'Don't say: Monsieur le pédagogue (the formally polite mode of reference, somewhat ironised by the substitution of 'pédagogue' for 'professeur'). Say: die, you bitch!' R. Viénet, *Enragés et situationnistes dans le mouvement des occupations* (Gallimard, 1968).

[61] Duteuil, *Nanterre 65–66–67–68*, 161.

> Quant à Godard, nous vivons depuis un mois dans son ombre. (. . .) Les enfants de Marx et du coca-cola[62] occupent le pavé; on ne joue pas encore Mozart dans les cours de ferme, mais au moins dans la cour de la Sorbonne; les voitures flambent comme dans *Pierrot* et *Weekend*. (. . .) Le Front de Libération de Seine-et-Oise figure bien la débauche présente de désaliénations. Tout ce monde de Godard: parodie, violences, irruptions de joie et de liberté, impasses, détours, paix entrevue, brutalité soudaine, c'est encore le nôtre.[63]

'Dérision' was the favoured term of the 'enragés' and the 'prositus' for the permanently renewed 'live' contestation, for example in lectures, when the lecturer would be challenged, pitilessly mocked, and often reduced to the state where they could not go on. 'Détournement de sens' is another situationist term for a range of denunciatory procedures holding meanings up for mockery and derision. One favoured mechanism was to appropriate bourgeois disapproval as approval: headings from newspapers condemning the behaviour of *les enragés* were plastered all over Nanterre. Similarly an extract from the judgement on the affair of the *De la misère* brochure at Strasbourg, which gained some notoriety for its accurate assessment of the issues and themes of the movement, was used on the back cover of the 1976 reprint in a typical gesture of 'détournement', turning a discourse of shame into a badge of honour.

Alain Touraine suggested that 'dérision' was the reaction of the protestors faced with the perceived non-sense of the world around them;[64] the laughter and anger of derision when faced with the absurd presented as logic, when the so-called rationality and morality of the established order is driven by the interests of profit and loss and the wealth of the few. This is at least the effect of the discourse of denunciation, to create its object, be it established ideas, ways of teaching, social relations, or whatever, as that which should be denounced. Witty, facetious, burlesque, shocking, violent, parodic, ironic, the walls, posters, and publications of Nanterre, and after them the Sorbonne and the streets of Paris, fully lived up to the situationist injunction: 'les révolutions prolétariennes seront des fêtes ou ne seront pas'.[65]

[62] One of the most famous captions of *La Chinoise*.
[63] 'As for Godard, we have been living for a month in his shadow. The children of Marx and Coca-cola are occupying the road; we are not playing Mozart in farmyards yet, but at least in the Sorbonne's courtyard we are; cars are burning as in *Pierrot* and *Weekend*. The Seine-et-Oise Liberation Front is a good figure of the current orgy of de-alienation. This whole world of Godard's, a world of parody, violence, eruptions of joy and freedom, dead ends, detours, glimpses of peace, sudden brutalities, is our world.' Paul Thibaud, 'Imaginons', *Esprit*, 36/372 (June–July 1968), 1032.
[64] Labro *et al.*, *Ce n'est qu'un début*, 44.
[65] *De la misère*, 56: 'Proletarian revolutions will be festivals or will not exist.'

3 Order and disorder: scenes of violence

In an interview for Philippe Labro's book on the May events: *Ce n'est qu'un début*[1] Alain Geismar, general secretary of SNESup until his resignation on 27 May, and one of the leading figures of May, talks of the impact which the miners' strike of 1963 had on him, 'le fait politique fondamental qui m'a servi personnellement de référence'.[2] It was a major strike which lasted for five weeks, and there was much public sympathy for the miners, but nothing was done; no one mobilized. Geismar deplored the passivity which led to failure, drawing the political lesson that inertia serves the status quo: 'le fait donc que ce mouvement ait pu pourrir dans l'isolement quand il était évident pour quiconque, homme politique ou syndicaliste, de bonne foi à l'époque, qu'il aurait suffi de déclencher la grève de la fonction publique pour qu'immédiatement ils obtiennent satisfaction, ceci m'a servi de révélateur'.[3] Much of the voluntarism and activism of 1968 is self-consciously acting out the Sartrean dictum that you cannot choose not to choose, that not to take a stand is as much an intervention as taking one, and Geismar learns the value of 'l'action directe'. Cohn-Bendit cites the large demonstrations in May 1958 in relation to events in Algeria as important for his political formation. In spite of the tens of thousands on the streets nothing changed, nothing was prevented.[4] This time the political lesson points to the limitations of traditional means of protest: strikes and demonstrations and the frustration with them as the state protects and the bourgeoisie defends its interests. To step over those limits is to meet with violence. These are the kinds of arguments which led to the terrorist tactics and assassinations of the Red Brigades and Red Army

---

[1] 'Ce n'est qu'un début, continuons le combat' ('This is only a beginning, let's keep up the struggle') is a phrase that was blasted out on car horns (long, long, short, short, long etc.), just as 'l'Algérie française' had been a decade earlier.

[2] Labro *et al.*, *Ce n'est qu'un début* (1968), 182: 'the basic political event which for me personally was a major reference'. Cf. also J. Kergoat in A. Artous (ed.), *Retours sur mai* (Montreuil: La Brèche-PEC, 1988) for a substantial discussion of this strike.

[3] 'The fact that the movement could slowly disintegrate in isolation when it was obvious to anyone, any politician or union leader, acting in good faith at the time, that all it would take was a strike in the public sector for their demands to be met immediately, that was a real revelation for me.' *Ce n'est qu'un début*, 182.

[4] *Magazine littéraire* (May, 1968), 20.

Faction in Italy and Germany.[5] The *Gauche prolétarienne* consistently argued for the necessity of violent tactics, but never turned into an armed terrorist group. None the less, the view that the social order was established and maintained by violence was widely shared on the left.

'De la contestation de l'université à la contestation de la société': countless student graffiti underlined the ambition of the protest movement, to change society totally. It was taken for granted that it could not be changed by peaceful means. That the police were brought onto the campus, at Nanterre and at the Sorbonne, was living proof that state violence, coercion, and repression were the social realities to be faced. The influential German militant Rudi Dutschke placed the German students protests exactly in this light: 'Pour la première fois depuis la fin de la guerre, une bonne partie des étudiants s'étaient dressés contre la structure de base, autoritaire, de la société allemande. Par leurs manifestations, ils l'avaient obligée à montrer son vrai visage, celui de l'autorité irrationnelle.'[6] Society is then indeed a spectacle, a spectacle of order, organization, and political tolerance serving the interests of the bourgeoisie and masking the ugly realities which any serious challenge immediately reveals: 'Rompre les règles du jeu propres à l'ordre capitaliste dominant ne peut avoir pour résultat que de démasquer pleinement le système en tant que "dictature de la violence".'[7] The whole point of this is to reveal where the key points of the system are, namely the institutions of the bourgeois state (justice, parliament, prisons, police stations) and business, to translate the moral force of the current unrest into organized opposition, to acknowledge the ever-increasing violence of international imperialism, including genocide in Vietnam, bombing of China, invasion of North Vietnam or South America, and to prepare for an escalation of the conflict, via 'des formes de lutte n'ayant plus qu'une ressemblance assez lointaine avec celles que nous employons à l'heure actuelle'.[8] Death and destruction are perceived as capitalism's weapons, and like must be met with like. It should be remembered that Dutschke himself was the object of an assassination attempt in 1968, and although he survived, he was very seriously injured. In France, direct action against American targets such

[5] See D. Cohn-Bendit, *Nous l'avons tant aimée, la révolution* (Seuil, 1986), iii. 'La Guerre', for interviews with former members of terrorist groups.

[6] 'For the first time since the end of the war, a large number of students had taken a stand against the basic authoritarian structure of German society. By their demonstrations, they had forced it to show its real face, the face of irrational authority.' 'Les Étudiants anti-autoritaires face aux contradictions présentes du capitalisme et face au tiers monde', U. Bergmann *et al.*, *La Révolte des étudiants allemands* (Gallimard, Idées, 1968), 174.

[7] 'Breaking the rules of the dominant capitalist order can only result in unmasking fully the system as a 'dictatorship of violence'. Ibid. 182.

[8] Ibid.: 'forms of struggle having only a distant ressemblance to those that we use at the moment'.

as the offices of American Express was one of the triggers of the Nanterre protest.

Student violence is therefore a resistance: against the forcible reimposition of 'order', that is, bourgeois disorder, against the harsh punishment meted out to those who take action, and against the occupation of the Sorbonne. The established social order has lost all moral authority, and it is difficult not to be reminded of the rhetoric of the 'non-conformists' of the early 1930s when right and left also shared the perception of society as facing imminent collapse, translated in the term 'le désordre établi'.

This may in part explain the apocalyptic side to the celebration of street violence in May. The violence of the street battles in the photographs and *Cinétracts* is a distanced, balletic violence of beautiful images: poised bodies, smoke, streetlights, flares, and dark shadows, accompanied by the deafening sounds of the gas canisters, and *pavés*. The trailer for *Cocktail Molotov*, directed by Diane Kurys, exploits this agression and tension. Starting with a scene from *Diabolo Menthe*, her previous and very successful film, it switches dramatically to a blank red screen, rapidly filling in horizontal lines with the famous image in black of a CRS, *matraque* raised above his head, accompanied by the sound of hands clapping harshly the rhythms of 'Ce n'est qu'un début, continuons le combat'. That 'Atelier populaire' poster is just one of the stylized portraits of CRS to be used, which recall some of the close-ups in the *Cinétracts*, and which are very powerful images in their own right. The aesthetics of violence celebrates the confrontation with the power of state and its machines, and finds its counterparts on the walls: 'La plus belle sculpture, c'est le pavé de grès'; 'Le lourd pavé critique c'est le pavé qu'on jette sur la gueule des flics'; 'Les tas (de flics) c'est moi';[9] 'Mettez un flic sous votre moteur';[10] 'Salaud, salaud, salaud, C.R.S. répondit l'écho.'[11]

There are therefore two closely entwined, mutually reinforcing strands to the May 68 social movements: the state and its institutions on the one hand, and society on the other. The bourgeois state is the institutional

[9] 'The finest sculpture is the paving stone in sandstone'; 'The heavy critical tome is the paving stone thrown in the face of the police' (pun on *pavé* which also means a large book); 'The pile of police is me': Besançon, *Les Murs*, 103, 15. 'Les tas' is a homonym of 'L'État', thus punning on Louis XIV's famous phrase 'L'État c'est moi'. It is in line with the accusation of personalized dictatorship that the phrase—or the variant 'L'État c'est lui'—is used on images of de Gaulle. *Le Canard enchaîné* had a long-running column on de Gaulle's administration as the 'ancien régime'.

[10] 'Put a policeman under your engine': Censier, *Miroir de l'histoire*, 24–5. Cf. the famous Esso campaign: 'mettez un tigre dans votre moteur' (put a tiger in your tank). For a recent discussion of the violence as symbolic rather than actual, see K. Reader, 'The Symbolic Violence of the May 1968 Events in France', in R. Günther and J. Windebank (eds.), *Violence and Conflict in Modern French Culture* (Sheffield Academic Press, 1994), 57–65.

[11] A chant of May 68, Jean-Louis Calvet, *La Production révolutionnaire Slogans, affiches, chansons* 'Bastard, bastard, bastard: "C.R.S.", came back the echo.' (Payot, 1976), 87.

structure keeping the bourgeoisie as class in power and reproducing the bourgeois social order. Much of the time they appear synonymous—the power of the state is maintained by the social and ideological forces of integration, for example; consumerism is both an economic order and a social-cultural phenomenon. But at times differences emerge, in the contradictions between them, contradictions between capitalism and social forces defending outmoded structures, contradictions in the dislike of the bourgeoisie for consumerism.

A rhetoric of violence also operates at times in the understanding of the functioning of ideology, culture, and mechanisms of integration and recuperation, reinforcing the representation of the social order as a virtually transparent veneer laid on the structures of a police state. Sartre argued consistently through the late 1960s and early 1970s that the state was violent and would only be overthrown by violence; those enlisted to its service were therefore keepers of the bourgeois 'peace', a situation which weighed particularly heavily on intellectuals, the living embodiments of the contradictions between the universalizing discourse and particularist interests of the bourgeoisie:

> Les étudiants qui sont déjà des techniciens du savoir pratique (. . .) ont senti immédiatement le vrai problème: on allait faire d'eux malgré tout des travailleurs salariés pour le capital ou des flics qui permettraient de mieux tenir une boîte. (. . .) Le fait d'apprendre à devenir un flic aux ordres de la bourgeoisie n'étaient pas compensé du tout par le fait d'appartenir à un comité de base pour le Viêt-nam.[12]

Chien blanc by Romain Gary, set in the United States and France, shares this perception of violence at the heart of the social order. The dog which Gary adopts, only to discover to his horror that it is a 'white dog' trained by the Southern police to attack blacks, is the metaphoric centre of this hybrid narrative which is part autobiography, using Gary himself and his wife Jean Seberg as characters, drawing on her work with civil rights movements. With its flippant tone and uncomfortable use of sarcasm, the novel is a dissection of the paranoia generated by race (anti-black and anti-Jewish) hatred and class hatred.[13] The America of McCarthyism obsessively sniffing out 'subversives' and of race riots, is juxtaposed to the

---

[12] 'Students, who are already technicians of practical knowledge, have immediately felt the real problem: they were going to be made, in spite of themselves, into salaried workers for capital, or into policemen who would enable a firm to run better. The fact of learning to become a policeman in the bourgeoisie's service was not compensated for at all by the fact of belonging to a Vietnam Committee.' *Situations VIII*, 460.

[13] For a reading which brings out the complex interweaving of themes of Jewishness, anti-Semitism, and the Holocaust in Gary's work, see Jeffrey Mehlman, *Genealogies of the Text: Literature, Psychoanalysis, and Politics in Modern France* (Cambridge, Cambridge University Press, 1995).

France of 68; to get away from the atmosphere in America, Gary goes off to have a look at the barricades and riots in Paris. One memorable incident has him drawn to a large black American by a large fire in front of the *Bon Marché* store, chanting Black Power slogans: *Burn, baby, burn!*

> **Il est toute la vérité, cet Américain, face à la flamme française. Car, pour moi, aucun doute: lorsque nos C.R.S. se jettent en avant, matraque au poing, à Sèvres-Babylone, c'est au ghetto américain qu'ils ont affaire, au Viêt-nam, au Biafra et à tout ce qui crève de faim sur la terre. La révolte de la jeunesse de Paris s'inscrit tout naturellement dans ce récit parce qu'elle ne vise aucune situation sociale spécifique: *elle les vise toutes*.[14]**

It also, via the mechanism of the trained dog, investigates the question of spontaneity; the dog has been trained to react automatically, Pavlov-like, with hostility at the sight of a black person. Can this learnt response be unlearnt? If our responses are learnt also, through social indoctrination, to what extent can one talk about freedom and difference? 'Un flic dort en chacun de nous, il faut le tuer.'[15] The social order is not only 'out there', but within us as well. The recognition of the social dimensions of power therefore has another important effect, in bringing into focus the way power structures are lived by the individual. The boundaries of public and private, of the political and the psychological, are becoming very blurred. Collective change and individual change go together: 'Construire une révolution, c'est aussi briser toutes les chaînes intérieures.'[16]

The violence of the streets contributes to the double discourse of revolutionary social change. All destruction is at one and the same time a construction, and the utopian discourse of access to a new order, a new reality, is a permanent feature: 'Sous les pavés, la plage'; 'fermez la barricade, ouvrez la voie'. It does not take much for the discreet charms of the state and the bourgeoisie to be replaced by the exercise of violent power, which is by definition, in its abandonment of reason and reason-ableness, irrational and illogical, a repression of desires that things be different. Boundaries between rational and irrational, transgression, subversion, and order, are also then becoming very blurred. Especially as, after 13 May, society comes to a stop:

---

[14] 'This American in front of the French fire is the whole truth. For me, there is no doubt; when the CRS rush forwards, wielding their truncheon, at the Sèvres-Babylone crossroads, it's the American ghetto they are dealing with, with Vietnam, with Biafra and with all who are dying of hunger on the earth. The revolt of Paris youth is quite naturally part of the story because it is not aiming at any specific social situation: *it is aiming at them all*.' *Chien blanc* (Gallimard, 1970), 176 folio edn.

[15] 'A cop sleeps in every one of us, he must be killed.' Besançon, *Les Murs*, 77.

[16] 'To build a revolution is to break all the internal chains also.' Marc Rohan, *Paris 68* (Impact Books, 1988), 90.

> Pour ceux qui les ont vécues, ces dix journées pendant lesquelles rien n'était impossible resteront gravées à jamais. Pour toute une génération, cette échappée belle d'un pays entier, cet effacement soudain de l'ennui quotidien seront une marque indélébile. On a eu peur, on s'est révulsé, on s'est passionné, on a cru à la prise de pouvoir par on ne sait qui, à la guerre civile hideuse ou à la révolution enchantée. Mais on a vécu. Ça ne s'oublie pas.[17]

The demonstration of 13 May, backed by all the unions, marked the start of the 'second phase' of the May events. The widespread view that the police had been excessively and dangerously violent in dealing with the students had forged a common political enemy, accompanied by a shared desire for social change. In the following days over ten million people went on strike and it looked as though the students' wish to be the detonators of revolution was to be met, especially when de Gaulle disappeared. And although not all the strikers were working-class strikers (significant numbers were teachers, civil servants, managers), the importance of working-class mobilization cannot be underestimated. An alliance between workers and students was one of the major themes of the campus protestors at Nanterre and the Sorbonne, of the *enragés*, of the situationists; a common cause could be forged through a focus on shared terms: youth, exclusion, exploitation, marginalization. Workers were invited in to the Sorbonne, students marched to occupied factories. The *établi* movement was into its second year, as students went to factory jobs, expressing both the ultimate rejection of the bourgeois path their studies had engaged them on, and the desire to put their political views into practical actions of solidarity, working at the cutting edge of the class struggle.

The *gauchiste* vision of society as a battleground for confrontation between bosses and workers owed much to readings in marxism, and particularly the theoretical work of Althusser. It is something of a shock to go from the views of the *gauchiste*s to the sociological work on class in the 1950s and 1960s. The sociologists had been considering the implications of modernization, changing practices in factories, developments of new technologies, and the attendant socio-political changes. It was widely accepted that one could no longer talk about 'a working class'; there were several, depending on age, education, type of industry, region. Post-68, work on participation in strikes suggested that the better qualified the worker, the more likely they were to have been on strike, confirming earlier theses on the mismatch between old practices and new forms

---

[17] 'For those who lived through them, those 10 days when nothing was impossible will remain for ever in their memories. For a whole generation, this fine escapade of a whole country, this sudden elimination of day-to-day ennui will be an indelible mark. We were afraid, disgusted, passionate. We believed in the take-over of power by we knew not who, in hideous civil war, in enchanted revolution. But we lived. It's unforgettable.' L. Joffrin, *Mai 68* (Seuil, 1987), 193.

of knowledge and technology. And while workers certainly registered their aspirations to education, and their sympathy with the student demands, there is strong evidence that this did not go so far as to welcome student presence at the workplace. Now, Althusser certainly differentiated between different kinds of worker and education, but the distinctions are all rather technical, expressions of the determinant role of the mode of reproduction subordinating society to the demands of the economic order, and not affecting the political discourse whereby *la bourgeoisie* and *le peuple* or *le prolétariat* are the opposing protagonists.[18] But if this seems rather simplistic in retrospect, it was deliberate, for the idea that the traditional working class might be an obsolete notion was explicitly dismissed as bourgeois recuperation. From 'Pourquoi des sociologues', to the absence of sociological reference deplored by Domenach, to graffiti, the clash between *gauchisme* and sociology is a constant: 'Quand le dernier des sociologues aura été étranglé avec les tripes du dernier bureaucrate, aurions-nous encore des "problèmes"?'[19]

Tout va bien: 'On a raison de séquestrer les patrons'[20]

However much the strikes are a major element of the period, pre-May, during May, and post-May, however much the participation of the workers was the key element turning student protest into a potential revolution, however much an alliance with the workers was a key plank of intellectuals' and student demand, it is none the less true that factories and workers tend to be conspicuous by their absence from the imaginative literature: 'Le thème des luttes ouvrières, pourtant mythologique, est absent des romans, c'est à peine un paradoxe. Cela s'explique certes, dans un premier temps, par des raisons esthétiques: le réalisme du XXe est caduc; et le monde prolétarien a déserté notre littérature.'[21] The relationship posited between

---

[18] See 'Appareils et appareils idéologiques d'État', *Positions* (Editions sociales, 1976), 86; 'La Philosophie comme arme de la révolution', ibid. 41–56.

[19] 'When the last sociologist has been strangled with the intestines of the last bureaucrat, would we still have 'problems'?' Besançon, *Les Murs*, 156.

[20] Slogan on banner hanging over the entrance to the factory as Susan and Jacques arrive. This is a *Gauche prolétarienne* slogan. See D. Drake, '*On a raison de se révolter*: The Response of *la Gauche Prolétarienne* to the Events of May–June 1968', in J. Windebank and R. Günther (eds.), *Violence and Conflict in the Politics and Society of Modern France* (Lewiston, Queenston, Lampeter, Edwin Mellen Press, 1995), 61–72.

[21] 'The mythological theme of workers' struggles is missing from the novels, but this is hardly a paradox. It is certainly explainable, firstly for aesthetic reasons: 20th century realism is finished, and the proletarian world has deserted our literature.' P. Combes, *La Littérature et le mouvement de mai 68* (Seghers, 1984), 178.

the aesthetics of realism and representation of the proletariat is certainly one that Godard would endorse. Twice in *Tout va bien* he parodies the conventional miserabilist description of a worker's lot, judging it to be based on a bourgeois moralism which disturbs society's structures not at all.[22]

By 1968, Godard already had a very high profile as a political film director, challenging the nature of society, art, and ideology as bourgeois. He appears to be the only film director to be insulted by the Situationists: 'Enfant de Mao et du coca-cola'; 'Le plus con des Suisses pro-chinois', the latter appearing also on the walls of the Sorbonne,[23] the former being a reference to the famous caption in *La Chinoise*, 'Enfants de Marx et du coca-cola', which has been endlessly recycled. His first feature film, *A bout de souffle* (1959), starring Jean Seberg and Jean-Paul Belmondo, met with immediate success. Although he had been writing and collaborating with others in the Nouvelle Vague ('new wave') for some time, this film established him for a wide public as a leading exponent. His following films tackled issues of contemporary society, particularly class, women, and cities, and problems with the censor were not infrequent: *Le Petit Soldat*, with its reference to Algeria, was banned. *La Femme mariée* had to be renamed *Une femme mariée* as the censor objected to the generalist implications of the use of the definite article in a film which portrayed a married woman as prostitute. Godard was publicly involved in opposing the American intervention in Vietnam, being one of the directors who participated in the collective *Loin du Viet-nam*.[24] *Tout va bien* is a collaborative work with Jean-Pierre Gorin, and the first film inspired by the agit-prop work which they undertook in May and afterwards in the Dziga-Vertov group to aim for a commercial audience. Like other Nouvelle Vague directors, Godard had a love affair with American film, though he became progressively anti-American. It is difficult to imagine a director with such roots, and such knowledge of American cinema, framing the scene with the factory boss in *Tout va bien* against a window

[22] In response to Combes's judgement on the traditional aesthetics of the May novel, Lynn Higgins presents a reading of *Tout va bien* based on 'May as subject of enunciation' in *New Novel, New Wave, New Politics* (Lincoln, Neb.: Univ. of Neb. Press, 1996), 116 ff. Her discussion of the film raises interesting points, but is undermined by her misreading of its politics. Astoundingly for someone writing on May 68, she misses the *gauchiste* denunciation of the PCF/CGT at its centre, and also describes the maoist 'commando' raiding the hypermarket as a group of shoppers. There are several other minor factual errors.

[23] Photographed inside the Sorbonne: R. Viénet, *Enragés et situationnistes dans le mouvement des occupations* (Gallimard, 1968), 101: 'The stupidest of the maoist Swiss.'

[24] *Tout va bien* will be followed by *Letter to Jane*, a long exposition of critical views of Jane Fonda's trip to Hanoï, using a famous photograph of the event, and which Higgins persuasively argues reveals unthinking reproduction of paternalist, reifying attitudes (238–9).

with a flashing neon sign, even if it is daylight and he does have his back to it, without 'quoting' the famous shot of Dick Powell at the beginning of *Farewell My Lovely*, possibly seeking to 'Americanize' this image of the capitalist. Godard's style, strongly influenced by previous critiques of 'bourgeois realism' such as Brecht, the Russian formalists, Dziga Vertov, became a very recognizable 'signature' in his political films of the 1960s, mixing short narrative sequences, scenes of the cities, 'captions', word games, political denunciation, actors talking to camera in a pseudo-interview which has become very conventional now in mainstream filming, but which was highly stylized at the time, as was his consistent failure to use the shot/reverse shot method to film dialogue 'naturalistically'.

The political mix is also very recognizable. On *Une ou deux choses que je sais d'elle*, Godard insisted that 'elle' was not the character played by Marina Vlady but Paris. However, the trailer for the film displayed the range of themes familiar to critics of consumer society at the time, a trailer which is also typical of Godard's use of non-narrative, non-realistic devices, as its message is conveyed by the use of 'cartons':

> SILENCE
> Apprenez en silence deux ou trois choses que je sais
> d'ELLE
> ELLE, la cruauté du capitalisme
> ELLE, la prostitution
> ELLE, la salle de bains que n'ont pas 70% des Français
> ELLE, la physique de l'amour
> ELLE, la vie d'aujourd'hui
> ELLE, la guerre du Vietnam
> ELLE, la call-girl moderne
> ELLE, la mort de la beauté moderne
> ELLE, la circulation des idées
> ELLE, la gestapo des structures[25]

The political themes of anti-capitalism, anti-colonialism, and anti-imperialism, together with the challenge to conventional sexuality and to conventional aesthetics as bourgeois, make Godard one of the prime articulators of *gauchisme* in the cultural sphere. Godard was actively involved in May, filming in the streets, the result of which were the *Cinétracts*, short agit-prop films. But almost immediately afterwards, he left for London to direct *One plus One* (*Sympathy for the Devil*) with the

---

[25] 'SILENCE/Learn in silence two or three things I know about HER/HER, the cruelty of capitalism/HER, prostitution/HER, the bathroom which 70% of the French do not have/HER, the physique of love/HER, life today/HER, the Vietnam war/HER, the modern call-girl/HER, the death of modern beauty/HER, the circulation of ideas/HER, the Gestapo of structures.' *2 ou 3 choses que je sais d'elle: Découpage intégral* (Seuil/Avant-Scène, 1971), 10.

Rolling Stones. Critics of *One plus One* have drawn attention to its root-lessness, the depoliticizing effect of creating scenes of the Black Panthers in London. It is a criticism which tends to recur through Godard's career, that he was more interested in political art for political art's sake than in political effectiveness.[26]

Godard has said that *Tout va bien* is not a film 'about' 68,[27] to which one can only respond: yes and no. The first image on the screen is 'MAI 1968', with MAI in white capitals, and 1968 in red beneath. It is followed by MAI, then MAI 1972. The relationship to May 68 is therefore a very immediate one. May is a political and historical frame and point of reference. On the other hand, there is no narrative sequence set in May 68, and no newsreel footage or recreation of the street fights or demonstrations. While there is a scene recalling the death of Gilles Tautin, the *lycée* student who drowned in June 1968 at a Renault-Flins demonstration, by portraying the recovery of his body from the river, it is in a very stylized manner (with a woman's voice reading a poem about Tautin in tribute), and towards the end of the film when the 'filmic' nature of it all has been very well established. As the CRS chase protestors in another of the scenes at the end, the shot of the riot policeman's pose, arm raised above his head, directly recalls the famous 'Atelier populaire' poster. May 68 is in quotation marks.

While frequently pointing to the filmic nature of its representations, *Tout va bien* does have several narrative sequences. The longest concerns the visit Susan de Witt (Jane Fonda), a reporter for ABS (American Broad-casting Services) makes to Samuli, a sausage factory, accompanied by her husband Jacques (Yves Montand), a film-maker. She has an appoint-ment with the managing director Marco Guidotti in order to interview him as part of a report on French management today. However, the workers have occupied the factory, and locked Guidotti in his office. The reporter and her husband are therefore locked in with him. The sequence at the factory is an important part of a wider diegetic development which one could call 'the political education of Susan and Jacques'. They are released after two days—the boss is held for five—and return to their work, which in Jacques's case is the filming of an advertisement for Dim tights. Susan is the one who has been most unsettled by the experience of the strike; she finds it impossible to submit the kinds of reports she used to do, and she challenges very strongly Jacques's attitudes towards sexuality and behaviour in their relationship. His acceptance of her analysis changes his view of the political situation in France; the rather

[26] Steve Cannon, 'Godard, the *Groupe Dziga Vertov* and the Myth of "Counter-Cinema"', *Nottingham French Studies*, 32/1 (Spring 1993), 74–83.

[27] Higgins, *New Novel*, 129.

self-satisfied, narcissistic persona of the previous 'statement to camera' about his work and aspirations is replaced by a more critical, and politically self-critical voice. Both realize the limitations of their previous understandings. The story of Susan and Jacques is thus a political fable. Contact with the workers has led them to review their own practices and attitudes.

In addition to the factory sequence and subsequent development for Jacques and Susan, and the narrative of Jacques's own development and political practice as a film-maker, there are many different scenes of France—protest being brutally repressed, protestors being arrested, the drowning of Gilles Tautin, Susan's journey north to cover the protest at the hypermarket, pictures of the countryside, of farmers dumping produce, images of the city, and of the wasteground at the end with the popular song: 'Il y a du soleil sur la France'. Through this variety of different locations, the targets of the film are revealed as multiple: not only the capitalist bosses who exploit the workers, but the PCF which helps them do so, male workers who exploit women, bourgeois men who exploit women, and intellectuals as *chiens de garde* of the bourgeoisie, which is presented as not so much philosophical legitimation of bourgeois ideology and power, as the legitimation of consumerism: Jacques directs advertisements to keep a roof over his head while preparing his political film on France, and the factory is complemented by the hypermarket as site of oppression. In addition to the political and cultural domination of the bourgeoisie, the communist CGT is systematically denounced at the sausage factory, at the scenes of violent clash and protest, and in the hypermarket. In each case it is offering active support for the status quo. The quotations of its denunciations of Geismar's *gauchistes* as objectively helping Gaullism are quite accurate,[28] and many more could have been used. The reply of Georges Séguy (general secretary of the CGT) when asked a question about Cohn-Bendit, 'qui est-ce?', was widely quoted at the time; the fact that *L'Humanité* was the only newspaper, apart from *Minute*, to talk about 'l'allemand Cohn-Bendit' when reporting the events at Nanterre, was widely deplored. Sartre's articles, 'Les Communistes ont peur de la révolution', express common views.[29]

The choice of the two international stars to play the lead roles may have been motivated by box-office considerations but is a significant political feature of the film. Both came with very loaded political agendas: Yves Montand's primary career was as a singer, from the 1950s on. He starred in some major political films (*La Guerre est finie*, *L'Aveu*)

[28] Cf. ' "L'Humanité" au jour le jour', a compilation of quotations from headlines and articles, as well as communiqués from the party and the CGT between 3 May and 8 June, *Mai 1968: Première phase de la révolution socialiste française*, special issue of *Quatrième internationale* (July 1968), 62–8.

[29] *Situations VIII*, 208–25.

and was associated with fellow travellers of the Communist Party. Jane Fonda started her film career in France. In the 1960s, she took a public stand against American intervention in Vietnam. Montand was of Italian origin: he was born Ivo Livi, and in fact created some embarrassment for his brother Julien Livi, a CGT organizer, by his role in *Tout va bien*, since Julien had been actively involved with the factory which was used for Samuli in the film.[30] Julien Livi contributed a small, eminently orthodox, article to the *Le Peuple*'s special issue on May 68—*Le Peuple* being the official CGT journal, it is not surprising that a leitmotiv of the conference around which it is based is the occultation of the role and importance of the CGT in histories of May.[31]

Tout va bien proclaims itself to be about France. The blue, white, and red of the flag colour the titles of the credits, which include the word 'FRANCE'. The sequence following the credits could almost be read as a direct response to the criticism of *One plus One*, as a child's voice admonishes the director that he must be more specific. The variety of scenes from country and city aim for a representation of the totality, or at least the totality as the *gauchistes* of May understood it: workers, *paysans*, students. The use of the cheerful lyrics of 'Il y a du soleil sur la France' as the camera pans over the wasteground is also an ironic statement on the state of France.[32] Yet there are many contradictions in this representation of France. Although Ivo Livi had been effaced by Yves Montand, international French film star and celebrated French singer, his non-French heritage echoes the foreignness of both the American Jane Fonda and the 'boss' Marco Guidotti. The rootlessness noted in relation to *One plus One* appears to resurface here. Why choose an Italian factory owner, and mock him for his command of French? (He tells us proudly that he has long been naturalized, has a French passport, and now passes for French—in an extraordinarily pronounced Italian accent.) The state of France in *Tout va bien* is the state of *gauchiste* analysis: it is because of the detour through maoist China that the *paysans* are represented, but the shot of the protest demonstration and the dumped, burning, produce, has no other resonance in the film; it just hangs there. Otherwise all the shots of France are the shots of the urban landscape which Godard has made his own just as much as John Ford colonized the landscape of the western: buildings being noisily demolished and rebuilt, the sounds and sight of machinery, lorries, dustcarts, and busy roads. The factory, and the hypermarket are

[30] Hervé Hamon and Patrick Rotman, *Tu vois, je n'ai pas oublié* (Seuil/Fayard, 1990), 619–20. Points edition.
[31] *Le Peuple*, 1041, special issue on May (1–15 July 1978), 38–9. The photograph of J. Livi shows a strong family resemblance.
[32] 'The sun is shining on France.' And an interesting echo of Ophuls's very effective use of Chevalier's songs in *Le Chagrin et la pitié*.

linked to the final view of the wasteground by the repetition of a very long tracking shot.

This stress on France today stems from the internationalist perspective of the politics of anti-imperialism and anti-capitalism, and produces a synchronic rather than a diachronic analysis. May is an absolute beginning which is not itself historicized, and is retrospectively collapsed into the present-day. While Jacques says that nothing was the same after May, it is the factory occupation which appears to realize the political project of May ('C'était un vrai début'), in the same way that a work on the Lip strike, *Il était une fois la révolution*, will proclaim that 'Lip 73 est la vérité de Mai 68'. Gaullism and anti-Gaullism have disappeared. The confrontations of bosses and workers have a certain timelessness, accentuated by the stylized cinematic language. Individuals—Jacques, Susan, Marco Guidotti— have a history, but France does not. We are exhorted to think historically, and Jacques and Susan are presented as having learnt to think about themselves historically in the final scene, but it is difficult to see what the content of that history might be. The confidence of the political discourse in the film has been achieved by focusing on staging the *gauchiste* script of May.

The final parts of the film, entitled 'Aujourd'hui 1', 'Aujourd'hui 2', 'Aujourd'hui 3', include short scenes of demonstrations outside Renault-Flins and fights with the riot police, the death of Gilles Tautin, short pieces showing two young men in a wood setting upon a solitary CRS and running away when his colleagues arrive, the commando tactics in the hypermarket, and the arrest of 'prisoners'. They can be read as *Cinétracts* of the moving image: the original *Cinétracts* are black and white, silent (apart from the noise of the street battles), and use photographs interspersed with captions. They are unsigned, and were produced as part of a collective project involving a range of people. They are very short, and each one has a clear political message. One is devoted to Gilles Tautin, and is part lament, part celebration, part protest.[33] Others focus on the student–worker alliance, or police repression. Although the format sounds very restrictive, it is not. The use of editing, the great variations in the speed at which photos are shown, the use of close-ups,[34] zoom shots, tracking shots, all make powerful statements about 68. Indeed, the images themselves, and the imaginative use of parts of them, are at times disquietingly

---

[33] An extract from it appears in Chris Marker's film, *Le Fond de l'air est rouge*.

[34] For example there is a very effective use of close-ups: a series of shots of a riot policeman's goggles, held for a long time, or of just one goggle, perfectly underline the message of dehumanization conveyed in so many posters; the funeral of Gilles Tautin is preceded by photo after photo of individual faces of young people, establishing a visual continuity with the pictures of the young *lycéen* which are carried, some poster size, some very large banner size, by the huge numbers at the funeral.

beautiful. These films are anonymous, but Godard's 'signature' was unmistakably all over his for anyone who knows his work. The hand-written 'titles', broken words, juxtaposition of images, continue the visual practices of *La Chinoise* (stills from which are used) and *Le Gai Savoir*. They have a much wider set of targets than other *Cinétracts*: knowledge, art, culture, advertising and consumer society, Vietnam, are all 'in the frame', as well as the nature of the cinematic representation.

The film is seeking to transmit a political message, as an example of 'le cinéma militant', politically committed cinema, and like the rest of Godard's work, obliges the spectator to think about cinematic images and processes of meaning. As well as underlying the techniques of non-realism, the politics of representation is thematized: Susan questions the fact that everything in the radio station seems to have been written by the same person, parodying the same voice (of bourgeois ideology). Since May, the kind of material she has wanted to write has not been acceptable. Jacques's involvement in May was minor, although he talks of the impact of a visit to Flins. Both register a lack of understanding of what is happening in France, and a sense of confusion when thinking about it. Both point to the necessity of new forms for a new content, transmitting a political message about the class war and the cultural war of cinematic process, signalled from the credit sequence as the captions change to the loud snap of the clapperboard.

This approach to political film-making associated with his Dziga-Vertov work, has been the subject of a good deal of debate: the critical distance it instals has been praised as Brechtian, and criticized as politically ineffective.[35] The combination involved in 'making political films politically', in Godard's famous phrase, has been criticized as politically eclectic and incoherent, as coherent only at the level of the image, or praised in its mobilization of May as discursive subject of enunciation, resulting in a disruptive, fragmented, multiple narrative.[36] My own view would be that in its combination of workerism, of contestation versus recuperation in relation to spectacle and consumerism, representation, knowledge and the intellectuals, of hostility to the PCF, the communist union the CGT (Confédération Générale du Travail), and all their works, of the violence of the state (the death of Tautin, attacks on demonstrators), and of sexual politics, it is dominated by its *gauchiste* politics. Its depiction of the factory and the later episodes outside Renault-Flins is a virtual restaging of the *Cause du peuple* special number: *Flins 1968: La Résistance*

[35] Peter Wollen, 'Godard and Counter-Cinema: *Vent d'Est*,' in *Readings and Writings: Semiotic Counter-Strategies* (Verso, 1982); Cannon, 'Godard, the *Groupe Dziga Vertov*'.
[36] Jill Forbes, *The Cinema in France after the New Wave* (Macmillan, 1992), 27; Lynn Higgins, *New Novel* 128.

prolétarienne.[37] At the level of the enunciation it has the coherence of a *Bildungsroman*, being a didactic lesson in political readings of France. From the 'Atelier populaire' to the *enragés* and situationists, this includes attacking bourgeois art. It also includes attacking bourgeois sexual repression and morality.

It is typical of post-May representations in the absence of anti-Gaullism, and in the fact that the politics of anti-repression has discovered patriarchy. One can compare it to *Il était une fois la révolution*, the collective work about Lip published by the symbolically named Éditions Gilles Tautin, which offers a very similar thematics to *Tout va bien*: denunciation of bosses, of political and sexual repressions. It is a patchwork text of cartoons, *bandes dessinées* extracts, autobiographical witness from a range of workers, women and men, photographs, bold reproductions of May 68 slogans, particularly situationist ones, investigation of image, spectacle, and repression of women, with a grand two-page reproduction of a Bas Dim advert, and also two comic-strip sequences around the sequestration[38] of the boss whose use of the WC is strictly controlled. In the exuberant variety of layout, design, and content, it is fun, as *La Chinoise* was fun.

Tout va bien is different, in its attempt to find a commercial audience. It is sparing in its use of titles; there are none of the word games. The scenes at the occupied factory are certainly stylized, as is the scene at the hypermarket. But in the first case, it is theatrical rather than a surface disturbance of the image or the diegesis, in the way the camera retreats to reveal the set with its rooms like so many boxes, then slowly pans to the right as the workers chant their song. The slow travelling shot along the long, long line of the check-out desks at the hypermarket reproduces the factory shot, again filming multiple scenes viewed in the hypermarket itself whose shelves replicate the divisions between the floors and rooms of the factory. None the less, in relation to the main characters, who have a private life, and professional lives, there is no unsettling of the notion of 'character'.[39]

---

[37] *La Cause du peuple*, 9 special (June 1969). It tells the story from 16 May to 10 June (death of Tautin) and beyond, with accounts of the students' battles against the violent CRS, and the reactionary brake of the unions, who call a short stoppage of work in solidarity, but the workers are not satisfied and decide to occupy (which is the scenario in *Tout va bien*). The unions have to support it to avoid being swept aside, but continue to manœuvre to limit its impact.

[38] There has been much perplexity as to why 'sequestration' became such a favoured tactic, one of the defining attributes of May and its aftermath; the student occupations will have been an encouragement. Others included heads of *lycées*, and the Rector of Vincennes for a while.

[39] See Dominique Noguez's criticism of the film on the grounds that these disparate styles and approaches are incompatible. 'Une distanciation véritable aurait consisté à "déréaliser" *aussi* les scènes Montand-Fonda.' (A genuine distancing effect would have led to 'derealizing' *also* the Montand–Fonda scenes.) *Le Cinéma, autrement* (Union Générale d'Editions 10/18, 1977), 65.

Montand did not quite see it like this. Godard applied his anti-realist technique to his character and, until Montand exploded that about it, gave him no information (and no script) to work on.[40] Peter Wollen considers that Godard does not like actors, since he appears to insist so often on them being filmed without a script, valorizing 'spontaneity' over 'acting'.[41] In fact, the obviously false nature of such spontaneity would seem to me to be grist to Godard's political mill. The well-known and possibly apocryphal anecdote about him, that he refused to use workers to play workers, since they would turn in imitations of Jean Gabin, is much more true to the politics of the image in his films and his acute awareness of the internalization of bourgeois culture. Like the situationists, Godard saw that spontaneity without political consciousness reproduces the doxa of convention and the dominant culture, just as his dramatization of the different modes of narration of social misfortune— lamentation contrasted to denunciation—highlights the former as endlessly recuperable.

Sex scenes: transgressions and subversions

Louis Malle's *Milou en mai* can usefully be contrasted to *Tout va bien*. It invites reflexion very explicitly on the question of disruption and disorder, albeit in primarily thematic terms. This is realism, tinged with the fantastic when the dead old lady walks up to watch the old retainer dig her grave, or when she dances with Milou after they have all left again at the end. This is a film interrogating bourgeois *mœurs*, not the republican state. Tradition, longevity, and hierarchy are marked as old-fashioned and contrasted to the aggressively modern values of the new bourgeoisie, represented particularly in the ambitious lawyer who hardly has time to fit in the funeral, and in the family debates on the advisability of selling the house: questions of money, property, economic interests, and sentimentality shift across the boundaries of old and new.

   In the introduction to his screen play for the film, Jean-Claude Carrière, a long-term collaborator of Luis Bunuel, and no stranger to the notion of disruption of the social order, writes that the family quarrels in the film would have no interest whatsoever without the resonance given to them through the use of the May events. There are two strands to the theme of 'May as disruption' in the film. First, May itself is a disruptive event, unleashing forces of disorder, of misrule destructive of bourgeois social

---

[40] Hamon and Rotman, *Tu vois* 614–17.   [41] *Readings and Writings*, 90.

order, and particularly in relation to sexuality. Secondly, May is revelatory, imposing a particular interpretation upon the family quarrels: because of the contemporary street battles and social contestation, the quarrels become typical of a society in turmoil. The family quarrels are read as society quarrels, between the old and the new order. They become exemplary. As such, the disorder and misrule of May are as much as anything the new order which is going to impose itself for the new generation and the new bourgeoisie, and the function of May is therefore to politicize the interpretation of the family quarrels.

The film shows a family gathering for the funeral of their mother and grandmother at the family home she shared with one of her children, Emile known as Milou (Michel Piccoli). May's effects are the result of happenings outside the narrative: the funeral has to be postponed as there is no petrol, for example. There is panic-buying in the shops. May itself is a series of narratives—events on the radio, from one of the grandchildren who is a student who has been occupying the Sorbonne, from the lorry-driver who gave him a lift down and who stays—as indeed it was for the participants, with radios on the barricades and hanging from buildings to allow everyone to follow the unfolding story.

From their intense questioning, it is clear that the Sorbonne is, for the family in the provinces, a place of rampant, uncensored sexuality. It is a classic theme of writings on May which André Glucksmann dubs the 'ship of fools': 'La Sorbonne "libre" devient une nouvelle "nef des fous", les honnêtes gens y logent toutes les perversions.'[42] Stories of the student milieu, be it *Derrière la vitre*, Bizot's *Les Déclassés*, or Ikor's *Le Tourniquet des innocents*, demonstrate the importance of the attack on sexual taboos. Alfred Willener notes in an interview with a retired engineer, carried out as part of his investigations into the relationship between imaginary and action, that he mispronounces Cohn-Bendit as Ben-Cohit, in Willener's view a highly Freudian slip of the tongue, especially as the interviewee's wife later stated that the young people were motivated by a 'volonté de jouir', by pleasure not work.[43] The celebration of sexuality as transgressive and subversive was indeed part of the *gauchiste* project, and Godard and others are following in well-worn tracks by the combination of class and sexual politics: 'Ceux qui parlent de luttes de classe, sans se référer explicitement à la vie quotidienne, sans comprendre ce qu'il y a de subversif

---

[42] 'The "free" Sorbonne becomes a new "ship of fools", and decent folk place every kind of perversion there.' *La Stratégie de la révolution* (Christian Bourgois, 1968), 82.

[43] A. Willener, *L'Image-action de la société* (Seuil, 1970); trans. by A. Sheridan-Smith as *The Action-Image of Society* (Tavistock, 1970), 322. Cohit is a homonym for coït, that is, coitus. Furthermore, the Arabic-sounding *Ben* Cohit reinforces the stereotype of dangerous sexuality, as well no doubt as picking up the 'foreignness/otherness' which was part of the right's denigration of Cohn-Bendit.

dans l'amour et de positif dans le refus des contraintes, ceux-là ont un cadavre dans la bouche.'[44]

Jean-Claude Carrière will have been all too familiar, from his work on Bunuel's films, with the nexus of sexuality, power, and class. Touraine suggested that it was because sexuality connoted immediacy and 'le naturel' that it was used as a weapon against the instrumentalism of bureaucracy.[45] This is surely part of it, yet it seems to diminish the complexity of the thinking on power, culture, and ideology, to reduce the contestation and exploitation of sexuality to a struggle with bureaucracy. Another significant current is the recognition of the commodification of sexuality in consumer society, the institutional hypocrisies contrasting prostitution and marriage, given the subordinate and powerless role of women in the latter, and the ambiguous nature of images of women in advertising and elsewhere, potentially disturbing and reified at one and the same time, as in the iconic images selling Dim tights. All this is Godard territory *par excellence*, and his representations of women did not only annoy the official censor: 'L'utilisation qu'il fait des personnages féminins, rend le cinéma de Godard détestable', wrote Françoise Audé, going on to exempt only Jane Fonda's character from the charge of misogyny.[46]

In *Tout va bien* there is much talk of sexuality, but no sex. The denunciation of the sexual politics of capitalism is an integral part of the social critique. After the visit to the factory, where the women have talked about their oppressive relationships—or their oppressive experiences of perfectly conventional male/female relationships—the action shifts to the living room of Jacques and Susan. Provoked by Jacques's comment that she was too tired to have sex the night before, Susan angrily dissects the pattern of their relationship: 'boulot, bouffe, baise' (work, food, sex). Holding a photograph of an erect penis held in a woman's hand, she angrily denounces the phallocentric order of things, and particularly the fact that male desires, male needs, are the unspoken context of their relationship.

The connection between the critique of sexuality and the critique of capitalism is created through the use of women workers at the factory denouncing their specific exploitation—or trying to negotiate their unequal domestic responsibilities so that they can continue in the strike,

---

[44] 'Those who talk of class struggles, without referring explicitly to daily life, without understanding how subversive love is, how positive the refusal of constraints is, they have a corpse in their mouths.' Besançon, *Les Murs*, 162.

[45] *Le Communisme utopique* (Seuil, 1968, 1972), 118.

[46] Françoise Aude, *Ciné-modèles, cinéma d'elles: Situations de femmes dans le cinéma français 1956–1979* (Lausanne, L'Age d'homme, 1981), 55. 'His use of women makes Godard's cinema detestable.' 53.

and through the representation of love and sexuality as alienated and alienating, in Susan's lesson. In both cases, narratives of love and relationships are part of the challenge and subversion which bringing the revolution into daily life entailed. And yet the clarity of the political text does not consistently stamp itself unambiguously on the cinematic text, which in turn raises questions about the politics.

'L'art est mort. Créons notre vie quotidienne.' (Sorbonne)[47]

The violence done to image, discourse, and representation in May is generated by the analysis of 'one-dimensionality' and the consequent elimination of any 'negation'. For the Frankfurt school, art is negative by definition, it is that which reality 'is not', but the all-encompassing spectacle of consumer society, the techniques of mass satisfaction and integration which recuperate all opposition, render art literally impossible:

> La misère réelle de la vie quotidienne étudiante trouve sa compensation immédiate, fantastique, dans son principal opium: la marchandise culturelle. (. . .) A une époque où *l'art est mort*, il reste le principal fidèle des théâtres et des ciné-clubs, et le plus avide consommateur de son cadavre congelé et diffusé sous cellophane dans les supermarchés pour les ménagères de l'abondance.[48]

Drastic means are necessary to shock the passive viewer of capitalism's cultural spectacle into a critical awareness. 'Anonymous, cheap and immediate, the use of graffiti in the May events epitomised the avant-garde dream of art realised in the practice of everyday life. A transformation of its environment, graffiti was as powerful a form of subversion and engagement as the larger *détournement* of the city it inspired and reported.'[49] However much they insulted him, the situationists knew Godard's work, and his demolition job on bourgeois culture and representation had been the air one breathed in his films for some time.

There are other roots too. Calvet records how, towards the end of the Algerian War, the UNEF started using graffiti against the FEN (Fédération des Étudiants Nationale which supported French Algeria), either changing the F of FEN into a swastika, or, by altering the F and adding IS, making

[47] 'Art is dead. Let's create our daily life.' Willener, *L'Image-action*, 239.
[48] 'The real poverty of student daily life finds immediate, fantastic compensation in its principal opium: cultural merchandise. At a time when *art is dead*, he remains the main faithful follower in theatres and cinema-clubs, and the keenest consumer of its frozen corpse distributed, wrapped in sellophane, in the supermarkets for the housewives of affluence.' *De la misère*, 19.
[49] Sadie Plant, *The Most Radical Gesture* (Routledge, 1992), 104.

the word PENIS. 'Dans les deux cas, qu'il s'agisse de dérision ou de spécification politique (de sous-titre en quelque sorte) le graphisme se lisait autant au niveau de la dénotation (Penis/Fen + nazi) que connotation. (. . .) Le graphisme connote aussi le détournement, le parasitage, et c'est ce détournement qui devient le message premier.'[50] This double structure of text and subtext, and of the process of contestation becoming the true subject of the image, narrative, or film, is highly pertinent to Godard's work.

The techniques of 'contestation' in *Tout va bien* are directed at breaking naïve identifications with the narrative or the characters, at introducing a critical distance, at recalling: this is a film. To quote a few examples: sequences do not unfurl smoothly, but start again, sometimes from a slightly different angle; a woman comes to clear up after Jacques and Susan in their 'home'; the camera or set is also revealed in the double framing of the Dim tights ad, at the factory.

The question is then whether Godard's political message is at variance with the cultural politics of the text. For unlike *Derrière la vitre*, there is here no failure of interpretation of History, and while there would be an assumption that a film of multiple narratives and fragmented diegesis is a film of playful, and unstable uncertainties, *Tout va bien* demonstrates that this is not necessarily the case. The individual stories are so many denunciations all working in the same direction, all underpinned by the didactic reading of contemporary France. Where there is uncertainty, however, is paradoxically in the area that has been criticized for its jarring realism, namely the character of Jacques. His self-criticism destabilizes the politics of the film, in that his insistence that he has abandoned his former aestheticism and is now engaged on political cinema inflects the way one views this film. Is this the kind of cinema Jacques is now seeking to make? Yet Jacques refuses to join Susan on her trip to cover the hypermarket protest, and it is from this sequence that the title of the film comes. Is this committed cinema or not? Or not yet? In which case, is *Tout va bien* unwittingly staging the impossibility, as some would have seen it, of the politics of the image escaping its recuperation as just another image of politics? 'L'art est mort, Godard n'y pourra rien.' (Sorbonne).[51]

[50] 'In both cases, through derision or political clarification (in a kind of subtitling), the handwritten element could be read at the level of both denotation (Penis/FEN + Nazi) and connotation. The handwritten element connotes also the diversion of meaning, its parasitical nature, and this diversion becomes the primary message.' Calvet, *La Production révolutionnaire*, 31.

[51] 'Art is dead. Godard can do nothing about it.' Besançon, *Les Murs*, 42.

4 Intellectual fictions

Et oui, ça se raconte, les intellectuels.

Bernard-Henri Lévy

Les Samouraïs was the first novel written by Julia Kristeva, who is internationally renowned for her theoretical work on linguistics, subjectivity, ideology, and psychoanalysis.[1] It is a '*roman-à-clef*' relating the trajectories of the structuralist group of intellectuals from the mid-1960s onwards, and therefore unavoidably takes a particular position in relation to the interminably vexed question of 1968 and epistemology. Published in 1990, it is a major reappraisal of the structuralist and *Tel Quel* writers, their hopes, interactions, and motivations. It is not the first retrospective narrative of the intellectual trajectories during and since 1968, but because Kristeva was a prominent member of the group which came to achieve international fame in the 1970s, it has a particular resonance. More recently Catherine Clément, an exponent of the work of Lévi-Strauss, and of Lacanian and feminist theory in the 1970s, published *La Putain du diable*, also a novel of intellectual history.[2]

May 68 was a fiercely intellectual moment: unless one recognizes the crucial role played by ideas it is impossible to make sense of it. It was the occasion of an extraordinary explosion of interest in the nature and definitions of knowledge. This is partly due to the importance of the rebellion within the universities, and the intense debates about knowledge, disciplines, and institutional structures which the critique of the university entailed, partly to the fact that the critique of society involved readings in political and cultural literatures which did not feature on humanities or social sciences programmes, and in which therefore the university's constitution of knowledge was *de facto* subjected to another critique, from outside itself, as it were. As Michel Butor, who welcomed the events 'avec un vif intérêt et une grande joie', commented at the time: 'Le problème de la transmission du savoir en France—ce qu'il y a de fondamental à l'intérieur d'une société: les étudiants et les enseignants sont les délégués à la culture pour l'ensemble de la population—devait

[1] Fayard, 1990.   [2] Flammarion, 1996.

être contesté.'[3] The sheer volume and intense concentration of reading, writing, studying, discussing, seems quite unprecedented. This social revolution saw demonstrations and the 'nights of the barricades' complemented by the production of new ideas, new systems, and new forms of knowledge. What did the students occupying the administrative tower on the night of 22 March do but set up commissions for a study day on 30 March. On 29 March, a group of students from Nanterre had gone to a meeting at the Sorbonne which the rector had decided to ban. None of the Sorbonne students was very sure what to do, and they were roundly admonished by Daniel Cohn-Bendit when they sought his guidance: 'Qu'est-ce que vous faites? hurle Cohn-Bendit, mais vous occupez, bon Dieu! Vous occupez. Discutez entre vous. Organisez des commissions, travaillez! Ne cédez pas!'[4] Bertolino describes the Nanterre militants going from nights of violence on the barricades in Paris to days of discussions out at Nanterre.

The seriousness of the intellectual commitment can be gauged by the document devoted to *Université critique*, produced in June 1968 by the Comité de grève de la Faculté de Droit.[5] 148 pages long, it gathered together the results of the deliberations of the study groups and 'commissions' working during May in the occupied premises of the Sorbonne, resulting in a whole social programme criticizing consumer society, capitalism, alienation, violence in the name of freedom, equality, and participation:

La création d'une Université Critique des Sciences de l'Homme est un fait politique.
1. *Nous refusons* l'actuelle organisation technique et idéologique des sciences dites humaines.
2. *Nous contestons* le découpage traditionnel de ces sciences: sociologie, économie, psychologie, droit, ethnologie, linguistique, psychanalyse, médecine, sciences politiques etc.,
3. *Nous dénonçons* ce découpage comme un découpage historique, contemporain de l'organisation capitaliste de la Société.[6]

---

[3] 'The problem of the transmission of knowledge—which is the fundamental element in any society: students and lecturers are the cultural delegates for society as a whole—had to be contested.' *Magazine littéraire* 19 (July 1968), 30.

[4] '"What should you do?" shouted Cohn-Bendit. "You occupy, for God's sake! You occupy. Have discussions. Organize study groups. Work! Do not give up!"' Bertolino, *Les Trublions* (Stock, 1968), 355.

[5] *Université critique*, report of the work of the strike committee of the Law Faculty (Paris, June 1968). Introduction reproduced in A. Schnapp and P. Vidal-Naquet, *Journal de la Commune étudiante* (Seuil, 1988), 679–81.

[6] 'The creation of a Critical University of the Social Sciences is a political fact. 1. *We reject* the current technical and ideological organization of the so-called human sciences. 2. *We challenge* the traditional divisions of these sciences into sociology, economy, psychology, law, ethnology, linguistics, psychoanalysis, medicine, political sciences etc., 3. *We denounce* this as a historical division which is part of the capitalist organization of Society.' *Université critique*, 15.

This statement is typical of much student writing on knowledge and its institutional boundaries. Interdisciplinarity is a theme which occurs time and again, as does the demand for new forms of knowledge, and keenly felt dissatisfaction with the perceived compartimentalization of knowledge. What is recognized as knowledge is that which is considered worthy of being taught, placing the university at the centre of society's self-knowledge. The social and political implications of that are a constant theme: 'La révolte des étudiants contre le système de l'enseignement touche au point vital du capitalisme, car il s'oppose au mécanisme fondamental du procès de reproduction des rapports de production: opposition travail manuel-travail intellectuel qui impose un monopole du savoir et constitue dans une société impérialiste le savoir comme monopole.'[7]

All this work was led by students and teaching assistants who were not starting from nothing, but had been reading and working for years, frustrated that the subjects and perspectives they were really interested in were not officially considered worthy of study. The same was equally true in English universities. If Brecht was not on the German Department's syllabus students set up their own Brecht study groups: the politically motivated were nothing if not propelled by intellectual curiosity. In the amphithéâtre Guizot at the Sorbonne, Krivine, Weber, and Bensaïd spoke on 'les grands problèmes politiques et les grandes périodes historiques de notre temps. Plus que de simples meetings, ce seront des séances de travail, sérieuses, appuyées sur une documentation solide, une sorte de jaillissement intellectuel, débordant d'idées, de faits, de détails, d'improvisations etc.'[8]

All this ferment had one real result in the foundation of Vincennes, the Centre universitaire expérimental, in September 1968, an establishment situated in the Bois de Vincennes (in eastern Paris) which grew directly out of 68 and which tried to bring together the institutional and epistemological aspirations of May to forge a new kind of university. Autogestion and cogestion were the principles for the running of departmental affairs, and it endeavoured to be the realization of the *Université critique* based on the critical apparatus of contestation. Michel Beauvais singles out three main tendancies at work in the elaboration of Vincennes'

---

[7] 'The students' revolt against the system of education hits the vital point of capitalism, for it challenges the basic mechanism of the process of the reproduction of relations of production, namely the division between manual and intellectual labour which imposes a monopoly of knowledge and constitutes knowledge as a monopoly in an imperialist society.' *Après mai 1968: Les Plans de la bourgeoisie et le mouvement révolutionnaire*, drawn up by the activists of the action committees of the Sorbonne, Vincennes, Nanterre, (Maspero, 1969), 8.

[8] Bertolino, *Les Trublions*, 109: 'the great political problems and the great historical periods of our time. More than mere meetings, these will be serious study periods, backed up by solid research, a kind of intellectual geyser overflowing with ideas, facts, details, speculation etc.'

programmes: criticism of academic knowledge, the creation of Vincennes as a counter-model of society (for example in its refusal of any kind of selection, not even by *baccalauréat*, for entry), and as a centre of political struggle to change society, which show how far it was a melting pot of May's themes: 'L'utopie vincennoise, c'est de refuser de choisir entre ces images contradictoires, de vouloir qu'elles coïncident.'[9]

Knowledge was, then, a major battleground. The fact that sociology students were so prominent in the initial unrest seemed to be something of a self-fulfilling prophecy. These students were by definition those who had been attracted to the subject by the wish to change the world. But other disciplines too, and not the most obviously sociologically aware ones, saw the interconnections between socially instituted knowledge and social objectives very clearly indeed. Students studying fine art for example, and architecture, subjects which led to independent freelance or practice-based work, were only too aware of the relationship between the work they produced and issues of economic viability and social value. They demanded new kinds of knowledge: 'on ne peut faire de l'architecture sans étudier la sociologie, l'urbanisme, des disciplines économiques et financières',[10] as well as an end to exploitative practices in an old-fashioned profession:

> Les élèves de l'École ont saisi la chance de mai. Ils occupent les locaux depuis le 14 mai. Un comité de grève siège en permanence, révocable devant l'Assemblée générale qui se tient chaque jour. Des commissions travaillent dont les noms sont révélateurs d'une tendance: 'Rôle objectif de L'École des Beaux-Arts', 'déféodalisation de la profession' . . . là tous les jours, professeurs, diplômés, étudiants syndicalistes, ouvriers du bâtiment viennent dialoguer.[11]

Finally, underlining the esteem accorded to intellectual prowess in student circles, knowledge was (sexual) power. Roumain Goupil's film *Mourir à trente ans*, about his friend and political colleague Michel Recanati, a young leader of the Jeunesse Communiste (marxiste-leniniste), relates the awesome power held by those who seemed to have 'read everything',

[9] 'Vincennes's utopia was to refuse to choose between these contradictory images, to want them to coincide.' *L'Université ouverte: Les Dossiers de Vincennes*, introduced by Michel Beauvais (Presses Universitaires de Grenoble, 1976), 7.

[10] 'You cannot do architecture without studying sociology, urbanism, and economic and financial disciplines.' *Revue politique et parlementaire, économique, financière*, special issue, *La Révolution des idées, les idées de la révolution* (May–June 1968), 60.

[11] 'The students of the School have seized the chance of May. They have been occupying the premises since 14 May. A strike committee is in permanent session, answerable to the General Meeting which is held every day. Study groups are at work, with revealing titles: "the objective role of the École des Beaux-Arts", "Ending the feudal system of the profession" . . . There, every day, teachers, graduates, students of the union, and building workers meet and discuss.' Ibid. 60.

which meant they had read the foundation texts of the new revolutionary politics, were able to quote them chapter and verse, and pour scorn on any whose knowledge and readings had failed to keep up. *Les Déclassés*[12] is an amusing novel about the emotional and intellectual development of Hugues, who suffocates in middle-class ennui in the 1960s until he becomes involved with trotskyist students. Acceptance involves reading lists: 'Je suppose que tu as déjà milité? Non? Ça s'apprend. Une lecture de Marx, c'est un début, mais il te faut Lénine. Tu vas commencer par *Que Faire?*'[13] The power games played between the militants with intellectual references as weapons—'la guerre des citations'—are nicely observed, as is the cultural range, from the films of the Nouvelle Vague to the 'happenings' of his friend Weltan Showung.[14] 'On échangeait des conseils: il fallait lire Nizan, et *Pour Marx* d'Althusser avec sa théorie de la surdétermination des contradictions. Hugues recommandait *Alphaville* de Godard qui venait de sortir. L'étudiant aimait Dolphy. Il disait: "Dolphy, c'est le bras armé du nouveau jazz." Maria cherchait à emprunter le disque des chants révolutionnaires cubains.'[15] But the cultural creativity of the Chicago Art Ensemble, the underground, Grateful Dead, the Fugs, Jefferson Airplane, experimental poetry, and the books (by Breton, Tzara, Camus, Lefebvre, Reich) on Hugues's shelves meet with no approval from the rather austere militant leader who recommends Mao and the Albanian leader Enver Hodja . . . Predictably enough, the Nanterre insurgents also fail his political test: 'ce sont des anars, bons à chahuter le Living Theatre et à revendiquer l'entrée dans les dortoirs des filles. Sans liaison avec les luttes concrètes des ouvriers, les étudiants ne pèsent pas lourd.'[16]

Le roman des intellectuels

There are various competing truisms on May 68 in intellectual history: May 68 was the sociologists' moment; May 68 was the structuralists'

[12] Jean-François Bizot, *Les Déclassés* (Le Sagittaire, 1976).
[13] Ibid. 118 (livre de poche, 1979): 'I suppose you've been politically active before. No? You can learn. Reading Marx is a start, but you need Lenin. You will begin with *What is to be Done?*'
[14] The cover of the livre de poche edn., with a Crumb cartoon of a characteristically hairy naked couple kissing, and superimposed on a photograph of a demure young couple kissing who could have walked out of a Nouvelle Vague film, renders the pre-May to post-May trajectory most effectively.
[15] Ibid. 122: 'They swopped tips: Nizan was a must, as was *For Marx* by Althusser for its theory of the overdetermination of contradictions. Hugues recommended *Alphaville* by Godard which had just come out. The student liked Dolphy. He would say: "Dolphy is the armed wing of new jazz." Maria asked to borrow the record of Cuban revolutionary songs.'
[16] Ibid. 164: 'They're anarchists, only good for heckling the Living Theatre and demanding right of entry to the girls' rooms. Without links to the real struggles of the workers, students have no weight.'

moment; May 68 defeated structuralism; May 68 defeated sociology. May has been something of a political football at the centre of arguments between intellectual currents vying for hegemony or establishing demonologies, as well as figuring in socio-political histories of the intellectuals.[17] Ferry and Renaut's much discussed work: *La Pensée 68: Essai sur l'anti-humanisme* established a firm relationship between the movements of May and the structuralist fashion which had been building up since the 1950s but which became the point of intellectual reference in a very public manner after 1968. Not only were academic and intellectual circles fired by debates about the new problematics and new methods, but their extension to a wider audience was evidence of the successful establishment of a new sensibility.[18] In 1967, François Furet wrote of 'une parenté spontanément ressentie par l'opinion intellectuelle' when looking at the works of Barthes, Foucault, and Lévi-Strauss.[19] Yet this does not in itself establish the necessary connection between May 68 and structuralism which Ferry and Renaut argue for.

It was the work of Lévi-Strauss, his development of structural anthropology, which had a crucial impact in establishing the importance of new perspectives on knowledge. Lévi-Strauss's work was concerned with the systems of meaning, particularly kinship systems, operating in 'primitive' societies, and he found the structural linguistics of Saussure, who argued that any units of language were only meaningful by their difference from other units in the whole linguistic system, an effective model for analysing complex cultural practices. By the late 1950s, structuralism was an intellectual talking point, and linguistics had become the linchpin of a new quasi-scientific approach to culture and society. One of the most controversial aspects of this was the relationship between structuralism and history, and its political implications.'Lévi-Strauss and his followers sought deep, transhistorical constants in human experience, buried structural "languages" common to all social life. Structuralism, like marxism, thus sought to decode social relationships and expose their basic logics. In contrast to marxism, however, the logics uncovered by structuralism were so profound that they made history disappear altogether.'[20]

In his influential article, 'Les Intellectuels et le structuralisme', François Furet traced the contradictions and difficulties of the French left, arguing

[17] See e.g. H. Hamon and P. Rotman, *Génération*, 2 vols. (Seuil, 1988) and the works by Judt, Rieffel, Khilnani, Hazareesingh, Chebel d'Appolonia, Lévy, listed in the bibliography. *Le Débat* has also devoted significant space to these issues.
[18] Christophe Prochasson, 'L'Historien aux prises avec les idées', *Le Débat*, 73, 'Le Structuralisme a-t-il une histoire?' (Jan.–Feb. 1993), 26.
[19] 'Les Intellectuels et le structuralisme', *Preuves* (Feb. 1967), 9.
[20] George Ross, 'Where have All the Sartres Gone? The French Intelligentsia Born Again', in James F. Hollifield and George Ross, *Searching for the New France* (New York and London, Routledge, 1991), 222.

that since the Dreyfus affair it had defined for France its universal values, it had seen its traditional enemies of the right falter in the postwar period after the triumph of anti-fascism, yet now disaffection with stalinism was producing a 'première diaspora des intellectuels communistes et progressistes'. Intellectuals' support for Third World independence movements, the 'messianisme de substitution', had also ended in tears, since their nationalisms and religious ideologies were impossible to integrate into the left's secular universalism. Furthermore, because of the lack of support for Third World struggles from the Communist Party and the French working class, the intellectuals were isolated by their revolutionary fervour for causes outside the borders of France, including Algeria. In other words, conditions were ripe for a theoretical approach which offered a rethinking of history:

> L'irruption dans l'histoire des nations du tiers-monde a contribué (. . .) à hâter la fin des idéologies dans la culture française contemporaine; ce qui, en surface et pour un instant semblait ranimer les grandes visées universalistes de transformation sociale, a discrédité en profondeur et durablement les philosophies de l'histoire du XIXe siècle: phénomène qu'on pourrait résumer grossièrement en disant que dans la vie intellectuelle française, si sensible à la conjoncture, et si prompte à la généralisation, l'ethnologie structurale a tiré une partie de son rayonnement de ce qu'elle offrait une *anti-histoire*.[21]

The fact that it met an ideological need, when the previous world-view driven by the Sartrean intellectual had failed, propelled Lévi-Strauss's work out of its highly specialist arena, much to the latter's surprise. 'Il y a en France trois structuralistes authentiques: Benveniste, Dumézil, et moi; et ceux que vous citez [Lacan, Foucault, Althusser] ne sont compris dans le nombre que par l'effet d'une aberration.'[22] But by the 1960s, structuralism had become a major reference point in the academic world; the remarkable success of difficult works by Lacan and Foucault in 1966 showed the intellectual readership was now a wide one.[23]

---

[21] 'The eruption into history of the nations of the Third World contributed to hastening the end of ideologies in contemporary French culture; that which, superficially and for a time, seemed to be reviving the great universalist perspectives of social transformation, was in depth and lastingly discrediting the 19th-century philosophies of history. One could crudely summarize the phenomenon by saying that in French intellectual life, which is so sensitive to the conjuncture and so ready to generalize, structural ethnology drew a part of its success from the fact that it was offering an *anti-history*.' Furet, 'Les Intellectuels', 5 (original emphasis).

[22] 'There are three authentic structuralists in France: Benveniste, Dumézil and me, and those you quote (Lacan, Foucault, Althusser) are only counted among them by a kind of aberration.' Quoted in Catherine Clément, '1966: Le Structuralisme', *1966–1996: La Passion des idées, Magazine littéraire* supplement (1996), 8. Benveniste was a linguist, Dumézil a specialist in myths.

[23] Clément records 50,000 copies sold of Lacan's *Écrits*, 20,000 of Foucault's *Les Mots et les choses*, in 1966 alone.

Paul Foulquié brought out a second edition of his *Dictionnaire philosophique* in 1969, which he presented as needing very few changes, apart from 'le structuralisme, évidemment'. The first edition of 1962 had not even had such an entry. The quotations illustrating the movement, which stress above all Lévi-Strauss, language, and psychology, include one from Domenach: 'Le structuralisme donne un bain froid à la mythologie existentialiste. Il nous rappelle que l'impersonnel est un élément structurant de l'univers personnel et que toute richesse ne vient pas de l'homme, et que ce n'est pas moi tout seul qui, à chaque instant, invente la vie.'[24] The opposition between structuralism and existentialism outside the Academy proper focused on man and individual human action (rather than set theory, or psychology), and painted existentialism into one particular corner of its own problematic, *le vécu*. Its anti-humanism, its complex theorizations of discourse and ideology, theorizations of the Other and of subjectivity, slipped out of view.

Sartre was the towering figure of the committed intellectual who both theorized political commitment as inevitable, and who acted it out in the public arena. In 1965, he argued again his case in three lectures delivered in Japan and later published as *Plaidoyer pour les intellectuels*, a title which itself suggests a defence has become necessary. His argument is, effectively, that the intellectual is made, not born, being produced by a critical awareness of the primary contradiction of intellectual work in a divided society. The bourgeoisie needs people to work on knowledge at all levels, and recruits and trains them through its universities and other institutions. But the contradiction which, according to Sartre, drives individuals either into bad faith or into the critical position of the intellectual, is the contradiction between the universal and the particular, which is both an ideological and an intellectual contradiction. In both cases, it is a profoundly political one. The bourgeoisie has long presented itself as the universal class (the class which stands for freedom for all) and the champion of universal humanism, but, as he and others had often argued before, bourgeois humanism is humanist in name only. The humanism of the bourgeoisie achieves its unspoken partisan ends by defining its enemies as non-human, and therefore excluding them from the human community. Imperialism, and colonialism show the extent to which its humanism is a false humanism: 'Tous les hommes sont égaux *sauf* les colonisés qui n'ont de l'homme que l'apparence. D'autres travaux établissaient de la même manière l'infériorité des femmes: l'humanité était

---

[24] 'Structuralism gives a cold bath to existentialist mythology. It reminds us that the impersonal is a structuring element of the personal world and that all richness does not come from man, and that it is not I alone who, in each moment, invents life.' P. Foulquié and R. Saint-Jean, *Dictionnaire de la langue philosophique* (Presses Universitaires de France, 1969), 694.

faite de bourgeois, blancs, et masculins.'[25] The same contradiction is found in relation to the work the 'technicien du savoir' will be carrying out, summed up in the phrase: 'universalisme de profession, particularisme de classe'.[26]

Sartre's texts are governed by the attempts to theorize the relationship between the individual and the collective, between the particular and the universal, which had dominated his work since *La Critique de la raison dialectique*. Arguing that the intellectual lives the contradictions and divisions of society, means that there is still a representative function for the intellectual, a mirror in which society can see itself. Yet there are many reasons why the representational function of the intellectual, speaking the true values of the true (Republican) nation, was indeed in crisis, and which many commentators related to the rise of structuralism. Sartre and Beauvoir were not alone in their views of it as the ahistorical and depoliticized ideology of the modern bourgeoisie. As we have seen, Furet pointed to the failure of the left's third-worldism to explain its attractions; Henri Lefebvre devoted many articles to structuralism and history, relating the former to the cybernetic, planified, Americanized, dehistoricized, developments in France.[27] On the other hand, he had always treated Sartre's work as the expression of the ideology of petit-bourgeois individualism, and therefore is also reinforcing that particular polarization between existentialism and structuralism.

Ferry and Renaut use anti-humanism as the basis to build a bridge between structuralism and 68. They gather statements from structuralists relating their work to the events and ideas of May, and argue that the apparent humanism of May was a humanism in appearance only, being no more than individualism run rampant.[28] But in fact, structuralism had a very low profile during the events themselves; very few structuralists had anything to say about them—Barthes's short piece in *Communications*, 12, is a notable exception. Epistémon presented May as the end of structuralism (Nanterre was notorious as a hotbed of anti-structuralism), as did participants in *Esprit*'s 'Table ronde' on May: 'Parmi les victimes de cette crise, il me semble qu'il faut placer au premier rang, je ne dis pas l'analyse structurale, mais certainement la métaphysique structurale' (Vidal-Naquet); 'Il n'y a pas que le structuralisme, ou un certain

---

[25] 'All men are equal *except* the colonized who are human only in appearance. Other work established in the same way the inferiority of women. Humanity was made up of male, white, bourgeois.' *Plaidoyer*, 28.

[26] Ibid. 77: 'professional universalism, class particularism'.

[27] See *Au-delà du structuralisme* (Anthropos, 1971).

[28] Luc Ferry and A. Renaut, *La Pensée 68: Essai sur l'anti-humanisme contemporain* (Gallimard, 1985); they pursued their arguments in *Itinéraires de l'individu* (Gallimard, 1987).

structuralisme, qui en a pris un coup, c'est toute la société technocratique.' (Julliard).[29] May is the 'event', the apotheosis of human action in
the world, which is sweeping aside the synchronic approaches associated
with structuralism. Sartre's star certainly rides high in May: he addresses
a huge audience in the occupied Sorbonne,[30] he publicly welcomes May
and his work is congruous with it. His arguments, particularly in relation
to the violence of the state and bourgeois repression, are those of the
gauchistes.

Yet the view that May was the last gasp of the committed intellectual has
some foundation too. The value accorded in political circles to the working class as fount of all knowledge isolates and devalues the intellectual.[31]
It is difficult to imagine the cold war intellectual thinking he could fulfil his
functions by becoming a factory worker in order to listen and learn, but
the *établi* movement argued just that. The post-May intellectuals like
Foucault and Deleuze no longer believed in a totalizing figure of the intellectual speaking for all, and stressed specific interventions in specific
campaigns. One might also see the value placed on *la dérision* as an intellectual weapon being at variance with classic intellectual modes, as in *Le
Débat*'s judgement on *Hara-kiri*: 'ces pionniers de l'irrespect ont davant-
age contribué à la gestation de l'esprit de 1968 que tous les coupeurs
épistémologiques de la rue d'Ulm réunis'.[32] After the dissolution of the
groupuscules, the illegal *Gauche prolétarienne* launched its paper *La
Cause du peuple*. When Le Dantec was jailed for this, Sartre and Beauvoir
took to the streets to sell it, to defy the state to arrest them too or recognize
the inequities in its law. They were left in peace. De Gaulle's retort to their
provocation reads like a most calculated insult dismissing Sartre's entire
project to reinvent the intellectual in the context of *gauchisme*. He is reported to have said: 'On n'arrête pas Voltaire.' ('You don't arrest Voltaire')

Julia Kristeva had been one of the leading structuralist intellectuals since
her dazzling entry into public intellectual life in Paris with the publication
of *Semiotiké: Recherches pour une sémanalyse*.[33] She was hailed as a quite
brilliant student of Goldmann, having come from Bulgaria in 1965. Her

[29] 'Among the victims of this crisis, it seems to me that at the very front one must put, well not
       structural analysis, but certainly structural metaphysics'; 'It's not only structuralism, or a certain
       structuralism which has been hit hard, it's the whole technocratic society.' 'Le Sens du mouvement',
       Esprit (June–July 1968), 1060, 1061.
[30] See the photograph in Hamon and Rotman, *Génération*, i.
[31] R. Rieffel, *Les Intellectuels sous la Ve République* (Calmann-Lévy/CNRS, 1993), i. 142.
[32] 'These pioneers of disrespect have done more for the creation of the spirit of 1968 than all the epis-
       temological breakers of the rue d'Ulm [École Normale Supérieure] together.' 'Illustres inconnus et
       inconnus illustres', *Le Débat* (May–Aug. 1988), 50, 245.
[33] Seuil, 1969.

work has gone through many phases in the past thirty years, and is associated with pioneering important concepts and approaches in structuralist linguistics, and structuralist poetics, through her reflection on intertextuality and signification, on power, on decentred subjectivity, and particularly her notion of 'le sujet en procès', reflecting the view that the subject is, from its very constitution, divided, and that subjectivity is a process, not a given. Her creation of the notion of the Semiotic, the stage which both precedes and coexists with the Symbolic, the realm of language, logic, and rationality, has been immensely important for theories of women's writing. Her ideas brought her for a time close to the feminist group 'Psychanalyse et politique': she published *Des chinoises* with them, which was the text which resulted from her journey to China with the *Tel Quel* group, and which is recounted in *Les Samouraïs*. She subsequently trained as an analyst, and her writings on love, maternity, and abjection have reflected that. She has now written several novels, yet her book on Proust shows that she sustains her critical interest in the literary text.

She has long been part of the circle around *Tel Quel* (renamed *L'Infini* in 1983), the journal most closely associated with the idea of revolutionary writing, writing which would change the world. Godard used the cover of *Tel Quel* as well as a picture of Sollers in his *Cinétracts*. Sollers's championing of a cultural politics which would revolutionize the expression of culture was clearly welcomed as a kindred kind of work by the cultural *gauchistes*, yet the strange paradox is that, while the stress on the production of meaning, the attack on realism, the combination with cultural revolution and subjectivity as sites of political action, mean that *Tel Quel* and Sollers are close to the ideological and cultural sensibilities of May, politically they are not, as they champion the cause of the Parti Communiste and the communist union the CGT. Although there were elements within the PCF trying to move the cultural debate forward, they did not have an easy time in a party still dominated by those who tended to think of literature in terms of the debates around socialist realism. And however much it preached class struggle and the dictatorship of the proletariat, the formal response of *Tel Quel* to May was to set up *Groupes d'analyse théorique*.[34] It also developed a passion for China, both as home of the cultural revolution and as home for different modes of representation and signification, although as first America then religion were substituted as objects of desire, the political core of this revolutionary project appeared increasingly hollow.

Les Samouraïs attracted a good deal of attention as a *roman-à-clef* about the group of intellectuals associated with structuralism and *Tel*

[34] Summer 1968: 4.

Quel, as well as an ironic rewriting of Simone de Beauvoir's famous novel *Les Mandarins*, which won the Prix Goncourt in 1954. Set in Paris, it opens as Olga Morena arrives at the airport one cold morning. She has come from *là-bas*, from Eastern Europe. Through her friend Ivan, she is quickly introduced to the Parisian scene: the Sorbonne is rubbish, she learns (in terminology which seems to belong to the 1980s rather than the 1960s: 'ringard, archi-ringard'), and the exciting place to be is Bréhal's seminar where Hervé Sinteuil has just delivered a brilliant exposé on Mallarmé. It is when she is advised to study with Edelman rather than Bréhal, because she is from 'là-bas' and because she is a marxist, that the double structure of the *roman-à-clef* probably becomes unmistakably clear; Edelman 'tutoyait tout le monde et ne cessait d'en découdre avec l'existentialisme, au profit de la raison dialectique revue et corrigée par l'expérience de Pascal—*Le Dieu caché*, l'aliénation, le Nouveau Roman'.[35] Lucien Goldmann, supervisor of Kristeva's thesis, author of books on Pascal, on marxism, the Nouveau Roman, is the identity being enacted through Edelman, and there are two pages of subsequent polemic from him about the hidden God, tragedy, Racine, and totalizing ideologies, in case the point had been missed. Many characters are identified by a short reference, such as Strich-Meyer's *cuisine du sens* unmasking the anthropologist Claude Lévi-Strauss. And thus slowly is the cast assembled: Barthes/Bréhal, Foucault/Scherner, Sollers/Sinteuil, Benveniste/Benserade, Pleynet/Brunet, François Wahl/Stanislas Weil, Lacan/Lauzun, the journal *Maintenant* edited by Sinteuil shadowing Sollers's *Tel Quel*. Other conventions of the historical novel, such as the mixing of both fictional and 'non-fictional' characters, are also used: the students Carole and Martin, the psycho-analyst Joëlle Cabarus, her husband Arnaud, are some of the characters without shadows in the 'real world'.

Kristeva imposes a fictional narrative upon a historical one; the 'nar-rative real' supports a 'historical real'. In *La Putain du diable*, Catherine Clément writes her intellectual history as fiction through such narrative conventions as use of dialogue, framing devices, the personalization of history through characters as intradiegetic narrators. Both approaches fictionalize history, both play with different levels of narration and modes of indexing reality, both implicitly suggest they are parallel narratives, in that they tend not to unsettle the notion of historical narrative itself. They both use fiction to particularize their account, yet the intertextual rela-tionships with historical (or biographical) narratives of the intellectuals authenticates their realism as real.

---

[35] *Les Samouraïs*, 19: 'said "tu" to everyone and never stopped arguing with existentialism, in favour of dialectical reason revised by the experience of Pascal—*The Hidden God*, alienation, the New Novel'.

On top of this, *Les Samouraïs* cultivates a hall of mirrors effect between history and fiction through its exploitation of Beauvoir's novel *Les Mandarins*[36] and the figures of Sartre and Beauvoir. When Beauvoir's story of intellectuals in the post-Liberation era, struggling to translate the certainties of the Resistance into the cold war, was published, two of her main characters were generally interpreted as transpositions of Sartre and Camus. Robert Dubreuilh (Sartre) was the committed intellectual, not afraid to get his hands dirty trying to broker political compromises, and who has launched a journal *Vigilance* (*Les Temps modernes*); Henri Perron (Camus) was more concerned to keep his journal *Espoir* (*Combat*) true to the moral principles of Resistance. Anne Dubreuilh, a psycho-analyst, had to be Beauvoir herself, in spite of the non-correspondance of profession, partly because of the relationship with Sartre, but also because she draws upon her relationship with the American novelist Nelson Algren for the episodes between Anne Dubreuilh and Lewis Brogan. In *Les Samouraïs*, Kristeva the psychoanalyst is indexed by Joëlle Cabarus; Olga Morena transposes Kristeva the writer and her marriage to the import-ant avant-garde literary figure, Sinteuil/Sollers. Through her liaison with the American Edward Dalloway she indexes Anne Dubreuilh, as does Joëlle Cabarus through her profession. The important intellectual Sinteuil often refers to is called Dubreuilh.

As author/autobiographer, Kristeva is shadowed by the figure of Beauvoir.[37] More specific to Morena/Cabarus is their relationship to France. Morena is 'in exile', culturally and philosophically. Like the Kristeva of *Des chinoises*, her position as other gives her an insight and access to otherness, an important element in the structures of cultural significa-tion, as that which is expelled and repressed in the (Symbolic) constitu-tion of identity. Cabarus on the other hand is French. Furthermore, she fantasizes a lineage with Thérèse Cabarrus, a figure in the French Revolution, and offering roots going back several generations. It is an intriguing dichotomy.

The novel follows Olga as she becomes part of the intellectual scene; her relationship with Sinteuil and its development, particularly through scenes with his family in Bordeaux; travels to China, to America, to American universities. It therefore has an episodic structure, offering a *mise en scène* of a range of different attitudes and ideas in that particular

---

[36] Published in 1954, it won the Prix Goncourt.

[37] See Paul Renard, 'Des *Mandarins* aux *Samouraïs*, ou de l'engagement existentialiste à l'individual-isme post-moderne', *Roman 20/50*, 13 (June 1992), 111–24, for a full exploration of the parallels between the two novels. Kristeva returns to May 68, and to the question of the importance of Sartre, in *Contre la dépression nationale*, conversation with Philippe Petit (Textuel, 1998).

milieu. Catherine Clément also uses a historical frame to discuss postwar history of ideas. She and her friend Julien have been commissioned to make a television programme entitled *Le Roman des intellectuels*, a scenario which allows her to juxtapose different narratives of the 1960s: the anecdotes and views of the two friends are often quite unpalatable to the producer who knows what he is expecting to hear. She gives a detailed picture of intellectual life revolving around seminars of the famous.

The story of Olga Moreno's involvement with France and its intellectuals starts in 1966/5, which means that the absence of any discussion of the Fourth Republic, its issues, and social movements, or the Algerian War and the birth of the Fifth Republic, should be perfectly logical. And of course it is, but its logic is a logic governed by the particular historiography of the intellectual in the postwar period shown in the novel, rather than by chronology and diegesis, for if the 1950s and early 1960s are absent, the war and postwar periods are very much part of the picture, through the references to Beauvoir's texts, and the use of Sartre and Céline in discussions of the intellectual and politics. Furthermore, after the May 68 episodes, contemporary France as social text does not reappear. Morena travels to China, to America, then returns to Bordeaux and Sinteuil's family. There is no further student or social unrest, no debates about immigration and the nation, no riots in the *banlieues*. So May is at one and the same time the focus of the production of the intellectual's committed politics, and the confrontation between the positions of Dubreuilh and Sinteuil. The logic of the confrontation is to reduce the existentialists to silence.[38]

In a series of exchanges, Sinteuil singles out Dubreuilh as the antithesis of his own project. Committed literature, and its corollary, a belief in the unitary, rational, logical consciousness, representing the repressive structures of power, is contrasted to the open pluralities of other modes of signification, including songs, dances, and writing, which stage relations of otherness. But the figure of Dubreuilh is in fact made up of a composite figure, the Sartre of the Resistance (committed literature), of the cold war ('il ne faut pas désespérer Billancourt'[39]), and of May 68 and its aftermath (speaking outside the Renault factory). Dubreuilh thus embodies a particular narrative of postwar literary history, of existentialism versus the

---

[38] Cf. M. Atack, 'The Silence of the Mandarins: Writing the Intellectual and May 68 in *Les Samouraïs*', *Paragraph*, 20/3 (1997), 240–57.

[39] 'We must not drive Billancourt to despair', a phrase which came to stand for the need to work with the Communist Party as the only mouthpiece and representative of the working class in France. Sartre never actually said the phrase, which is a variation on a line taken from his play *Nekrassov*. Bernard-Henri Lévy describes the paradoxical status of the non-provenance of this famous saying in *Aventures de la liberté: Une histoire subjective des intellectuels* (Grasset, 1991), 257–8.

Nouveau Roman, *Tel Quel*, and structuralism, or of political literature (naïve and simplistic) versus textuality (complex and knowing). But the depoliticization of the narratives of the *nouveaux romanciers* and their descendants, and the detextualization of committed literature, does no service to either. It is a division which completely distorts the writings of May, but it was real enough. This narrative dominated the apprehension of literary history from the 1970s onwards. At a conference on the novel since 1945, held in 1970, Michel Mansuy noted, in his conclusion to the proceedings, the absence of even the names of Sartre and Camus during the preceding days:

> **Tout le roman actuel doit être envisagé dans l'éclairage du Nouveau Roman et mesuré à son aune. (. . .) L'année 1945, si importante en politique, ne sera probablement pas retenue comme une date-clé de notre histoire littéraire. Le vrai tournant se situera quelque huit ans plus tard, vers le moment où paraissent *le Voyeur, l'Emploi du temps, Portrait d'un inconnu*.**[40]

The hint of sarcasm seems to have been his only revenge, as he went on to enumerate the literary riches which might have been discussed.

La Putain du diable also presents structuralism as putting an end to existentialism. In its historical scenario, the publication of *La Pensée sauvage*, the final section of which is devoted to Sartre, is a moment of release for the existentialist generation:

> **Dans les années soixante, Sartre nous apparaît comme un vieux jeune homme décati, Camus comme un raseur languissant, leur langage nous semble bavard, on suffoque. L'aliénation nous embête, l'existence et le phénomène nous barbent, Sartre est illisible. (. . .) Entre 1955 et 1960, le Nouveau Roman, *Tel Quel*, la Nouvelle Vague, le structuralisme, tout est en germe, tout est né. On veut notre Libération. Il ont eu la leur, c'est à nous maintenant.**[41]

In other words, it's a generational thing:

> **—Le structuralisme comme révolte, c'est bizarre, tu ne trouves pas? objecte Julien prudemment.**

[40] 'The novel today should be seen in the light of the New Novel and measured against it. The year 1945, so politically important, will probably not be retained as a key date in literary history. The real turning-point will be situated some eight years later, around the time when *Le Voyeur* [Robbe-Grillet], *L'Emploi du temps* [Butor], *Portrait d'un inconnu* [Sarraute] appear.' Michel Mansuy (ed.), *Positions et oppositions sur le roman contemporain* (Klincksieck, 1971), 230.

[41] 'In the 1960s, Sartre seemed like a decrepit old young man, Camus was a bore and running out of steam, their language seemed like verbiage, we were suffocating. Alienation irritated us, existence and phenomenon bored us, Sartre was unreadable. Between 1955 and 1960, the New Novel, *Tel Quel*, the New Wave, structuralism, it was all there, it was all being born. We wanted our Liberation. They had had theirs, it was our turn.' Clément, *La Putain du diable*, 44.

—Mais c'est la seule explication de son succès ravageur. Parce que nous avions vingt ans, parce que c'était notre moment unique. Chaque génération a le sien ou devrait l'avoir.⁴²

In contrast, *Les Samouraïs*'s stress on May 68 as psychodrama shifts the focus from the collective to the individual, from the political to the psychological, redefining the political in psychological, individual terms. *Les Samouraïs* is not a paeon to individualism, but the key role accorded to subjectivity in its political and cultural systems effectively creates a focus of individualism. The interpretation of May's protest as a psychodrama also has many antecedents, from Raymond Aron's *La Révolution introuvable*, to the psychological studies of Andre Stéphane (*L'Univers contestationnaire*), and Gérard Mendel (*La Révolte contre le père* and *La Crise des générations*). The revolt against authority derives its force from other revolts, considered more fundamental since rooted in unconscious battles. Kristeva's analysis is drawing upon concepts familiar from other works by her, particularly *Pouvoirs de l'horreur*. Unlike Stéphane and Mendel, she does not see the conflict in terms of generation and paternal authority, and indeed ironizes more 'conventional' psychoanalytical interpretations, particularly 'le pénis anal'. Joëlle Cabarus sees the involvement of her patients as an inability to come to terms with their own abjection; their efforts to expel it outside of themselves are intimately bound up in their wish to smash The System. It is interesting to note that they return to her couch *to speak*, as though *la prise de la parole* were on the side of the individual, not of protest. In fact, in terms of the representation of May 68, the duality/doubling of the central narrative commentators into Morena and Cabarus serves to reinforce the individual at the expense of the collective in two separate spheres. With her knowledge of the socialist future being called for, Morena points to its suppression of all the freedoms which the protestors already enjoy.⁴³ Of course, for the *gauchistes* at the time, the Soviet Union and the Eastern bloc were far from being a model to aspire to, were not considered in any way 'true socialism'; that Kristeva presents it in these terms is again symptomatic of the displacement of the PCF from its actual situation of raging angrily in the margins until it reimposed itself on the workers, to being at the

⁴² Clément, *La Putain du diable*, 58: '"The idea of structuralism as a revolt is rather odd, don't you think?" objected Julian carefully. "But it's the only explanation for its extraordinary success. Because we were 20, because it was our unique moment. Each generation has its own, or should have."'
⁴³ In this she is close to views expounded many years earlier by Stéphane in *L'Univers contestationnaire*. He tells of a colleague recently arrived from Eastern Europe who comments that such protests could only exist in a democracy.

centre of the protests. Added to Morena's political critique, Cabarus's psychoanalytical critique serves to reinforce the presentation of the May movements as wrong-headed and ineffective.

The other important strand to the critique of rationality in the history of the intellectuals is the French Revolution and the Enlightenment. However much the Dreyfus affair casts the intellectual, seemingly definitively, within the Republican mould, there is no doubt that the Enlightenment's elaboration of human rationality, of social progress, which Sartre would see as bound up with the political project of the bourgeoisie as universal class, is an ever-present part of the intellectuals' baggage, and of the dissection of their role. In recent years, arguments over the fragmentation of the intellectual, representation, and politics have been explicitly related to the project of the Enlightenment and its apotheosis in the French Revolution. That Kristeva intertwines her account of May 68 with reflection on the Revolution is a further sign of the text's critical distance towards the project of the 'classic intellectual'. Joëlle Cabarus has discovered the existence of papers relating to a Thérèse Cabarrus, who was imprisoned during the Terreur. Drawn by the coincidence of names, speculating that a 'r' could easily have been dropped at a later date from a name pointing to one of her own ancestors, Cabarus reflects on death and pleasure in 1789/93 and 1968, on the dynamics of jouissance and death at the limits of rationality.

It has been argued that Kristeva and Barthes saw May as a political impasse, leading them to redefine politics on the new terrain of culture and subjectivity.[44] The question of how 'contestatory' this new structuralist terrain was remains ambiguous. One academic argued that in the Sorbonne, the dominance of established knowledge meant that structuralism represented a contestation of knowledge,[45] although this is less true of the sociological marxists of Nanterre. Others, like Jacques Rancière, have more acerbic views: 'Lagarde et Michard s'appelleraient désormais Barthes et Kristeva.'[46]

It is difficult to disentangle histories of intellectuals and ideas from the willed coherence inherent in any narrative project. Georges Lapassade, a sociologist of note, and organizer of the Writers Centre in May, put it succinctly in relation to the sociology department at Vincennes where he

---

[44] Peter Starr, *Logics of Failed Revolt: French Theory after May 68* (Stanford: Stanford University Press, 1995).

[45] Jean-François Fosse, *Histoire du structuralisme*, 2 vols. (Editions La Découverte, 1992), i. 227.

[46] 'Lagarde and Michard [authors of standard illustrated literary textbooks] would from now on be called Barthes and Kristeva', 'La Légende des philosophes (les intellectuels et la traversée du gauchisme)', *Révoltes logiques,* special issue on May (1978), 9.

had hoped to move. It was explained this was not possible since the team there believed their work had a 'cohérence epistémologique' which they did not wish to disturb, and which he described as a 'phantasme d'une cohérence qui n'existe nulle part, ni dans la sociologie, ni ailleurs dans ce qu'enseigne l'Université'.[47] *Les Samouraïs*'s coherence is a fantasy, in its representation of May 68 without the vocabularies or motivations of *gauchisme*, and indeed without Vincennes, where Foucault, Deleuze, Lyotard, Lacan, Miller, and Cixous taught, and where the contestation of knowledge rivalled anything in May. Rifts in the Department of Psychoanalysis have become legendary, and the transcript of a seminar held by Lacan makes for extraordinary reading now, combining 'discussion' of psychoanalysis as a body of knowledge, institutional questions, and theoretical questions, with what appears to be a real contempt for his public, and particularly for women—he even replies to one question in a falsetto voice: 'C'est justement ce que je vais expliquer Mademoiselle.'[48]

What is absolutely missing from *Les Samouraïs* is the sense of other trajectories, which were intersecting in important ways with the structuralist one. The postwar surge in the social sciences is a well-established fact of intellectual history, though at its beginnings there did not always seem to be such a grandiose destiny for it.[49] But by the early 1960s, sociology dominated the intellectual field. More strikingly, the arguments and differences between the various currents were being widely debated. Lévi-Strauss devoted seminars to Sartre's *Critique* (and saw numbers rise dramatically when he did so); Lefebvre discussed Barthes, language, Saussure, Lacan, as well as launching immensely influential studies on modernity, on everyday life, and on the city. Structuralists were contributing to *Arguments*, which was also introducing the Frankfurt School, Lukacs, and Marcuse. *Les Temps modernes* and *Esprit* were also publishing a wide range of theoretical work. Furthermore, one cannot abstract their stances on Algeria, their hostility to colonialism and racism, from these politico-theoretical debates. Cohn-Bendit considered that *Socialisme et barbarie*, where Castoriadis, Lefort, and Lyotard, were regular contributors, should be a co-signatory of his *La Maladie infantile du communisme*. The late 1950s and 1960s were the most extraordinarily exciting time.

[47]   *L'Université ouverte*, 219: 'fantasy of a coherence which does not exist anywhere, neither in sociology, nor in any other University discipline'.

[48]   Beauvais, *L'Université ouverte*, 268: 'That's just what I am about to explain.'

[49]   See Alain Touraine, *Un désir d'histoire* (Stock, 1977); Alain Drouard, 'Réflexions sur une chronologie: Le Développement des sciences sociales en France de 1945 à la fin des années soixante', *Revue française de sociologie*, 23 (1982), 55–85.

As Kristeva herself says, *Les Samouraïs* is an ironic text. But its irony bears particularly on its intertextual references[50] rather than on history, which is a key difference between *Les Samouraïs* and earlier texts of the intellectuals such as *Les Mandarins*, Nizan's *La Conspiration*, and *Les Justes Causes* by Jean-Louis Curtis. In the last three, the historical gap between *énoncé* and *énonciation* is crucial to the structure of irony. Nizan's students are conspiring ineffectively in the late 1920s to change the world. The historical present of the text and its narration is the late 1930s, and the gap between their aspirations and reality, as well as the superior knowledge of reader and narrator, mean that the naivety of the students informs every word of the way it is related. A similar device is apparent in *Les Justes Causes* and *Les Mandarins*, where the intellectuals are trying to build a new world after the Second World War, with no means of its realization. History is used to leave them stranded. In *Les Samouraïs*, however, there is no shadowing of the plot by its failure. And so it makes perfect narrative sense for the story to develop without any backward glances at May: it is an episode which allows the question of revolutionary changes in culture, politics, and subjectivity to be redefined.

May was a moment of great political upheaval: the question as to which of the intellectual movements could therefore best be considered to be responding to it, which one could theorize the junction of history, politics, and sociology, was important. The attack on established knowledge went hand in hand with a theorization of the event and the intellectual as public go-between. Intellectuals were both the subject and object of many of the books. As Certeau points out, the importance of the university, its role in the nation, the role and function of research and its relation to industry and government, university in the regions, relations between students and workers are all involving one of the key issues of the relations between intellectuals and politics.[51] The way structuralism focused on power, signification, language, class and ideology, and the problematization of knowledge itself, was perfectly in tune with the debates going on in the occupied campuses, as was the combination of *Tel Quel*'s cultural revolution, of althusserianism, of emphasis upon meaning, process, mechanisms, and the political agenda of anti-nature, anti-naturalizing, anti-bourgeois. In the aftermath of May, they achieved a hegemonic intellectual position. But during May, *gauchisme* and structuralism were not synonymous. The extent to which the problematic of the *enragés* and

---

[50] One of the examples of textuality and irony lies in the designation of the May chapter of intellectual effervescence as 'Saint André des Arts'. In his pastiches of May 68, Jean-Louis Curtis had used this in his Proust chapter to designate Saint Germain des Prés.

[51] Michel de Certeau, *La Prise de la parole* (Seuil, 1994), 113.

others was formed by the overlapping problematics of existentialism, sociology, situationism, and marxism is evident in the following announcement (on 30 May 1968) of a debate organized by the Mouvement du 22 mars:

Nous vous proposons le programme suivant:
   A) Toute conscience est critique
   B) Toute critique est politique

A)	1) Engagement
Introduction:	2) Contestation, Responsabilité, Liberté, Culture-Travail
	3) Aliénation: Loisir-Travail

B)   Spectacle-Consommation.[52]

It is one of the great paradoxes of cultural history, that Sartre, who had such a wide popular audience up to and including 68, whose conceptual framework of philosophical and ideological critique of the bourgeoisie, its class, and its culture, with its corollary of permanent revolution and permanent contestation as values, was virtually swept aside by the structuralist tide with which he had been arguing for nearly a decade, when it was his world-view which stressed the theorization of human agency and the possibility of political action in the world. The perspectives of *Les Samouraïs* certainly demonstrate one part of that process, as well as being eloquent testimony to the constant rewritings and superimposed scripts, lived and projected, of the intellectuals.

---

[52] 'We suggest the following programme. A) All consciousness is critical. B) All criticism is political. A) 1) Commitment 2) Contestation, Responsibility, Freedom, Culture-Work 3) Alienation Leisure-Work B) Spectacle-Consumerism.' J.-P. Simon (ed.), *La Révolution par elle-même* (Albin Michel, 1968), 55.

5 Perturbation, ma sœur

Linguistics was the foundation stone of structuralist theory. Gradually, language filled the intellectual field and the complex interplay of language and silence became, as Certeau saw in May 68, the royal road to social understanding. In sociological, political, cinematic, and literary terms, May 68 triggered a renewed focus on new kinds of language and writing, and also new theorizations of being where language and writing were central. *Les Mots pour le dire*, by Marie Cardinal, articulates this 'rush to language', examines the complex social and political dimensions of the language/silence dialectic, in the social and political contexts of gender and women's identity, and exemplifies the perspectives which will become associated with 'French feminism'. The relationship of the novel to May 68 is thematic and, in terms of the text, structural.

Until recent editions started printing the last two chapters on the same page, it had been known for the importance of May 68 in *Les Mots pour le dire* to pass unnoticed by a reader, as it is superficially confined to the final chapter of the book. Already chapter 17 is less than a page long, and can give the impression of being a coda to the book, as the narrator leaves the psychiatrist's room for the last time, closes the door of the house behind her, and gazes out on the world metaphorically opening before her: 'Devant moi, l'impasse, la rue, la ville, le pays, la terre et un goût de vivre et de construire gros comme elle.'[1] It is understandable that readers might react to this as the closure, the optimistic closure, to the novel, ending symmetrically as it began, with the impasse and the journeys to and from the psychiatrist, and so fail to turn one more page to read the seven words of the final chapter: 'Quelques jours plus tard c'était Mai 68.'[2]

It is a truth universally acknowledged that one of the major legacies of May 68, if not *the* major legacy, was the women's movement. The May 68 generation of women had the impression of inventing feminism, as they discovered the oppressions and repressions of gender—although as their work progressed, as they delved into history to rehabilitate women's

---

[1] 'In front of me, the *impasse,* the road, the town, the country, the earth and an appetite for living and building as large as it is.' Marie Cardinal, *Les Mots pour le dire* (Grasset et Fasquelle, 1975), 343.

[2] Ibid. 345. 'A few days later it was May 68.'

stories, to redress there too the pro-male bias they were finding in every-thing, then they unearthed the long, rich history of women's organiza-tions and individual women's work to challenge sexism. But their sense of charting new territory, of inventing a collective women's movement, was real. They were faced with extraordinarily powerful negative images of women and sexist discourse, political quietism, and the over-arching dominance of left-wing thinking which gave clear priority to class and workers' liberation. The socialist revolution would free all.

In fact, rather than see feminism and the women's movement as a legacy of 68, I would argue that it is the single clearest encapsulation of what 'May 68' has come to mean. If May stands for new attitudes, new ideas, new artistic practices, and new forms of writing challenging exist-ing aesthetic and literary norms; a social, political, and philosophical reappraisal of modern life; a questioning of epistemology and the estab-lished boundaries of knowledge; new understandings of society, class, history, cultural politics, and sexual politics, in combination with com-mitted political and social action, in order to change life intellectually, politically, and practically, then feminism and the women's movement are its most complete expression, in a way that *autogestion*, ecology, pri-soners' movements, regionalism, or anti-psychiatry, are not. Many of the slogans of the month of May aspire to such total change, yet it is in the years of the aftermath of May through the continuing social and political challenges, accompanied by the intellectual work, that the aspirations begin to be lived experience. But the origin, inspiration, and context of May's expressions of change are *gauchiste*, situationist, anarchist: the liberation of women is not in their sights at all. One indication of this is revealed in the fact that sexual violence against women is an acceptable metaphor for the expression of contestatory violence: 'Violez votre Alma Mater' (Sorbonne); 'Vive le viol et la violence!' (Nanterre).[3] On a notice-board at Nanterre, the announcement of the meeting of the 'Commission Culture et Créativité' ('Lisez le Bulletin du mouvement du 22 MARS et préparez vos cocktails MOLOTOV'[4]) is next to a large picture of a naked 'Miss September' reclining on a bed, alongside which is the following handwritten poster:

C'EST A
L'ECOLE DE
LA POESIE ET
DE LA JOUISSANCE

---

[3] 'Rape your alma mater', 'Long live rape and violence', J. Besançon (ed.), *Les Murs ont la parole* (Claude Tchou, 1968), 142, 83. On the latter graffiti, someone had written 'Non', someone else had added 'Si'.
[4] 'Read the Bulletin of the *mouvement du 22 mars* and prepare your Molotov cocktails.'

SEXUELLE QUE LES
NOUVEAUX REVOLUTION
NAIRES APPRENDRONT
LEUR VIOLENCE.

LA REVOLUTION COMMEN
CE OÙ COMMENCE LE
PLAISIR
LE PLAISIR COMMENCE
OÙ FINIT LE POUVOIR
TELLE EST LEUR THEO
RIE.
CREER EST LEUR SEUL
BUT[5]

It is hardly surprising that representations of women will be a major political battleground for feminism.

In August 1970, there was a demonstration by nine women at the tomb
of the unknown warrior, which is under the Arc de Triomphe at the head
of the Champs-Elysées in Paris. They tried to lay flowers—'A la femme
inconnue du Soldat'—and two banners on the tomb: 'Un homme sur
deux est une femme', 'Il y a plus inconnu encore que le Soldat: sa femme',[6]
but were prevented by the police. The demonstration had significant
press coverage, with *France-Soir* putting the story on its front page the
next day, and is generally recognized now as the first public manifestion
of the women's movement in France, dubbed 'mouvement de libération
des femmes' after 'Women's lib' in America, a press designation much
hated by feminists.[7] This was followed by an increasingly public campaign for the liberalization of abortion and contraception: Simone de
Beauvoir recounts that she was contacted at the end of 1970 by feminists
hoping for her support in the attempt to improve what they saw as a very
weak bill coming before Parliament; this produced in April 1971 the
'Manifeste des 343', a declaration that they had had an abortion signed
by 343 women, including Beauvoir, Colette Audry, Simone Signoret,
Delphine Seyrig, Catherine Deneuve, Françoise Sagan, Monique Wittig,
Hélène de Beauvoir, Anne Wiazemsky, Ariane Mnouchkine, Christiane

[5] 'It is at the school of poetry and orgasmic pleasure that the new revolutionaries will learn their violence. The revolution begins where pleasure begins. Pleasure begins where power ends. This is their
theory. Their sole aim is to create.' J.-P. Duteuil, *Nanterre 1965–66–67–68* (Mauléon, Association
Acratie, 1988), 193. Duteuil's uncritical caption to the photograph of this noticeboard: 'La Commission
Culture et Créativité s'en donne à cœur joie!' suggests that some things do not change.
[6] 'To the unknown wife of the Soldier', 'Every second man is a woman', 'It is possible to be even more
unknown than the Soldier: his wife'.
[7] Anne Tristan and Annie de Pisan, *Histoires du MLF* (Calmann-Levy, 1977), 55.

Rochefort, Marguerite Duras, and many other famous women, as well as many unknown ones.[8] May 1971 saw the first edition of the feminist newspaper *Le Torchon brûle*, and literary and critical magazines such as *Sorcières*, and *Cahiers du Grif* would follow. *Les Temps modernes* started a column, 'Le sexisme ordinaire'. Issues of sexual violence, rape, battered women, women and work, women and sexuality, heterosexuality and heterosexism, pornography, sexual discrimination became part of the left's political agenda as feminism and gay liberation recast the whole issue of sexual politics away from 'sexual liberation' quickly perceived as exploitative and heterosexist.[9] During May, *gauchisme* had been even more hostile to attempts to raise homosexuality as a political and cultural question. Posters of 'le Comité d'Action Pédérastique Révolutionnaire de la Sorbonne' in the occupied Sorbonne were immediately torn down, 'arrachées par des militants gauchistes qui trouvaient qu'elles salissaient la noble cause de la révolution'.[10]

Anne Tristan writes of a meeting for women's revolution held in the occupied Sorbonne, and a tract addressed to women is reproduced in the *Journal de la Commune étudiante*: 'Aucune voix ne s'élève pour déclarer que le changement des rapports entre les hommes implique aussi le changement des rapports entre les hommes et les femmes'; 'Il faut que la société qui va se construire soit l'œuvre des femmes aussi bien que des hommes',[11] but in the middle of the hundreds and hundreds of other documents, this is hardly a presence at all. This absence of women's issues in the written *revendications* is matched by the relative invisibility of women in the iconography of May. They are present, there are young women's faces in the crowds on the demonstrations, but they are few: the public face of May is overwhelmingly male. The student leaders are male, the CRS are male, the union leaders are male, the politicians are male, the demonstrating farmers (*les paysans*) are male.

In contemporary iconography of the street battles, demonstrations, occupations, and meetings, patterns emerge in the representation of

---

[8] See Claudine Monteil, *Simone de Beauvoir, Le Mouvement des Femmes: Mémoires d'une jeune fille rebelle* (Montreal: Ed Stanké, 1995), for an account of the first actions of the feminist movement.

[9] Claire Duchen, *Women's Rights and Women's Lives in France* (Routledge, 1994), 198.

[10] Jacques Girard, *Le Mouvement homosexuel en France 1945–1980* (Ed Syros, 1981), 80: 'torn down by *gauchiste* activists who felt they besmirched the noble cause of the revolution'.

[11] 'No voice is raised to declare that the change in relations between men implies a change in relations between men and women.' 'The society which is going to be built must be the work of women as well as of men.' A. Schnapp and P. Vidal-Nacquet, *Journal de la Commune étudiante* (Seuil, 1988), 604–5. The tract is signed: 'Mouvement démocratique féminin', although Tristan refers to FMA (Féminin, Masculin, Avenir). There is no mention of women at all in the documents gathered in *La Sorbonne par elle-même*.

women. First, there are often no women.[12] The photos in the May number of *Partisans*, the *gauchisant* journal published by Maspero, are of (understandably) poor quality, but there is not one single woman. (An indication of the shift from the imaginary of May itself which will none the less be attributed to May is the fact that *Partisans* published one of the first collections of the women's movement in 1970 as a special issue: *Libération des femmes: Année zéro*.[13]) In the whole volume of *Les Barricades*, which contains 115 photographs and hundreds of individuals, twelve women are clearly seen without an effort to see if the photo contains women.[14] The *Cinétracts* are another case in point. As they cut from group to individual close-up, the faces we see repeatedly are faces of men.[15] In the aerial shots containing hundreds of people, women do not stand out. An aerial shot at the stade Charléty, a remarkable picture where the whole crowd appears to fan around Pierre Mendès France in the lower centre, one has to search to find women at all.[16]

Where women are visible, it is not as fighters. A famous photograph of a group of people dancing in the road on the way to Charléty shows more women than men, and as many women in the crowd watching as there are men. In the street battles, women are present as victims. There may well be pictures of women hurling *pavés*, but I can recall none. Yet the photograph of a woman carried on a stretcher with a bleeding leg is used in several *Cinétracts*; there is a much-used photograph of a woman with a knitted bag being helped across a road, obviously hurt, having lost a shoe, and later lying on the ground.[17] *Les Barricades* includes a famous photo of a woman lying face down in the road, with a CRS looking at her, as well as the women dancing to Charléty. Women and the elderly figure prominently in images of those looking at the debris, going about their business, the morning after the nights of street fights. Overall, the underlying text is clear: women participate, particularly in seminars, and in demonstrations, but in support roles, in nearly all cases. In the iconography (and the imaginary) of May, representations of women are subordinated to the

[12] Women are more numerous in the books of contemporary photos produced later, although the patterns of representation described above still pertain. The combination of close-ups of male student leaders and distance shots of crowded amphithéâtres to represent student activism significantly affects the representation of women. (See photographs 19–34 in *Générations*, i, original edn., for a typical example.)

[13] *Histoires du MLF*, 53–4.

[14] There are: one woman face down on the road, three in a group of five dancing on the way to Charléty, two older women looking at damage, the back of one older woman next to upturned trees, one younger woman shopper in the street with her bread, looking very bemused, three out of a group of five on a barricade, smiling at the camera, one in a daytime group including Cohn-Bendit.

[15] The photograph of the grey-haired man reproduced in G. Caron *et al.*, *Sous les pavés la plage* (La Sirène, 1993), 102, is a particular favourite in the *Cinétracts*.

[16] Ibid. 84–5.   [17] Ibid. 20, 40.

gauchiste theses on the police state, and its violent repression: the images of injured women reinforce the lesson about police brutality, especially in the absence of women being shown actively fighting. Otherwise they are onlookers.

One notable exception to the relative absence of women is *Cinétract 003*, devoted to the funeral of Gilles Tautin in June 1968, and which opens with several close-ups of young women's faces, followed by the face of one woman whom we then see standing next to something which is revealed to be a banner about the death. At the head of the demonstration are young women, presumably *lycée* students, each holding a photograph of him.[18] This sudden prominence of women can only be explained by the situation: this is not typical protest but a lament. Another exception, interestingly enough, is the relative prominence of women in the May special issue of *Le Peuple*, the journal of the communist union the CGT. The emphasis here is not on the student demonstrations, or the pitched battles on the streets, but on the strikes and marches of workers, and although there are many large group photographs of occupations with no women, such as the final one at Citroën, women workers are none the less clearly present in the foreground of many others, including demonstrations and meetings on occupied sites.[19] Women are also shown as the main subjects in a range of other activities: selling newspapers outside occupied premises, or leading a delegation.[20]

The last photograph in *Barricades* shows a group walking towards the camera, at Charléty, with a young woman carried on a young man's shoulders and brandishing a flag.[21] *Miroir de l'histoire* has a photo of the same group, though the woman, still brandishing her flag, is on a different pair of shoulders. Gilles Caron caught another young woman being borne on a young man's shoulders, holding her flag high, at the Gaullist demonstration of 30 May,[22] though it is true that their posh clothes are something of a shock to behold after all the other pictures. The appearance on the streets of the 'minets' and 'minettes' of the bourgeoisie was much commented upon at the time.[23] What they are doing is acting out the Delacroix

---

[18] Some of this can be seen in the film *Mai 68: Il y a 25 ans*. Photograph 34 in *Générations*, i, shows the huge enlargements of the picture of Gilles Tautin.

[19] It must also be recognized that the women are older and therefore more distinctively dressed than their male counterparts. Their dresses, their skirts, their hairstyles help them stand out more when towards the front of a demonstration or in a meeting. The students tend to all be dressed in jumpers and jeans. However, the women photographed as victims of violence mentioned above are without exception quite conventionally dressed in skirts.

[20] *Le Peuple, La Grève générale de mai* (15 May to 30 June 1968).

[21] *Les Barricades*, 110.   [22] *Sous les pavés la plage*, 108.

[23] She is wearing the short skirt, tiny fitting jumper, and knee-high white socks which were so fashionable in 1966–8.

painting 'Liberty at the Barricades' with its iconic image of a woman holding aloft the flag of the Republic, an image which, as part of the Republican tradition, is available and, as May shows, used by right and by left. Simone de Beauvoir has demonstrated the extent to which 'Woman' has been the mythical centre of cultural discourses on society and the human condition, a projection of hopes, fantasies, and fears, in relation to which women have to situate themselves somehow or other. With its juxtaposition of Woman as symbol of the Revolution, and the marginalization of women, figures in other narratives, May is a typical example. Remembering Barthes's mythological analysis of the black soldier saluting the French flag, one might say that the choice of this image (a photograph of another young woman carrying the anarchist flag surrounded by a sea of red flags at one of the large demonstrations) for the front cover of Joffrin's historical account, and the way it is framed to place her at the visual centre of things, is governed by the presence/absence of women and feminism in May and *l'après-mai*. May shows the complex interconnections of gender, politics, and discourse, written and visual, in shaping the very nature of the events; and this is the terrain that feminism will stake out as its own from that very first demonstration in Paris.

Anne Tristan relates that the women who demonstrated at the Arc de Triomphe were criticized on the left for carrying out a 'petit-bourgeois' action, purely 'spectacular'. But these critics had not only failed to understand the nature of reality, including political reality, in the society of spectacle, they were also trying to adhere to a vision of politics which the women's movement would definitely shift. The angry mainstream reaction against this particular event also shows that the idea of tackling one of the sacred sites of the Republic was an inspired choice, ideologically.

Nation and nationality are inseparably bound up with war and military endeavour to defend the frontiers. In France, this also resonates with the republican tradition from the French Revolution onwards; the defeat of the foreign armies at Valmy was one of its glorious moments, often recalled during the Resistance for example. Defence of France is also defence of the Republic: political history and national history are intertwined and transmitted through its monuments and ceremonies. There is also an intense emotional charge associated with the Unknown Warrior and the First World War, due to the anger and suffering caused by the mass slaughter of millions of young men. Like Liberty on the Barricades, like Joan of Arc, these symbolizations of national identity are not stable, but are continually being reinvented and reinvested, written anew into different contexts. The women's demonstration is doing precisely that, as it points to the representation of the people as representation of men.

Drawing attention to that exclusion, with flowers for the Unknown Soldier's unknown wife, was properly scandalous.

Women discovered their marginalization within the very political movements which had been carrying their hopes of change. Simone de Beauvoir's shift from the perspective that a socialist revolution would liberate women, to the espousal of a separate struggle, and separate organization, for women's rights and freedom, sums up this political critique of mainstream left politics. There was perceived to be a specific dynamic to the oppression and hierarchies of gender which necessitated a separate response in order to be effective. *La prise de la parole* is as much a theme of women's texts as it is in May generally, although May comes seen to be part of women's silence.

The relationship of gender and language poses, with particular acuity, issues of universalism and power. Just as the Soldier represents the Nation in War, so language has been inflected to invest the masculine with a universal import, standing for male and female. The arguments about 'man', 'chairman', *Madame le ministre*, *écrivain* or *écrivaine*, have been important for the public face of male power and female exclusion. But this is just one aspect of the immensely rich approach to gender characteristic of the feminist movement. In philosophy, sociology, literature, politics, and political activism, new views and new practices were forged. The demand that women must break out of the silence in which they were imprisoned was a constant theme translated in an immediate way in the explosion of texts, activities, meetings, newspapers, devoted to women and by women, and in the elaboration of powerful and influential theories establishing the silence of women as a pillar of Western culture, effectively redefining 'language' as 'men's language'. Women were not only to write, they needed to write differently if their language was to be theirs, and not a disempowered echoing of men's language. 'Je suis celle qui n'a pas de langage, celle qui n'a pas de visage; celle qui n'existe pas; nul n'entend mes cris; mes cris silencieux' are the phrases highlighted on the cover of the second issue of *Le Torchon brûle*.[24] 'Le Rire de la méduse', *La Venue à l'écriture*, *La Jeune Née*, *Parole de femme*, *Les Femmes s'entêtent*, are proof that the interplay of speech and silence affecting all aspects of women's existence is central to the proliferating number of feminist texts.[25] By its

[24] 'I am the one who has no language, the one who has no face; the one who does not exist; no one hears my cries; my silent cries.'

[25] Hélène Cixous, 'Le Rire de la méduse', in L'Arc, *Simone de Beauvoir ou la lutte des femmes* (1975); H. Cixous, M. Gagnon, and A. Leclerc, *La Venue à l'écriture* (10/18, 1977); H. Cixous and C. Clément, *La Jeune Née* (10/18, 1975); Annie Leclerc, *Parole de femme* (Grasset et Fasquelle, 1974); *Les Femmes s'entêtent* (Gallimard, 1975).

very title, *Les Mots pour le dire* puts the quest for language at the heart of the narrator's crisis of being.

In relating the story of a woman who goes in desperation to see a psychoanalyst after years of medical treatment for her incessant menstrual bleeding and her 'madness', who undertakes a journey of self-discovery which allows her to analyse 'la chose' as she calls the bundle of psychological and physical symptoms of her deterioration, to resituate her pain socially, and start her life anew, Cardinal shares some of the key supports of feminism's cultural revolution: language, subjectivity, discourse, body, madness, and power, as a contemporary flyer from the 'Psychanalyse et politique' group shows:

> A partir de la réactivation de la lutte des classes en mai 68, des femmes en révolte ont pris la parole. (. . .) A partir de l'histoire de chacune, de notre parole singulière et subjective, nous avons commencé l'analyse politique de nos contradictions et de notre lutte de femmes en travaillant sur divers thèmes qui se recoupent et s'articulent: la sexualité, le viol, l'inceste, l'homosexualité, l'hystérie, le rapport à la mère, le corps et les symptômes, le rapport des femmes et de l'écriture, les rapport[s] entre nous . . . (. . .) Nous avons commencé à transformer, chacune et toutes ensemble, notre rapport au pouvoir, à la masculinité, au savoir—là où ils nous oppriment et là où nous les reproduisons —à l'intégration, pour faire apparaître dans leur spécificité, leur différence, leur pluriel, nos corps, nos discours, nos textes de femmes . . .[26]

Cardinal's themes are the mother/daughter relationship, family relationships, the links between the personal and the social, the affirmation of self and experience. The narrator moves from a situation of acute distress to one of strength and confidence as her analysis allows her to face what for her had been quite 'unfaceable', the knowledge that her mother had tried to abort her. There is a classic Freudian structure to the description of her changing relation to herself: the 'talking cure' demands just that, that the patient talks, explores associations of ideas, images, and feelings to unlock the unconscious repression of threatening material, and although many feminists became highly critical of the psychoanalytical model,

[26] 'After the reactivation of the class struggle in May 68, women in revolt started speaking up. Starting with the story of each one, with our singular and subjective speech, we began the political analysis of our contradictions and of our struggle as women, working on various themes which connect and interact: sexuality, rape, incest, homosexuality, hysteria, the relation to the mother, the body and its symptoms, the relation of women and writing, the relation(s) between us. We began to change, separately and together, our relation to power, to masculinity, to knowledge—where they oppress us and where we reproduce them—and to integration, to reveal in their specificity and their difference, their plurality, our female bodies, our female discourses, our female texts.' 'Politique et Psychanalyse: Mouvement de Libération des Femmes', undated statement. The Librairie des femmes bookshop opened in May 1974, and this typed sheet is a statement of their aims and objectives.

in its reliance on the male as the norm from which the female deviates, psychoanalytical theory, particularly Lacanian theory, was central to feminist theories of language, subjectivity, and writing at the time. The narrator moves from a lack of awareness, which is translated by an obsession with the wrong things, the symptoms of the problem and not the problem itself, to awareness of the personal and social dynamics of her 'illness'. Her discovery of the right words is a 'prise de conscience'.

Although her first four novels had not been very successful, *La Clé sur la porte*, a story of adolescence, changed all that, and *Les Mots pour le dire* was a runaway bestseller and critical success.[27] There was clearly a large audience for a novel devoted to 'women's issues': Cardinal offered an honest examination of the difficulties and complexities of language, sexuality, the body, and the mother–daughter relationship through her portrayal of tortured family relationships and mutilations of repressive social discourse. Moreover, there had been intense coverage of such issues in the national press in relation to Gabrielle Russier, 'une affaire qui fut exemplaire de l'après-mai 68 à bien des égards (le rôle répressif de la famille, de la justice, de la psychiatrie)'.[28] Russier was a *lycée* teacher who developed a relationship during 68 with one of her students, Christian, aged 16. His family set legal proceedings in motion, she was tried and imprisoned. She committed suicide in 1969. For many, this story illustrated only too graphically the damagingly repressive nature of the state, governing the most intimate aspects of people's lives in the name of bourgeois morality.[29] Similarly, the annual deaths and injuries from backstreet abortions were, in many women's eyes, proof of the violence done to women's bodies subordinated to state control. The violence of state and bourgeoisie familiar from *gauchiste* analysis is therefore shared in feminist analysis, but it is lived in the supposedly peaceful spheres of the domestic, the emotional, the private, the personal.[30] *Les Mots pour le dire* is absolutely of its times.

The novel is (almost) framed by the narrator's analysis. The first pages describe *l'impasse* where the psychoanalyst whom she refers to as the

---

[27] It was awarded the Prix Renaudot.

[28] '... an affair which was typical of "l'après-mai 68" in many respects (the repressive role of the family, of the legal system, of psychiatry).' *CinémAction*, 25, 60–80: *Vingt ans d'utopies au cinéma* (1982), 38.

[29] 'La Répression dans la vie privée', L'École émancipée, *La Répression dans l'enseignement* (Maspero, 1972), 63–8.

[30] Cf. 'La famille occidentale moderne—un cannibalisme psycho-sexuel entre trois ou quatre affamés ficelés dans le même sac' ('The modern Western family—psycho-sexual cannibalism of 3 or 4 starving people tied in the same bag'), a quotation from Tony Duvert placed at the beginning of *Dans le mitan du lit*, a novel about emotions and gender within a couple (and written by a couple, Evelyne and Claude Gutman) in the aftermath of 68 (des femmes, 1974).

doctor has his cabinet; at the end of the analysis, she is 'cured', she has talked her way through her life and its agonies, and has understood the hallucinations and physical symptoms which were making her ill. After lengthy gynaecological treatment and psychiatric treatment for her permanent menstrual bleeding, the prospect of an operation causes her such anguish that she engineers an 'escape' from the hospital to search for a different treatment. The psychoanalyst takes her on straightaway, and the story of her life slowly unfolds. Her parents divorce in her childhood, and her father dies during her adolescence. Several key moments structure the gradual revelation of the traumas and experiences, some of which she has repressed but still suffers from: her father's coffin being carried up/down the stairs; her first orgasm when she created a 'paper tap' to be able to urinate standing up, like a boy; her father filming her when squatting down to urinate; her distress at being forced to eat the soup she had vomited; her mother recounting how she had tried to abort the narrator when she was in the process of divorcing and horrified to find herself pregnant; her mother's devotion to the memory of her older sister who died from tuberculosis as a child, an illness which her father also had and whom her mother blamed for the child's death. Her mother's bitter unkindness to, even hatred of, the unwanted daughter is the leitmotiv of the narrator's development through childhood. As an adult, she marries, has three children. She starts falling ill, becomes totally obsessed with her bleeding and other symptoms, and undertakes the analysis as an absolutely last chance for survival. As an old woman, her mother becomes overwhelmed by her alcoholism and dies. In one of the final scenes recalling her mother's tender care of her sister's grave, the narrator finds a kind of peace at her mother's grave. She also, through a number of nightmares, unlocks her hidden fears in relation to society, gender, and (male) power, enabling her to develop a critical attitude towards the analysis and its concentration upon the individual, and to face the wider world. The turn to May 68 at the end is therefore anticipated in the final stages of her emancipation which becomes increasingly political.

The account of the analysis, the unravelling of her old self and the creation of the new self, is structured through a series of resistances and revelations, of euphoria being replaced yet again by despair. As she says more than once, it goes through phases, first restoring her to health, secondly tackling the psychological traumas and rebuilding her character, thirdly situating her experiences within social constructions of gender and difference. Each revelation has to be fought hard for, as it entails a re-emergence of acute fears and sorrows; the triumph of discovery is always short-lived, as a new resistance, a new stage to go through, returns the narrator to feelings of sadness and defeat. A great deal of critical attention has focused on the traumatic revelation about the abortion attempt which occupies chapter 7 and is at the centre of the story. In fact she makes it clear that it is not the mother's wish to rid herself of the child she was carrying that the narrator calls 'la saloperie de ma mère', but the decision to tell her about it later, to discharge herself of the hatred on the living person. At the end of the chapter, however, the narrator has, in the pattern of the rest of the book, gone through this difficulty and accepted even 'la saloperie'; but this is not the 'cure', there are several more years of talking to come before she leaves the doctor's house for the last time, and it is not easy to decide how determinant this episode is. On the one hand, the insistent vocabulary of birth and rebirth throughout the text could be seen to be translating its overarching importance. On the other, it is located in the chronology of her recovery: it appears to be anguish about the abortion attempt which is finding expression through the bleeding, but the bleeding stops after the first session, and the account of the 'saloperie' is itself a staging post towards the most buried revelation of all, that of the narrator's own violence. Sexuality and attitudes to it may be more insidiously destructive.

Towards the end of the novel, the narrator returns home to find her mother, who is living with her, in a lamentable state: 'Elle était là, en face de moi, assise sur son lit comme d'habitude. Sa chemise de nuit relevée sur son ventre, si bien que je voyais son sexe pelé. Elle avait fait sous elle et sa merde dégoulinait jusque par terre.' She is quite drunk, and the narrator is unequivocal: 'Elle était ignoble.'[31] The scene is important, not only because she has enough distance, as a result of the analysis, to articulate to herself and to her mother what the problem is, that her mother is an alcoholic, but also because it is reproducing scenes which the narrator herself has already lived through. She described her monstrous madness before the analysis started in the following terms: 'Un courant de vie putréfiée m'entraînait, que je le veuille ou non, vers la mort absolument obligatoire qui était l'horreur même. Cela m'inspirait une peur épouvant- able, insupportable. Puisqu'il n'y avait pas d'autre destin pour moi que de tomber *dans le ventre ignoble de l'infect*, autant y tomber le plus vite possible. Je voulais me suicider, me finir.'[32] Her immediate reaction on

---

[31] 'She was there, in front of me, sitting on her bed, as usual. Her nightshirt had ridden up over her stomach, so I could see her now bare genitals. She had done her business where she was sitting and the shit was running down to the ground.' 'She was sordid.' (p. 329)

[32] *Les Mots pour le dire*, 40: 'A current of putrefied life was pulling me, whether I liked it or not, towards an absolutely unavoidable death which was horror itself. It inspired a terrifying, unbearable fear within me. Since there was no other fate for me than falling *into the sordid belly of the unclean*, it would be better to fall as quickly as possibly. I wanted to kill myself, to finish it all.' Emphasis added.

seeing her mother offering a kind of mirror image of her own abjection is that, without the analysis, she would have killed her.

The narrator describes her inner turmoil and physical symptoms of her illness as 'rottenness', 'decomposition', and the novel is full of scenes or description where bodily fluids, excrement, decomposing horrors, escape from their fine apparently clean exteriors. And this affects her, her mother, and her father. On one occasion, the narrator as a young girl is visiting her father, and decides she has to urinate in the lift, which she stops between floors for this purpose. Like her mother so many years later (and the coincidence of vocabulary, 'le sexe pelé' and the 'tapis-brosse tout pelé' is one reason for juxtaposing the two scenes), she loses control: 'Mais, horreur, mes déversements avaient traversé le tapis-brosse tout pelé, avaient franchi le plancher et se répandaient en cascade de gouttelettes.'[33] She remembers this incident when her father's coffin is being carried up the same five flights of stairs. The elegant surroundings, the profusion of flowers, of fine clothes, is no preparation for the sudden bad smell from the coffin, betraying the rotting flesh inside (pp. 74–5). Even when alive, her father's body, with its dandified exterior and rotten, tuberculous interior, partakes of this terrifying dichotomy of the clean and unclean; it is this deceit which his wife cannot forgive him. Having broken with his family, he had lived a rather dissolute life—'Dieu sait où il a traîné avant d'aboutir ici' (p. 145). But he copied the fine manners, adopted the elegant ways of the bourgeoisie to get himself a fine wife, and she had no hint of the 'uncleanliness' within, the hidden tuberculosis with which, she said, he killed her daughter. The narrator herself is isolated by her uncleanliness. 'Comment jeter le pont qui joindrait l'intense au calme, le clair à l'obscur, qui enjamberait l'égout, le fleuve gros de matières en décomposition, le courant méchant de la peur?'[34] 'La chose' is not only blood, it is 'le sang, la sueur, la merde, la morve, la salive, le pus, le vomi'.[35] Even her rather bovaryesque identifications with religious passions end up reproducing the same opposition as she contemplates the clean 'mort du chrétien' (Christian death) compared to the dirty 'mort du pécheur' (sinner's death). And it is the shame, the sinfulness, which helps hold the key to the obsessional nature of the fears associated with dirt. She is 'la petite-fille étron' (the little turd girl), who could not be killed, whom her mother passed out of her own body as she would pass a motion. She

[33] 'But what horror, my outpourings had gone through the threadbare rug, had crossed the floorboards and were spreading in a cascade of droplets.' (p. 68)

[34] Ibid. 9: 'How can I build the bridge which would join intensity and calmness, light and dark, which would cross over the sewer, the river full of decomposing matter, the wicked current of fear?'

[35] Ibid. 25: 'blood, sweat, shit, snot, saliva, pus, and vomit'.

is 'laide comme un pou' (ugly as sin), she is a 'souillon' (slut), she is filth. For a time, she hoped to mask her inner turmoil and filth by keeping up appearances, outwardly. But her body, her dreams, her fears, her obsessions, everything lets her down. There is no control.

This psychological dynamic finds its counterpart in the world outside, in the hierarchies of class and race. Just as her father was contaminated by something indeterminate, since they didn't know 'where he'd been' ('Dieu sait où il a traîné'), so the working class and Algeria too represent danger. A nightmare of being attacked by an Algerian precedes her memory of being attacked in the lift. Her mother undertakes charitable work, and battles to impose health, cleanliness, and order on the 'plaies infectées' (infected wounds), driven by the complicated motivations of Christian charity, forever needing the dirt to be dirty (p. 112, p. 154). As with Algeria, so with her daughter whose illness is, in some senses, needed. The configurations of the personal and social levels of the text are therefore replicated at the level of national discourse. The narrator's family leaves Algeria at the time of the war of independence, and the portrayal of Algeria and France—the former 'la vraie mère' (p. 112), the latter 'le pays-chef détesté' (p. 319)—is also informed by the vocabulary and tensions of family and gender which are the novel's subject.

At one of the centres of these tensions stands the profoundly ambiguous figure of the narrator's father. At one point she comments: 'Mon père est un inconnu total qui n'a jamais fait partie de ma vie.'[36] Even though she is here expressing the view that her mother dominated her perception of her father, robbing him of any real existence for her, it still is a bewildering phrase, undermined by the metaphorical structures of filth and rottenness to which he is crucial. If one associates the scenes of the young girl urinating, the scenes of the watchful eyes, the network of associations with illness, decomposition, death, and the implicit or explicit sexuality in all this, he is present to it all. It is disturbing to read a long passage devoted to his seductive charms and power with women followed by her unease in his presence:

> **Chaque fois que je le rencontrais il était heureux de me voir. *Trop heureux.* Il me regardait en riant, il me serrait contre lui, il était attentif à mes mouvements, à mes paroles. Il détaillait les traits de mon visage: 'Ton nez, tes yeux, tes mains . . . les mêmes que moi! Tu me ressembles, petit loup!' Ça le faisait rire encore plus. Quand j'étais là plus rien n'existait que moi. Cela me gênait.[37]**

---

[36] *Les Mots pour le dire*, 78: 'My father is a complete stranger who has never been part of my life.'
[37] Ibid. 146: 'Each time I met him he was happy to see me. *Too happy.* With a laugh he looked at me, held me to him, he was attentive to my movements, to my words. He scrutinised my face: "Your nose, your eyes, your hands . . . the same as me! You look like me, little wolf!" That made him laugh even more. When I was there, nothing else existed for him. It made me feel awkward.' Emphasis added.

Yet looking at a photograph of him, she has a different reaction: 'A voir les belles mains qu'il avait, son sourire éclatant, son corps mince et musclé, je crois qu'il m'aurait plu.' She hastens to add, again strangely: 'Il ne m'a jamais blessée, jamais marquée, jamais touchée.'[38] Yet she was sexually attacked, in a lift; she urinates in the lift going up to her father's flat, an experience described in unmistakably sexual, phallic terms, having for the first time seen her parents as sexual beings. Her father is attractive; he is too attractive. She finds him attractive, she finds him repulsive. It is all her mother's manipulation anyway. She is at times like Little Red Riding Hood, surrounded by sexualized monsters disguised as parents about to devour her. The uncleanliness of illness, of sexuality, of female sexuality, devours her from within. Violent aggression and repulsion are her experience of both parents, and dispensed also through a range of other figures.

In its vocabulary and themes, its portrait of a woman trying to overcome the self-hatred and disgust which has been taught to her, *Les Mots* is at one with the feminist press. *Le Torchon brûle* was even prosecuted for obscenity for its issue on the vagina and female sexuality. The endless lists of negative, dirty, obscene words for women, especially women as sexual beings, the taboos of dirt and filth surrounding menstruation,[39] are a leitmotiv of feminist writing. Women's bodies are more than marginalized; if language, culture and society depend on processes of identification within a male symbolic order, then the exclusion of the female, and the female body, are its very mainstay. Celebration of femininity, of female physicality, of blood and milk (*Le Torchon brûle* was a 'menstruel', not 'mensuel'), cannot be accommodated within that order. Just as *Tel Quel* reconfigures subjectivity and the processes of writing which constitute individuality as the most powerful site of political struggle, so much feminist writing frames femininity as permanent and irrecuperable contestation. 'Perturbation ma sœur' are the words with which Simone de Beauvoir begins her preface to the multifaceted, multivocal *Les Femmes s'entêtent*.

The revaluation of the sexual politics of bourgeois morality from a woman-centred point of view, that is to say, breaking also with the *gauchiste* libertarian sexuality of disruptive violence and excess at women's expense, found a strong ally in the movement for gay liberation, which shared many of feminism's targets and themes. After early involvement in pro-abortion demonstrations,[40] the first public event was the disruption of the screening of a popular television programme by Gay Liberation and lesbian MLF

---

[38] *Les Mots pour le dire*, 80: 'Looking at the beautiful hands he had, his dazzling smile, his slim, muscled body, I think I would have been attracted to him.' 'He never hurt me, never left a mark on me, never touched me.'

[39] Cf. *Les Mots pour le dire*, p. 138.   [40] Abortion was legalized in 1974.

militants shouting: 'A bas l'homosexualité de papa'.[41] Guy Hocquenhem's articles in the aftermath of May express anger at the damage of enforced invisibility of homosexuality, and at the mechanisms of shame and disgust projected and internalized:

> Avez-vous jamais pensé à ce que nous ressentons, quand vous mettez à la suite ces mots: 'Salaud, ordure, tapette, pédé'? Quand vous dites à une fille: 'Sale gouine'?
> Vous protégez vos filles et vos fils de notre présence comme si nous étions des pestiférés.
> Vous êtes individuellement responsables de l'ignoble mutilation que vous nous avez fait subir ennous reprochant notre désir.[42]

Les Mots pour le dire is realist fiction, not experimental fiction. It tells a clear story, uses the structure of the *Bildungsroman*, taking the heroine through trials to the discovery of the self. It is a first-person narrative which explores the conventions of autobiography, as well as the difference, in knowledge particularly, between 'la folle' and the narrator, who is looking from the horizons formed by May 1968. The narrator is neither silent nor invisible at the beginning of her story. On the most banal level, as narrator she is the central figure in the autobiographical structure, ignorant of the outcome which has in fact produced the self as narrator. 'La folle' may be a victim, yet the narrator herself is not. She has taken charge and is in a position of power in the text, structurally and metaphorically.[43] In her earlier 'dialogues' with doctors, she is subsumed under the language of the body which the doctors appropriate. Women's bodies are not their own. Hysterical symptoms are all too visible and eloquent: like Laurence in *Les Belles Images*, her body is speaking for her.[44] The symptoms have to be rendered invisible for the narrator to be able to speak. The first reaction of her psychoanalyst to her story is: 'Parlez-moi d'autre chose.' (p. 42). Her knowledge brings her to understand her illness. The boundaries between madness and lucidity shift as the madness is

---

[41] See F. Martel, *Le Rose et le noir* (Seuil, 1996), 59–79.

[42] 'Have you even thought what we feel, when you run off these words one after the other: "Bastard, filth, queen, queer"? When you say "filthy dyke to a girl"? You protect your daughters and sons from our presence as if we had the plague. You are individually responsible for the sordid mutilation you made us undergo by reproaching us with our desire.' G. Hocquenhem, *L'Après-mai des faunes*, 145. See also Girard, *Le Mouvement homosexuel*, 89 ff.: 'Notre trou du cul est révolutionnaire', for further discussion of the issue of appropriation and revalorization of terms of abuse.

[43] Through the metaphors of sight and filming. It is now the narrator who, we are told, is the all-seeing eye on her parents, who is wielding the camera recording them (p. 20).

[44] Cardinal worked with Godard on the screenplay of *2 ou 3 choses que je sais d'elle*; be it coincidence or overdetermined by *Tout va bien*, her choice of image for the woman who takes control of her body, and no longer feels it to be either negative or out of control, is to compare it to an advert for Dim tights. (*Les Mots pour le dire*, 188.)

shown to be reasonable and to make sense; conventional reason is on the side of repression, ignorance, destruction, and madness. *Les Mots pour le dire* has a clear social message in relation to woman and society, and women and identity, detailing how society, how her family, how her mother made her ill: how the lively, confident, angry, sexual, little girl became a fearful, conventional, and very sick, woman.

There is much here that is close to what became known as 'French feminist theory', and its use of psychoanalysis to dismantle gendered norms. Phil Powrie describes the novel as: 'a poetic representation of the mother–daughter relationship illustrating the matrix described by Irigaray; it is an account of the repositioning of the protagonist as a subject within language, as well as an exploration of the mother–daughter bond which can be illuminated by the psychoanalytical grid of abjection as defined by Kristeva'.[45] Yet it is also an enactment of the trajectory which Beauvoir describes as 'on ne naît pas femme, on le devient', with its infrastructure of social values, choices, and interests situating women as 'other'. Indeed, one of the clearest refutations of the thesis that '68 thought' is based on a division, at the level of content, between structuralism and existentialism, is the importance of *Le Deuxième Sexe*, alongside the proliferating works of structuralist-inspired theorizations of gender and culture, in the constitution of women's writing at this time. In fact there are many feminisms in dialogue and argument in the aftermath of 68, with different emphases, on patriarchy, on class, or on *écriture féminine*, in order to account for and struggle against the power relations in society. And many nuances within particular positions—for example, the workerism of the Lacanian *Psych et po*—have been largely forgotten. *Les Mots pour le dire* demonstrates the artificiality of legislating too rigidly on the incompatibilities of the theoretical approaches, with its configuration of signification, language, gender, psychoanalysis, and the politics of nationality and colonialism, in conjunction with the fabrication and production of female identity through the story of one individual's lived experience.

[45] 'Reading for Pleasure: Marie Cardinal's *Les Mots pour le dire* and the Text as (Re)play of Oedipal Configurations', 164–5. In M. Atack and P. Powrie (eds.), *Contemporary French Fiction by Women: Feminist Perspectives* (Manchester University Press, 1990).

6 Nation/History: repenser la France

The instincts which led the feminist group to stage a demonstration at the tomb of the Unknown Warrior were very sound ones. They could hardly have chosen a more appropriate site to signal the new cultural politics and the challenge to established discourses of gender, especially as it had featured prominently in May's ideological battles. On 30 May 1968, André Malraux, Minister of Culture, acclaimed author and Resistance hero, was at the head of the Gaullist demonstration which marched from la Place de la Concorde the length of the Champs-Elysées to the Arc de Triomphe. Malraux, Michel Debré, François Mauriac, and the Gaullist hierarchy paid homage to the Unknown Soldier, reclaiming the site from an earlier student demonstration.[1] 'Devant la dalle sacrée jaillit la Marseillaise' captions *Miroir de l'histoire*.[2] This is their eternal France, the France of Resistance, of patriotism, of defence of the nation. It is a people's France too—albeit a different people from in the earlier demonstrations.

Monuments are the physical supports of complex discourses bearing historical and national identities, and just as the city of Paris itself has been described as a symbolization of the past, so too can the monument be a palimpsest,[3] for its meanings are similarly subject to processes of change and reinscription. The feminist demonstration reproduced in microcosm one of the most significant aspects of the May revolution which showed such a sophisticated understanding of the cultural: the cultural history of Gaullist France was to be shaken to its roots in the process. As *Le Chagrin et la pitié*, a four-hour long television documentary on the Occupation made in 1969, took its place alongside Modiano's *La Place de l'étoile* (1968), the cement holding together the post-1964 Gaullist model of the historical nation would start to crumble rapidly.

Le Chagrin threw open doors onto the 1940–4 years in a way that had not been done before, but in so doing it knocked many other things out of

---

[1] L. Rioux and R. Backmann, *L'Explosion de mai, 11 mai 1968* (Robert Laffont, 1968), 469.

[2] 'Before the sacred flagstone bursts forth La Marseillaise', *Miroir de l'histoire, Mai 68* (June–July 1973), 116–17.

[3] See Patricia Parkhurst Ferguson, *Paris as Revolution: Writing the Nineteenth Century City* (Berkeley, Calif., University of Calif. Press, 1994), 198. A palimpsest is a parchment prepared for writing on, and wiping out again, like a slate, and is often used as a useful metaphor for the cultural rewritings of memory, history, and intertextuality.

view. The fact that it was such a powerful film had the effect of turning everyone's attention onto the picture it revealed to the exclusion of all that lay outside the frame. Not much detailed thought has been given to its own inheritance. May 68 is one part of that story, for a close look at May and the historiography of the war not only reveals how complex is the relation of May to history, but also how important is *Le Chagrin*'s relationship to its own immediate history.

Général nous voilà![4]

> Les barricades parisiennes d'août 44 ont une fonction symbolique, commémorative. Elles affichent les retrouvailles avec le passé sacralisé des insurrections populaires, elles présentent un *miracle*, celui du Peuple retrouvé, peuple fraternel, égalitaire, héroïque et combattant, peuple exemplaire qui, sous le regard du monde entier, forge l'Histoire, en ces moments sublimes que sont 1789, 1830, 1848, 1871.[5]
>
> A vingt ans ils n'avaient pas connu Alger, encore moins la libération de Paris. Ils apprennent et ils n'oublieront pas.[6]

May was saturated with history, yet history was also being spontaneously rediscovered and relived, for the first time, by a new generation. Every element resonated with its antecedents in an often knowingly self-conscious relation to history. If, as is suggested above, a barricade in 1944 is as much a symbolic as a functional object, then this is all the more true of 1968. The sacred site of May is the street, in the revolutionary city *par excellence*, as throughout the nineteenth century, as in 1944: 'Avec les barricades, c'est toute la mystique du Paris insurrectionnel qui revient, du Paris porteur du grand message de l'émancipation humaine aussi.'[7] Mitterrand's

---

[4] Front page of *Action* (4 Sept. 1968), reproduced Marc Rohan, *Paris 68* (Impact Books, 1988), 56. 'Maréchal nous voilà' was the title/first line of the song celebrating Pétain taught to schoolchildren during the Occupation.

[5] 'The barricades in Paris in August 1944 have a symbolic, commemorative function. They proclaim the links with the sacred past of popular insurrections, they present a *miracle*, that of the reunion with the People, the fraternal, egalitarian, heroic and fighting people, the exemplary people who, under the gaze of the whole world, is making History, in those sublime moments of 1789 [French Revolution], 1830 [revolutionary movements, installation of Louis-Philippe as constitutional monarch], 1848 [revolutionary movements, proclamation of the Second Republic], 1871 [Paris Commune].' Alain Brossat, *Libération fête folle* (Autrement, 1994), 113.

[6] 'They were 20, and they had not known Algiers, even less the Liberation of Paris. They are learning and will not forget.' Caption to photograph of 24 May, P. Labro, *Les Barricades de mai* (Solar, 1968).

[7] 'With the barricades, it is the mystique of revolutionary Paris which returns, of Paris bearing the great message of human emancipation also.' Brossat, *Libération fête folle*, 113.

reaction to de Gaulle's radio speech of 30 May is classic in its use of the past: 'La voix que nous venons d'entendre, elle vient de loin dans notre histoire. C'est la voix du 18 brumaire, c'est la voix du 2 décembre, c'est la voix du 13 mai . . .'.[8] 1936, the year of the Popular Front and of a mass strike movement, is frequently evoked, as is the history of fascism and anti-fascism. We shall see the importance of the latter, and of Algeria, in the political historicization of May.

This great original, unrepeatable, unforeseeable event is, therefore, as historicized as it is immediate, and this is not new. The Resistance continually invoked the French Revolution, the defeat of foreign armies at Valmy, 1870, and the Paris Commune, to frame its own political projects. The historical can also be more than a reference: for example, representations of the phoney war, in journalism and in literature, owe everything to accounts of the First World War. Similarly with May, history is more than a reference. History is founding the event as such: the new, the immediate, is situated, effectively mediated, by the antecedents it is given. The historical dimension has an ontological role: 'Sans le poids des traditions, les incertitudes du printemps sont difficilement décryptables.'[9] 'Le risque existe que la crise de mai 68 soit—*elle l'est déjà*, mesurée à l'aune du passé, réduite aux significations et aux catégories déjà disponibles.'[10] The corollary of the very immediacy of May was the immediacy of historical referent. Experience abhors a representational vacuum.

May's cultural revolution played an important part in making the cultural itself, the symbolization of an event, an object of study. Earlier work on cultural myths (Barthes, *Mythologies*; Beauvoir, *Le Deuxième Sexe*) found a new audience, as structuralism and particularly the perspectives on knowledge associated with Foucault and his work on what is 'knowable' at a particular historical conjuncture, encouraged the study of ideologies and cultural structures. By overturning what it saw as the dominant view of 'the nation at war' during the Occupation, *Le Chagrin et la pitié* brought that view into focus, and it became a phenomenon in its own

---

[8] 'The voice we have just heard is the voice of 18 Brumaire [Napoleon Bonaparte takes power in 1799], the voice of the 2 December [Louis-Napoleon takes power in 1851], the voice of 13 May [the *putsch* of the French generals in Algiers in 1958]' Quoted in Rioux and Backmann, *L'Explosion de mai*, 466.

[9] 'Without the weight of tradition, the uncertainties of the spring are difficult to decipher.' A. Percheron and R. Mouriaux, 'Mai 68 entre la répétition et l'invention', in R. Mouriaux *et al.*, *1968: Exploration du mai français*, ii (L'Harmattan, 1992), 11.

[10] 'The risk exists that the crisis of May 68 might be—it *already is being*—measured against the past, reduced to meanings and categories that are already available.' J.-M. Coudray, in E. Morin *et al.*, *La Brèche* (Fayard, 1968), 127. Emphasis added.

right. In that sense, there are two narratives at work in the film, a narrative of the years 1940–4, and at one and the same time a narrative of the post-war period, which emerges as a narrative of false consciousness, or myth.

That 68 had a direct impact on representations of France through the reappraisal of the historiography of the Occupation which *Le Chagrin et la pitié* set rolling in 1969 is well established. Stanley Hoffmann considered that the film would not have been the same if made in 1967.[11] Filmed in 1969, commissioned by Swiss television, *Le Chagrin et la pitié* was available for viewing in 1971. As French television had not commissioned it, they did not literally 'ban' it, but the effect of their refusal to buy it was the same. This was the longest, most serious investigation of Vichy France on film, a major television programme, yet France would not see it. It was shown to packed houses in a Paris cinema; symbolically, it would be under the Mitterrand government that it finally was screened on French television. Symptomatic of the complex relationship between the French state, memory of the war, and representation, is the fact that by the end of his presidency in 1995, Mitterrand himself was severely judged for complicity with the Vichy State, revealed, appropriately enough, in yet another television interview.

Le Chagrin et la pitié was treated as a magisterial blast against a glorious cover-up. Its anti-heroic *parti-pris* is evident in the very choice of title: for a film about the nation and the Resistance under Vichy to be dubbed a story of sorrow and pity showed from the outset how different it was going to be. It raised a storm of controversy, and has generally been held to be the trigger for the outpouring of memory and reappraisal which soon came to be called the *mode rétro*.[12] Patrick Modiano's *La Place de l'étoile* was a major literary event which again brought the issues of youth and generation to the fore, since the author was born after the war; in 1974, Modiano wrote the screenplay for Louis Malle's *Lacombe Lucien*, a film which came much closer to defining the *mode rétro* vision of France as a nation of spineless, self-serving hypocrites pushed around by wilful collaborating degenerates. Over the past thirty years, the interrogation of collaboration and pro-Vichy sentiments has been combined with that of French complicity in the deportation of tens of thousands of Jews to the death camps, as the works of imagination become intertwined with highly public, mediatized events: the Barbie trial, the Touvier trial, the

---

[11] 'In the Looking Glass', preface to the screenplay of *The Sorrow and the Pity* (Paladin, 1975), xi.
[12] Although now used to designate the literary and cinematic texts which took the Occupation as their subject in the 1970s, it did initially have a more frivolous side, typified by Serge Gainsbourg's show 'Rock around the Bunker'.

killing of René Bousquet, Mitterrand's interview, the Papon trial.[13] It has also become something of a critical commonplace that until *Le Chagrin* started the whole process, representations of the war and the Occupation had been dominated by the Gaullist (or communist) myths of a nation united in Resistance behind its glorious leadership. However, a look at May 68 and its prehistory shows that such a view is, at very best, highly misleading.

Le Chagrin et la pitié starts with a wedding in Germany. It transpires that the father of the bride, Helmut Tausend, was stationed in Clermont-Ferrand during the Occupation. He contrasts the present with the experiences of himself and his wife, remembering their early married life in wartime. All this takes place in German with French subtitles, before cutting to an aerial view of Clermont-Ferrand as the voice-over lists its statistics, its distance in kilometres from Paris. The film therefore starts by framing the story of Clermont-Ferrand within the context of the war, the Franco-German war, and Tausend is filmed with hostility throughout the film. Given that it is 'la guerre franco-française' which is the exclusive subject of *la mode rétro*, this point is worth stressing. After the impersonal details about Clermont-Ferrand, the personal stories which form the substance of the film, take over. Marcel Verdier is sitting in a room explaining to his children, who are of student age, what life was like under the Occupation, and that the dominant emotions he associates with the time are 'le chagrin et la pitié'. At this point the film cuts to footage of Maurice Chevalier entertaining French prisoners of war in Germany with a jokey song about soldiers, and the credits roll. The choice of subtitle: 'Chronique d'une ville française sous l'occupation allemande' is intriguing, recalling as it does Camus's *La Peste* and its well-known claim to be a chronicle, not a novel. The effect is similar here, suggesting a refusal of fiction in the name of truth, which is however narratively constructed. The technique of the film, and its use of montage, made a great impression at the time, and is considered an essential support of the way it investigates the issue of memory and personal evasions, juxtaposing documents of the time with direct interviews.

Thirty-five people are interviewed in the film, covering a gamut of positions and experiences: politicians such as Pierre Mendès France and

---

[13] Klaus Barbie was brought back from Bolivia to face trial for crimes against humanity in relation to his activities as the senior SS officer in Lyons during the Occupation. Paul Touvier was tried for collaboration. René Bousquet was shot before his trial for his part in the deportations could take place. Mitterrand acknowledged his friendship with him in his television interview in 1994 where he also spoke about his position at Vichy before he became involved in Resistance work. This almost coincided with Patrick Péan's biography of him which revealed details of his time at Vichy to a wide public. Maurice Papon, an official in the Vichy government, was tried for crimes against humanity in 1997–8.

Georges Bidault, Resisters from the region like the Grave brothers, and from Resistance movements, including Emmanuel d'Astier de la Vigerie who devoted a special issue of his journal *L'Événement* to the May events and welcomed them enthusiastically as a continuation of the Resistance,[14] 'ordinary people' (such as Marcel Verdier the chemist, Madame Solange the hairdresser), a committed collaborator who fought on the Eastern Front in German uniform (Christian de la Mazière), and Colonel de Chambord, son-in-law of Pierre Laval who had two spells as prime minister in Pétain's government and who was executed for treason after the war. There are German military and businessmen, and also British witnesses: Anthony Eden speaking an impressive if heavily accented French, Major-General Sir Edward Spiers speaking flawless French, Denis Rake of the Special Operations Executive who was parachuted into France. The anti-heroic message which the film hammers home concerns the humiliation of the military rout and collapse of France, the level of support for Pétain, the pervasive anti-Semitism, both official (in the Vichy government and its actions, or in the anti-Semitic exhibitions and films such as *Le Juif Süss*, an extract from which closes the first half of the film) and unofficial, memorable particularly in the interview with the shopkeeper M. Klein who advertised to his 'aimable clientèle' that he was pleased to tell them he was not Jewish.

To the May activists, the anti-Semitism would hardly come as a surprise. It was a politician of the right who apparently dismissed Cohn-Bendit as a 'juif allemand', leading to one of the most famous of the May slogans: 'Nous sommes tous des juifs allemands'. Cohn-Bendit's past paralleled that of Marcel Ophuls. The son of German refugees from Nazism, he was born in France, though he spent part of his childhood in Germany. Ophuls's father, the director Max Ophuls, also had to leave Germany when Marcel was 12. Knowledge of the war and the political realities of Nazism was something they had both grown up with. Virulent anti-Semitic abuse was a feature of May. *Mourir à trente ans* includes footage of an orator addressing a right-wing meeting during May, saying with studied deliberation, and to rapturous acclaim: 'Nous ne sommes *pas* . . . des juifs allemands!' 'Cohn-Bendit à Dachau' was heard on the Gaullist march of 30 May; he himself says that on his arrest on 3 May a policeman said: 'Mon petit père tu vas payer. Dommage que tu n'aies crevé à Auschwitz avec tes parents comme ça, on n'aurait pas à le faire pas aujourd'hui.'[15]

---

[14] *L'Événement, Première histoire de la révolution de mai* (June 1968), 17.

[15] 'Well little fellow, you are going to pay. What a pity you didn't die in Auschwitz with your parents, as then we wouldn't have to do it today.' *Le Grand Bazar* (Pierre Belfond, 1975), 33.

La France des souvenirs

In 1964, André Malraux, Resistance hero, welcomed to the Panthéon the ashes of Jean Moulin, the supreme Resistance hero, the man sent from London by de Gaulle to unify the Resistance movements and who died under torture at the hands of Klaus Barbie. As Malraux delivered his extraordinarily powerful speech, at his side stood de Gaulle 'immense dans l'immense capote de campagne qui l'enveloppe jusqu'aux pieds, comme au temps de la bataille des Ardennes'.[16] The crowd joins in with 'Le Chant des partisans' at its end. Two years after the bitter end of the Algerian War, marked by violent divisions between the French (including an attempted *putsch* by some of the French military), the Gaullist establishment which had massively participated in the Resistance had a grand state occasion to celebrate, to draw together nation, people, and state in a shared identification in Resistance heroism. De Gaulle himself was the incarnation of Resistance; the man who broadcast a message of Resistance to the nation from London on 18 June 1940 after the rout of the French Army (the day after Pétain's broadcast informing the French that he was seeking an Armistice), who led the Free French in London, and the Provisional Government in Algiers after the Allies had landed in North Africa, and whose triumphal walk down the Champs-Elysées in August 1944 before a crowd of nearly a million people is one of the truly extraordinary moments of French history. But by the mid-1960s, another generation had grown up whose knowledge of the war was at best hazy. *Hitler connais pas* was the title of Bernard Blier's 1963 documentary on the young.

On 30 May 1968, de Gaulle addressed the nation in a radio broadcast. This was his second address, the first having been televised on 24 May. Its effect had been to reinforce the impression of an old man, out of touch with events, and out of his depth. It had done nothing to slow down the momentum of the social unrest. By the time of the meeting at the Charléty stadium on 28 May, when Mitterrand proposed the setting up of a provisional government headed by Mendès France, the conviction that the regime was finished was widespread. It was for these reasons that de Gaulle's 'disappearance' on 29 May had such a resonance. The vacuum of power was apparently a statement of fact. It emerged fairly quickly however that de Gaulle has been to 's'assurer l'armée' (get the backing of the army), visiting General Massu (who had commanded the first French troops sent into Algiers for the Battle of Algiers in 1957) at Baden-Baden.

---

[16] J. Lacouture, *Malraux: Une vie dans le siècle* (Seuil, 1973, coll. Points), 394; 'huge in his huge military coat covering him from head to toe, like at the time of the Ardennes battle'.

At 4.30 p.m. on 30 May the broadcast to the nation took place, and by all accounts, the nation was listening, this time.[17]

De Gaulle's preference for radio over television may indeed have had practical reasons, given the state of things at the ORTF,[18] but it also very knowingly evoked the famous 18 June broadcast from London in 1940. The saviour of the nation is once again calling the nation to arms. As well as recalling the revolutionary days of 1848, Mitterrand's call at Charléty for a provisional government had been a studied insult to the former head of the provisional government in Algiers and the symbol of national Resistance against the Vichy government. Now it was being suggested that rejection of de Gaulle was the patriot's position. De Gaulle's speech, shot through with the language of national crisis and resistance, is about power, and refers obliquely by its vocabulary to that previous fall of a Republic: 'Français, Françaises, étant le détenteur de la légitimité nationale et républicaine, j'ai envisagé depuis vingt-quatre heures toutes les éventualités sans exception qui me permettraient de la maintenir.'[19] He announces the dissolution of the Assemblée Nationale, the calling of elections, and the measures to be taken if democratic elections are prevented, such as the organization of 'l'action civique', the establishment of 'commissaires de la république'. The threat to be countered is that of a communist take-over: 'Et bien! non, la République n'abdiquera pas, le peuple se ressaisira.'[20] Republican legitimacy and republican power will not crumble this time, and he will continue, as in 1940, to embody them. Less than four years after the ceremony for Jean Moulin, where the republican Resistance discourse aimed in part, as Rousso puts it, to eliminate civil war by mentioning only the foreign (German) enemy, de Gaulle was playing the Resistance card as a call to arms. The reactions show that the message was heard: students, workers, politicians, all agreed, this was 'un appel à la guerre civile'. Totalitarian communism was certainly an alien enemy in Gaullist discourse; none the less, as during the Occupation itself, the call to rally around the patriotic figure is implicitly pointing to the divided nation.

At 6 p.m., Gaullist France was gathering for its demonstration on the Place de la Concorde. Anxiety about possible turn-out led the organizers to call upon organizations of veterans and political sympathizers. In the event, it was an impressive show of force for the established order.

---

[17] *Le Chagrin et la pitié* made it clear, a fact copiously confirmed since, that very few people actually heard de Gaulle's broadcast in 1940.

[18] A large number of journalists at the state-owned television network had been on strike since 25 May.

[19] 'Frenchmen, Frenchwomen, being the one who safeguards Republican and national legitimacy, I have in the last 24 hours considered all the options without exception which would enable me to uphold it.' Rioux and Backmann, *L'Explosion de mai*, 464.

[20] Ibid. 465: 'Well no! the Republic will not abdicate, the people will rally itself.'

Commentators agree that it was not the usual kind of demonstrator: small shopkeepers, the France of the petite-bourgeoisie, managing directors, young people too, the 'fils à papa', the 'minets' and 'minettes' of the bourgeoisie, beautifully turned out. The reference to Algeria is strong with the large number of paratroopers in uniform participating. Thibaudeau's radio play, *Mai 68*, underlines the car horns banging out the rhythms of 'Al-gé-rie fran-çaise'.[21] Slogans recall Vichy France too: 'La France aux Français', and notoriously 'Cohn-Bendit à Dachau'. 'C'est la France des souvenirs' was one reaction.

But the France which had demonstrated on 13 May was also remembering: 'Dix ans ça suffit' was their slogan. 13 May 1958 was the date of the *putsch* of the generals in Algiers, when a military *coup* was seriously feared. De Gaulle had left government in 1947, but the leaders of the Fourth Republic appealed to the one man they thought would be able to bring stability to a volatile situation. As a general, de Gaulle could pacify the revolting generals; as a Resistance hero, de Gaulle had credibility in claiming to represent the interests of the nation. He did not, however, pacify the left, and the fears of a military dictatorship were strong indeed, particularly as he used the situation to bring about the constitutional reforms he had tried unsuccessfully to initiate after the Liberation: the presidential Fifth Republic was about to be born. Opposition to de Gaulle and to Gaullism are quite fundamental to May, as the choice of 13 May for the great mobilization of workers and students, and their banners on the day, show:

13 MAI 1958
L'émeute d'Alger a amené
de Gaulle au pouvoir

13 MAI 1968
LA LUTTE ET LES BARRICADES
DES ETUDIANTS
l'ont ébranlé et
MONTRENT LA VOIE
pour l'en chasser.
Bon anniversaire,
mon général![22]

The politics of the Algerian War is a crucial strand in the politics of May proper. And in both 1958 and 1968, the vocabulary of Resistance and Occupation is an important mediator of political clashes.

---

[21] Jean Thibaudeau, *Mai 68 en France* (Seuil, 1970), 115–16.
[22] '13 May 1958, the riot in Algiers brought de Gaulle to power. 13 May 1968, the struggle and the barricades of the students have shaken him and show the way to expel him from it. Happy anniversary, General.' *Miroir de l'histoire* (June–July 1973), 33.

Ni fleurs ni Charonne

In relation to representations of Vichy and the Occupation, two funda-mental changes occurred with the Algerian War: first, the French were assimilated to the position of occupying oppressors. They were now the torturers (there was extensive documentary and eye-witness evidence on the use of torture by French paratroopers) and this had significant reper-cussions for the positioning of the Resistance, with leading Resistance figures like de Gaulle and Malraux in the government. Secondly, reference to the Occupation and to Vichy had become inextricably entwined with events and polemics of the Algerian War.[23] Simone de Beauvoir's discus-sion of the Algerian demonstration of 17 October 1961 in Paris, when the police opened fire, when 11,000 Algerians were arrested later that same day, when bodies of Algerians were discovered floating in the Seine and in the Bois de Boulogne, is a case in point. 'J'ai entendu l'interview de Frey et ses mensonges reposés: deux morts, alors qu'on en avait déjà dénombré plus de cinquante. Dix mille Algériens étaient parqués au Vel' d'Hiv, comme autrefois les Juifs à Drancy.'[24]

> A la Chambre (. . .), Claudius Petit dit à Frey: 'Nous savons maintenant ce que ça signifiait d'être allemands pendant le nazisme!'; ses paroles sombrèrent dans un silence de mort. Il y avait plus de cinq ans que Marrou avait évoqué Buchenwald et la Gestapo; pendant des années, les Français avaient accepté les mêmes complicités que les Allemands sous le régime nazi; le malaise tardif que certains en éprouvaient ne me réconciliaient pas avec eux.[25]

Roger Frey was the Minister of the Interior in October 1961, and the Prefect of Police in Paris was Maurice Papon, although his connection with Vichy appears to have gone unremarked during May.

'Ni fleurs ni Charonne', a play on 'Ni fleurs ni couronnes' (no flowers or wreaths) was one of the banners at the huge 13 May demonstration, recalling the nine dead in the Charonne métro station in February 1962

---

[23] Philip Dine, 'The Inescapable Allusion: The Occupation and the Resistance in French Fiction and Film of the Algerian War', in R. Kedward and N. Wood, *The Liberation of France: Image and Event* (Oxford: Berg, 1995), 269–82.

[24] 'I heard the interview with Frey and his repeated lies: 2 dead, when they had already counted more than 50. Ten thousand Algerians were held at the Vel' d'Hiv [Vélodrome d'Hiver] like the Jews at Drancy in the past.' *La Force des choses* (Gallimard, 1963), ii. 435 livre de poche edition.

[25] 'In the Chamber Claudius Petit said to Frey: "We now know what it meant to be German under the Nazis!"; his words were met by a deathly silence. More than five years ago, Marrou had recalled Buchenwald and the Gestapo; for years, the French had been accepting the same compromises as the Germans under the Nazi regime; the belated unease that some were feeling about it did not reconcile me to them.' Ibid. 436–7.

at a communist anti-OAS demonstration.[26] Posters of May 68 attack
Roger Frey, showing him as a sinister figure wearing a badge: 'Chef des
indics ASSASSIN DE CHARONNE Patron des briseurs de grève', or as a sabre-
toothed pig-like animal.[27] In the articles of *Le Canard de mai*, the edition
of the satirical newspaper *Le Canard enchaîné* devoted to the events,[28]
hostility to de Gaulle is the overriding theme, and particularly the supposed deal with the generals to offer an amnesty to the still imprisoned
members of the OAS. The legend '"Merci Cohn-Bendit" signé: Salan'
appears on the top right-hand corner of the front page.[29] De Gaulle is
presented here as in alliance with the anti-democratic extreme right who
only ten years previously had tried to take over in Algeria (and assassinate
him). In other words, Algeria is an important historical reference for May,
underlining the role played by older students, teaching assistants, and
UNEF. In Schnapp and Vidal-Naquet's index of historical references, the
number of entries for Algeria outweighs the number for the Second World
War.[30]

It all went to prove the thesis that the bourgeois state was a fascist state,
showing itself again in May under its true colours as violently repressive.
The iconography and history of Occupation and Resistance, were also
repeatedly used, both to index fascism/anti-fascism as the historically
authenticated reality of the events, and to attack de Gaulle, through the
connection in his person of Resistance and the ideology of the bourgeois
state (together with the iconoclastic enjoyment of reversal, showing the
Resister in his true colours as fascist): 'Halte à la fascisation' shows a
protestor being shot and a Croix de Lorraine, symbol of 'La France libre',
the Resistance movement de Gaulle founded in London, in the smoke
from the gun. The Gaullist Comités d'Action Civique are routinely depicted
as fascist assassins. There are many graphic reminders of the wartime
past of the General: an 'Appel du 18 juin 1968' reproduces the blue-
bordered sheet of La France libre, and parodies de Gaulle's text, but is
signed La Révolution.[31] 'NON au fascisme GAULLISTE' shows de Gaulle with
Hitler moustache and lock of hair, wearing a swastika, arm raised in a

---

[26] From footage of the demonstration in *Mai 68: Il y a 25 ans.*
[27] 'Head of the informers Assassin of Charonne Boss of the strike breakers.' *500 Affiches de mai*, 38. (Frey
was still a Minister of State in Pompidou's government in 1968.)
[28] Published in June.
[29] Cf. 'De Gaulle libère son copain Salan et interdit les nôtres' ('De Gaulle frees his pal Salan and bans
ours'), headline of *Action* (14 June 1968), reproduced Rohan, *Paris 68*, 35.
[30] A. Schnapp and P. Vidal-Naquet (eds.), *Journal de la Commune étudiante* (Seuil, 1988), 875. In
Reberioux *et al.*, *La Sorbonne par elle-même*, *Le Mouvement social* (1969), the Popular Front is the
most important historical reference.
[31] *500 Affiches de mai* 19.

fascist salute.[32] There are many substitutions of Pétain for de Gaulle: the poster 'Français, me voilà' plays on 'Maréchal nous voilà' and shows the general, hands raised, behind two mighty tank tracks. The situationist journal *Archibras*, whose twin enemies are the Gaullists and the communists, both pillars of the fascist state in its view, calls for a civil war, and recalls constantly both the Occupation and Algeria in order to attack de Gaulle. It even suggests, in a most telling parallel, that he would be ill-advised to draw comfort from the 'foule boutiquière du 30 mai', since 'elle vaut ce que valait celle qui acclamait Pétain à Paris, au printemps de 1944'.[33] This small item appeared under the large headline: 'A poor lonesome cowboy' which fans of the *bande dessinée* Lucky Luke will recognize, since its last caption was always in English: 'I'm a poor lonesome cowboy and a long way from home.' This lack of respect towards de Gaulle from the 68 generation found its supreme expression at his death, with the incomparable and very famous headline of *Hara-kiri*: 'Bal tragique à Colombey: un mort', a headline which earned the publication an official repression, with all publicity, advertising, and public display forbidden.

Blier's film may have been entitled *Hitler connais pas*, but the May activists were all too aware of the political history of Gaullism. Aron's contemporary judgement, that the 'enragés' were ignorant of history, is sadly misplaced.[34] But their history was not his, namely the denunciations of mirror-image totalitarianism (stalinism/communism and Nazism), denunciations of the *épuration*, defence of the traditions of bourgeois liberalism; their history was the political history of battles with the state and fascism: Spain, 1936, Vichy, 1944, 13 May 1958, and Charonne.[35] May was a great amalgam of historical and political references, as an eloquent photograph of placards at the gates of an occupied factory show: '700,000 chômeurs, capitalisme de malheur'; '1936=1968 Vive le prolétariat', 'Vive

[32] *500 Affiches de mai*, 108. See also p. 38.
[33] 'crowd of shopkeepers of May 30', 'it is worth what the crowd which greeted Petain was worth, in the spring of 1944': *Archibras: Le Surréalisme* (18 June 1968), 4, supplement, p. 15. The reference on its first page to de Gaulle's radio broadcast: 'la voix sénile qui exprime l'abdomen nationale a chevroté ses injures et ses menaces' (the senile voice which is giving expression to the national belly bleated its insults and its menaces) irresistibly recalls another 'voix chevrotante', a common phrase identifying Pétain in his broadcast of 17 June 1940.
[34] 'La génération des "enragés" semble avoir en commun, de Berlin à Berkeley, la même ignorance du passé, la grande dépression, Hitler, Staline, "connais pas".' (The generation of the 'enragés' seem to share, from Berlin to Berkeley, the same ignorance of the past, the great depression, Hitler, Stalin, 'never heard of them'.) *Opium des intellectuels*, 13. The German SDS were more than a little aware of the Nazi past, too.
[35] The extent to which the massacre of 17 Oct. 1961 in Paris was forgotten, and the persistence in some circles of the memory of Charonne, is by now well documented. The mention of Charonne by the communist character Jaumet in *Derrière la vitre*, and his remark that none of them knew what he was talking about, is an excellent example of both.

le Front Populaire/Papon souviens toi de Charonnes [*sic*] (9 morts) A'SS'A'SS'IN'.[36]

The notion of the 'Resistance myth', that Gaullist Resistance triumphalism was the dominant discourse on the Occupation from the moment of Liberation until *Le Chagrin* must therefore be treated with great caution. It is a fact that Vichy and Algeria were constants of political and cultural discourse during the Fourth and Fifth Republics, because the Resistance is consistently invoked to justify opposition to the Algerian War and to the use of torture, because the right-wing insurrectionists had, virtually to a man, impeccable Resistance credentials and were also fighting in the name of Resistance and loyalty to the true France,[37] and because Vichy, Pétain, and the realities of political and cultural discourse under Vichy, had not been forgotten.

The post-1964 fusion of Resistance, nation, and state in Gaullism also has very specific political effects. Gaullist discourse depoliticized Resistance; *gauchiste* discourse can therefore repoliticize it. A member of the Mouvement du 22 mars explains the tactics of the Comités de Vietnam de Base in terms which are typical of this: 'identifier, au début de l'année 1968, la lutte des Vietnamiens avec la lutte des Français pendant la Résistance',[38] and he goes on to explain the importance of anti-fascism to the CVB, creating links with the prewar struggles and the politics of the Communist Party until the signing of the Germano-Soviet Pact.[39] The combination of anti-fascism and anti-colonial freedom movements means that the Resistance is just waiting to be claimed for *gauchisme*. Jean-Pierre Simon concludes his collection of tracts of May, *La Révolution par elle-même*, with a presentation of the Occupation which is utterly typical of the *gauchiste* attitude to it, but one which would have been recognized by many in the Resistance as well as inspiring a younger generation:

> Il y a vingt-cinq ans, au fond de la cave d'une école de l'Alsace occupée, protégés par des écrans de cartes géographiques, nous 'tirions' des tracts anti-nazis. C.A.L avant la lettre, nous luttions pour l'avènement d'un âge nouveau, pour la justice sociale, la solidarité et la fraternité humaines. (. . .) Cette ambiance de ferveur révolutionnaire, de foi ardente dans laquelle nous travaillions alors, je l'ai retrouvée à la 'ronéo' de Censier, véritable fabrique de tracts révolutionnaires. Après l'immense déception de la libération, que nous aurions voulue révolution, après les trop longues années de compromission avec l'État bourgeois, l'idéologie dominante et la société de consommation,

---

[36] *Miroir de l'histoire*, 74.
[37] See the biographies at the end of *O.A.S. parle* (Julliard, coll. Archives, 1964), 343–50.
[38] 'identify, at the beginning of 1968, the struggle of the Vietnamese with the struggle of the French during the Resistance.' Labro *et al.*, *Ce n'est qu'un début*, 53.
[39] Ibid. 54. The pact of non-aggression between Germany and the Soviet Union was signed in 1939.

années de découragement et de résignation, le mouvement étudiant et ouvrier de Mai redonnait enfin à la Révolution un visage français.[40]

He ends with words which form part of the political context—and the political subtext—of *Le Chagrin*: 'car de la résistance anti-nazie à la Révolution, c'est le même combat qui continue'.[41] It is not surprising, when de Gaulle throws down the gauntlet to the nation in the terms of a military Resistance leader in a war, that eventually the political opposition should take a serious look at this Glorious Past moment which is invoked so often. It is also difficult to avoid the conclusion that the connection suggested by *Archibras*, between the masses who turned out for the status quo of an oppressive regime on 30 May 1968 and the crowds cheering Pétain, is implicitly part of the background to a film which frequently points to the 'ordinary fascism' of the ordinary supporter of order and the Maréchal.

Le Chagrin has a very clear political message about the realities of the Occupation: that the French state was defeated by the German state because the French state was a bourgeois state, and the bourgeoisie had a kind of admiration for Hitler. The bourgeois state failed the nation. And while there were bourgeois Resistants like Colonel Gaspar, on the whole it was the grassroots, the people, which stood up to Vichy, the collaborationist, anti-Semitic, defeatist bourgeois state, since the Resistance was dissidence, and stood for revolutionary social change. 'De la résistance à la révolution' was the subheading of the Resistance journal *Combat*, edited from 1943 by Camus. Maurice Clavel uses the same banner for the collection of his articles for May, and it sums up the left-wing view of the Resistance, a *gauchiste* view by 1968, that the French resistance was part of a revolutionary project.[42] Class analysis of the resistance is first voiced in the film by Pierre Mendès France, when he explains that the bourgeoisie had no stomach for a fight in 1940, recalling the hostility to the Popular

---

[40] 'Twenty-five years ago, at the back of a cave in occupied Alsace, protected by screens of geographical maps, we "ran off" anti-nazi tracts. C.A.L [Comités d'action lycéens, formed in May] before the event, we were fighting for the arrival of a new age, for social justice, for human solidarity and fraternity. I have rediscovered the atmosphere of revolutionary fervour and burning faith in which we worked then, in the "stencil" at Censier, a real production line of revolutionary tracts. After the immense disappointment of the Liberation, which we wanted to be a Revolution, after the overlong years of compromise with the bourgeois state, dominant ideology and consumer society, years of discouragement and resignation, the workers' and students' movement of May was at last giving a French face to the Revolution.' *La Révolution par elle-même*, 226.

[41] 'for from the anti-nazi Resistance to the Revolution, it is the same fight which goes on.' Ibid.

[42] Resistance as revolutionary movement is a leitmotiv of Clavel's articles in May itself (collected in *Combat de franc-tireur pour une libération*) and subsequently (*Combat: De la résistance à la révolution 1968–1970*).

Front of 1936 and its Jewish Prime Minister expressed in the slogan: 'Plutôt Hitler que Léon Blum'.[43] Paradoxically, it is the very *gauchisme* of *Le Chagrin* which leads it to depict the Communist Party as the only resistance movement, a fact which angered many. In the 1940s, the PCF still espoused a revolutionary rhetoric, and was certainly perceived as dangerous by London and La France libre, in a way that other resistance movements were not. It can therefore carry the banner for the grassroots 'resistance to revolution'. And the theme of Resistance as transgression reappears time and again throughout the film as the Grave brothers, Gaspar, and the others, emphasize that the Resistance was 'mal vue'; Emmanuel d'Astier de la Vigerie particularly develops his theory that it was the social misfits in bourgeois France who were attracted to Resistance.

It is often remarked that *Le Chagrin*'s claims to authenticity are marred by the absence of de Gaulle from the film, but he literally cannot fit into its Resistance frame. As a character in the novel *Les Grands de ce monde* remarks: 'Dommage qu'il se soit condamné au public de l'Étoile au lieu de garder celui de Charléty qui était le sien quand en 1940 il jouait les Cohn-Bendit à la B.B.C.';[44] the novel includes the thesis, enthusiastically endorsed by Maurice Clavel and others, that the young of 68 are the true heirs of the young Resisters of 1940, which necessarily leaves de Gaulle to pick up the role of Pétain. But because part of *Le Chagrin*'s aim is to 'rediscover' Pétain and Pétainism, the *gauchiste* commonplaces that de Gaulle = Pétain, that the right is the heir of Vichy and has embraced Gaullism and its Resistance figures, belong to an incompatible discourse. There is no place in *Le Chagrin* for de Gaulle as either hero or villain.

An even more obvious omission is André Malraux. His role in placing the Resistance as a central pillar of the Gaullist state cannot be underestimated, in 1964, and in 1968. He was the living symbol of political recuperation, much more so than de Gaulle, who had always been right-wing, Catholic, and military, very suspicious of democracy, and sharing the hatred of republican politicians (inevitably called 'politiciens') forged in the Third Republic that was axiomatic on the right. Malraux, on the other hand, was believed to have authentic revolutionary credentials, and his novels were still widely read and admired. However much he protested that he could not have written what he had written and condone torture, he was singled out with de Gaulle during the Algerian War for particular censure. Jean Lacouture quotes Graham Greene's open letter, published

[43] 'Rather Hitler than Blum Blum was subsequently tried and deported by Vichy]'.

[44] 'What a pity that he condemned himself to the audience at the Étoile rather than keeping that of Charléty which had been his in 1940 when he was doing his Cohn-Bendit act at the B.B.C.' Poirot-Delpech, *Les Grands de ce monde*, 235.

in *Le Monde*, which summed up the position of many: 'Il est difficile de croire que semblable tribunal puisse exister alors que le chef de la France libre est à la tête du gouvernement et que l'auteur de *la Condition humaine* est l'un des ministres.'[45] As Minister of Culture, it was Malraux who was attacked for the banning of Jacques Rivette's film *La Religieuse*. Godard wrote a famous letter of protest to him, where he referred to Spain, Budapest, Auschwitz, and Charonne, and concluded: 'Comment pourriez-vous m'entendre, André Malraux, moi qui vous téléphone de l'extérieur, d'un pays lointain, la France libre.'[46] Malraux was the living embodiment and justification of the *gauchiste* line that the Resistance had to be reappropriated from Gaullism.

Another excellent indicator of the *gauchiste* position of the film is the absence of women. Rousso pointed out that only one of the interviewees is a woman. As Sian Reynolds demonstrated, she stands alone for 'ordinary collaboration', and the interview with her makes for uncomfortable viewing. Her story is that she has been imprisoned because of a letter of denunciation written by the wife of a friend, and that she had done nothing. Questioning elicits her support for Pétain, and then implies clearly that this was crime enough, an anti-Resistance position. It is one of the weaknesses of the film that it has no nuanced analysis of Vichy, and that it conflates public opinion and the public expression of opinion. There is no Occupation footage of crowds cheering on the Resistance; this means that there is nothing to counterbalance the crowds waiting for Pétain, or, in Paris in 1944, cheering Pétain; the crowds in Paris cheering de Gaulle must therefore be turncoats. There is no basis on which it might be posited that anti-German, pro-Pétain, and pro-de Gaulle feelings, might not necessarily be mutually exclusive.

Many analyses of *la mode rétro* uncritically follow Foucault, who argued very influentially that the election of Giscard d'Estaing signalled the death of Gaullism, creating a new ideological climate in which the war could be re-examined. P. Bonitzer and S. Toubiana set out this scenario in order to discuss it with Foucault: 'Depuis le film de Marcel Ophuls, *Le Chagrin et la pitié*, des vannes ont été ouvertes. Quelque chose qui avait été jusqu'alors soit complètement refoulé, soit interdit, déferle. Pourquoi?'[47]

[45] 'It is difficult to believe that such a tribunal can exist when the head of the Free French is leading the government and when the author of *La Condition humaine* is one of its ministers.' *Malraux*, 379.

[46] 'How would you be able to hear me, André Malraux, for I am calling you from outside, from a far-off country, Free France.' *Cahiers du cinéma* (Apr. 1966), 8–9.

[47] 'Since the film by Marcel Ophuls, *Le Chagrin et la pitié*, the floodgates had been opened. Something which up till then had been completely repressed, or banned, is unleashed. Why?', 'Anti-Rétro' (conversations with P. Bonitzer and S. Toubiana), *Cahiers du cinéma*, 251–2 (July–Aug. 1974), 6–15, repr. in Michel Foucault, *Dits et écrits 1954–1988*, ii. *1974–1975*, 646–60.

Unfortunately Foucault's replies suggest an almost total ignorance of Gaullist history and the recent past. 'L'histoire de la guerre (. . .) n'a jamais été inscrite vraiment ailleurs que dans des histoires tout à fait officielles.'[48] This really is an extraordinary statement, given the large numbers of essays, novels, memoirs, newspaper articles, attacking Resistance historiography during the first ten years after the war, the public debates in the early 1950s surrounding the amnesty for collaborators, and the well-established return of the right from those years. De Gaulle himself was, of course, in the political wilderness at the time. Foucault continues: 'Ces histoires officielles étaient essentiellement centrées autour du gaullisme qui (. . .) était la seule manière de faire intervenir comme personnage de l'histoire le Grand Homme, l'homme de droite, l'homme des vieux nationalismes du XIXe siècle.'[49] The Algerian War must have slipped Foucault's memory, for it is difficult to imagine how a man like de Gaulle, whom the extreme right had tried to assassinate several times for his policy on Algeria, and in the name of loyalty to the Resistance to boot, could unproblematically represent the nationalist right. But part of the difficulty with this discussion is precisely the unnuanced use of 'la droite', as though there were this single entity which collaborated during the war, and later stood solidly behind de Gaulle for its own rehabilitation. This corresponds not one jot to the political history of the Occupation or of the postwar periods. Similarly, one wonders how recently the participants in this debate had seen *Le Chagrin*, which according to them is an anti-Resistance film with no heroes: 'Est-il possible actuellement de faire un film *positif* sur les luttes de la Résistance? Eh bien! on s'aperçoit que non'[50] which throws a strange light on the Grave brothers, Colonel Gaspar and his fellow Resisters, Dennis Rake's praise of the solid Resistance attitudes of the communists and parish priests, Emmanuel d'Astier of *Combat*, and so on. However, the second half of the interview is devoted to the films *Lacombe Lucien* and *Portier de Nuit*,[51] each of which is governed by a very different politics. The negative portrayal of the Resistance and the French does indeed apply to Malle's film, and this is one of the clearest examples of *Le Chagrin* being subsumed under the very different problematic of *la mode rétro*.

---

[48] 'The history of the war has never been inscribed anywhere other than in completely official histories.' 646.

[49] 'Those official histories were essentially centred on gaullism which was the only way to have the Great Man, the man of the right, the man of the old 19th-century nationalisms, intervene as a character in history.' 646–7.

[50] 'Is it possible at the moment to make a *positive* film about the struggles of the Resistance? Well, one can see the answer is no.' 649.

[51] *Night Porter*: Cavanni's film of an erotic relationship which develops in a concentration camp between an SS (Dirk Bogarde) and an inmate (Charlotte Rampling).

It would therefore be tempting to say that *Le Chagrin* was depoliticized by the post-May return to the Occupation which it had itself sought to initiate, and in one sense this would be true. On the other hand, *Le Chagrin*'s own relationship to political history is quite a problematic one, and most specifically its exclusion of the Fifth Republic from the overt narrative of the politics which is framing it.

In its multiple interviews and its use of montage, *Le Chagrin* bears the marks of 68's *prise de la parole*. Apart from the statistics at the beginning, there is no commentary explaining what we should think, it is the choice of material and editing that has to do this work. The montage of images during the delivery of Pétain's speech of 17 June 1940, in part taken from contemporary footage, is not unlike the *Cinétracts*, in its juxtaposition of disparate images, its use of close-ups against a specific background, an old man's voice this time, rather than the gas canisters and *pavés*. What this method relies on is synchronicity. The faces are set against each other, and against this background (which they may or may not have been aware of). The figures around a radio set, and then the close-ups of their faces, are directly related to the speech we are hearing. The close-ups of Mendès France and Helmut Tausend also, though we cannot be sure that the relationship is internal to the narrative itself; it may rather belong to the director's narrative. Certainly the expression on Tausend's face suggests this is probably an image from the wedding rather than a man listening to a historic speech. In other words, the use of montage gives great power to the director's narrative, at the expense of any narrative the images may be taken from; it also inscribes them into a present, namely the story the film is telling, at the expense of their own internal history. Images are being decontextualized and recontextualized in another order. Ophuls uses incongruous juxtaposition to undermine officialdom, be it Tausend looking smug, drawing on his cigar, as Pétain speaks, or the frozen shot of the smiling faces of French prisoners of war (who were laughing at Chevalier) with the words 'le chagrin et la pitié' across the screen.

This reinscription of *then* into the *here and now* of the film can also be traced at the level of political discourse. Some of the people interviewed are important political figures who bring a complex history to the screen. Mendès France talks about leaving France on the *Massilia* in 1940, his arrest and subsequent trial under Vichy. That he had had multiple confrontations with de Gaulle over the years, particularly in relation to Algeria, but also May 68, is never mentioned. Georges Bidault was in London with de Gaulle, and that is his contribution. But he had played a prominent part in the OAS, had only returned from exile in 1965, and had even written most supportively that same year, driven by his hatred of de Gaulle, to followers of Pétain trying to have his ashes transferred. It was noted that the film drew upon anti-Gaullist politicians. More importantly, the film concentrates on talking *now* about *then*, as if the twenty-five year gap had not happened. Because it passes over the postwar period and fails to locate the 'Resistance myth' within the dynamics of the Fifth Republic, it creates Resistantialist triumphalism as a feature of the whole postwar period. And yet *Le Chagrin* could be said to owe its existence to the shift effected in representations of the Occupation by the substitution of the French for the Germans during the Algerian War, a shift that was continued and strengthened during May, and which sustained a political perspective on the Resistance as anti-fascism within a contemporary context. *Le Chagrin* repoliticizes the Resistance for a new generation, but depoliticizes narration. The film is effacing its own problematic; the narrative of the enunciation creates itself as a neutral space by dehistoricizing itself.

This is therefore not the neutral narrative spoken from outside history which its self-description as a chronicle suggests; it is a very political narrative. As the title and subtitles ('L'Effondrement' and 'Le Choix') indicate, it examines the Occupation in the name of an ethics of moral choice and moral turpitude. It is ironic that it is a representative of the so-called philosophy of the individual, Simone de Beauvoir, who criticizes *Le Chagrin* precisely because of its emphasis on individual choice and a failure to weigh in the balance the pressure of events and the logic of situations: 'Avoir été résistant ou collabo, cela semblait une affaire d'opinion, alors que des monceaux de cadavres séparaient les deux camps.'[52] The perspective of *Le Chagrin* tends to highlight the Occupation as psychodrama: its juxtapositions of multiple memories and newsreels highlight individual hypocrisy, and failures of memory. In the absence of any examination of postwar political use of the Occupation, these individual failures conjure up a collective one.

While its internal values of approval and disapproval allow it to demonize 'middle France' as supportive of oppression and collaboration, its dehistoricized perspective, and the moralizing nature of its approach, make it perhaps less surprising that it becomes elided with films such as *Lacombe Lucien* which tackle issues of moral turpitude with no class base, no touchstone of approved behaviour. The complex configurations of Fifth Republic Gaullism had indeed tried to throw a mantle of Resistance over all civil conflict, and in the process stake a claim for ownership of the Resistance heritage and the interpretation of the Occupation. Like the

---

[52] 'Whether one was a resister or a collaborator appeared to be a matter of opinion, whereas piles of corpses separated the two camps.' *Tout compte fait*, 261. Her overall assessment of the film is very positive.

militants of May, Ophuls was having none of it, and he was right to have none of it. Yet somehow, in the very fact that this immensely important and powerful film unfurls in a total historical vacuum, leaving Algeria, the OAS, internal massacres, and all the postwar reconfigurations of the ideological Resistance and anti-Resistance positions out of account in order precisely to show that the Gaullist state had no clothes, it is as though the universalist pretentions of Gaullism ensnared him in the end.[53]

L'archaïque et le moderne

The demonstration of the women at the Arc de Triomphe was prompted by actions of American feminists. 'Nous n'avons rien à faire avec la mémoire du monde: nous sommes l'avenir!'[54] proclaimed Claudine Monteil. But the processes of history are not that simple. Alain Brossat summed it up nicely in *Libération fête folle*: 'La libération brouille les pistes en entrelaçant l'archaïque et le moderne.'[55] So did May 68. Indeed, it is difficult to see photos of the Liberation of Paris without being reminded of May and the aesthetics of youth and stylish beauty. Richard Kuisel's persuasive correlation of a fading anti-Americanism and the return to the French past means that history and modernity are intimately linked. Claire Duchen also argues a link between depoliticization and modernization in relation to May. The political crisis, anti-Gaullism, and even the workers' revolt have faded in the collective memory while the students and the 'crisis of civilization' (in Malraux's phrase) have gained in significance. As May was depoliticized in memory, so it was increasingly considered as a 'stage in the modernization of France'.[56]

As inspiration, as reference, and as foundational to the event as event, history is central to May. It is infused with the energy of the revolutions and liberations it is re-enacting. Already in 1944, building a barricade was dusting off nineteenth century history, and women were brandishing flags of freedom;[57] in 1968 the sense of building a set for a Revolution is becoming rather acute: hence the proliferation of metaphors of 'jouer la comédie', of repetitions, of imitation, of simulacres of Revolution. And yet

---

[53] It is worth noting that the 68/44 structure occurs in novels such as Ikor's *Le Tourniquet des innocents*, where the students' parents were young in the 1930s, and fought in the war. Most of the students were too young to know about Algeria, and most of the parents too old. When thinking to their own student days, it is the late 30s/early 40s which are the point of comparison.

[54] 'We have nothing to do with the world's memory: we are the future!'

[55] 'The Liberation blurred the lines by interweaving the archaic and the modern.' 20.

[56] Duchen, *Women's Rights*, 192.   [57] *Libération fête folle*, 80.

what May also teaches is that the implicit distinctions operating here, between 'true' revolutions and revolutionary 'games', is a false one. There is no escape from the symbolizations of history, and these appear to be all the more tyrannical when the event is at its least repetititve. Listing the myriad and overlapping references of revolutionary and political history in 1968 and elsewhere, Schnapp and Vidal-Naquet conclude: 'Le langage des révolutions n'est senti comme neuf que lorsqu'elles sont terminées! C'est mai 68 qui servira désormais de modèle.'[58]

[58] *Journal de la Commune étudiante*, 46: 'The language of revolutions is only felt to be new when they are over! It's May 68 which will from now on be the model.'

7 *Le néo-polar*: behind enemy lines

Des enfants de mai 1968 et de la Série noire[1]

Black Exit to 68 was the title of a collection of short stories about May by leading exponents of *le roman noir* and *le polar*, issued as part of the twentieth-anniversary celebrations of May, and although *Le Monde* gave it a mixed review, its very existence is exemplary of the influence of May on the development of the political thriller, and the importance of the thriller in France as a vehicle for social comment.[2] Jean-Patrick Manchette's *Nada* has been described as the 'consécration du "néo-polar" genre subversif',[3] a renewal of the genre directly related to 1968 and the themes of protest: the power of the state, police brutality, the need for social and political change. In 1973 the film of the book appeared, directed by Claude Chabrol, with screenplay by Manchette, which neatly encapsulates the interdependence of film and novel in the creation and development of the genre.

The one thing this particular field does not lack is terminology: suspense, gangster, detective, thriller, *roman policier, polar, néo-polar, roman noir*: the proliferation of terms reflects the diversity of a field of popular fiction with a range of different but overlapping genres, and works by A.D.G., Jean Amila, Claude Aveline, René Belletto, Didier Daeninckx, José Giovanni, André Héléna, Hervé Jaouen, Sébastien Japrisot, Auguste Le Breton, Jean-Pierre Magnan, Jean-Patrick Manchette, Jean-Claude Izzo, Jean-Bernard Pouy, Francis Ryck, San-Antonio, Georges Simenon, Albert Simonin, Pierre Siniac, Jean Vautrin, Jean-François Vilar, should be familiar enough to enthusiasts of postwar literary culture, though not perhaps to students following university syllabuses. The linguistic pyrotechnics of many of these authors must be partly to blame: the cultivation of slang and the jargons of criminality, together with a gleeful exploitation of the intertextualities of pun, quotation, reference, and register, across linguistic and literary fields, are part of the stock-in-trade of the genre regularly

---

[1] Jean-Pierre Deloux, 'Le Noir new-look', *Magazine littéraire*, 194 (Apr. 1993), 21.
[2] *Black Exit to 68* (La Brèche, 1988); *Le Monde des livres* (13 May 1988).
[3] A. Simonin and H. Clastres (eds.), *Les Idées en France 1945–1988: Une chronologie* (Gallimard, 1989), 289.

referred to as 'intello-populo'. The other reason of course is that popular bestselling fiction has always had an antagonistic relationship to mainstream literary culture. The argument that the Zolas, Balzacs, and Dickens of today will have to wait for their literary talents to be recognized is a very well-worn one, and the literary canon has traditionally resisted genre writing. However, the cross-over between literary and popular fiction in this area with the publication of Daeninckx, Japrisot, Magnan, and others in mainstream rather than generic lists has been a feature of recent years, due no doubt not only to the increased attention given to textuality and narrative structuration in 'high culture', from the Nouveau Roman to Borges to Perec for example, and to the role of 68 in providing a context for renewal of the genre, but also to the way in which the articulation of French national identity and modernity, a subject which has always run like a thread through *le roman noir* and its partner in crime, *le film noir*, has become an issue of increasing cultural importance in the past three decades. It is no accident that exploration of the psycho-dramas of wars and social conflict have been the subject of complex thrillers, and that in recent years the authors such as Japrisot and Daeninckx who have crossed into mainstream editions have been particularly associated with these themes.[4]

There are many strands to the complex and overlapping thematics of *roman noir*, detective fiction, and thriller: the mystery to be elucidated is both intellectual puzzle and access to the sombre otherness of violence, criminality, and murder, a psychological dimension which has been particularly important in the French tradition. 'The darkness that fills the mirror of the past, which lurks in a dark corner or obscures a dark passage out of the oppressively dark city, is not merely the key adjective of so many *film noir* titles but the obvious metaphor for the condition of the protagonist's mind.'[5] Such emphasis on darkness characterizes many other parts of this wide field. The exploration of a psychology of transgression is the hallmark of Georges Simenon, the rural or provincial stories of Claude Aveline, Pierre Véry, and more recently Pierre Magnan, and films such as Clouzot's *Le Corbeau*. The interchangeability of investigator and investigated, of hunter and hunted, is a frequent theme: both exist in the realm of the outlaw, of transgression; both obey codes of honour, and although the nature of their experience renders innocence forever inaccessible to

[4] e.g. D. Daeninckx, *Meurtres pour mémoire* (Gallimard, 1984: on 17 Oct. 1961 and Occupation); *La Mort ne s'oublie pas* (Paris, 1989: Resistance and collaboration). S. Japrisot, *Un long dimanche de fiançailles* (Denoël, 1991: First World War) and *L'Été meurtrier* (Denoël, 1977: Occupation).
[5] Alan Silver and Elizabeth Ward, quoted Elizabeth Cowie, 'Film Noir and Women', in Joan Copjec, *Shades of Noir: A Reader* (London, Verso, 1993), 132.

them, they may well have a lucid and tragic awareness of this, and of the inevitable doom which awaits them in a world governed by laws of violence and death.

The importance of the detective thriller in cinema to French national consciousness has long been recognized. Jill Forbes notes the frequency with which it is a vehicle for political discussion at times of crisis;[6] Patrick Raynal argues that the whole of twentieth-century history could still be reconstituted if the 'Série noire' were all that survived: 'Ils trouveront là toute l'histoire du siècle. Il y a tout: les conséquences de la Première Guerre mondiale, de la Seconde Guerre mondiale, de la guerre du Vietnam, de Corée, d'Algérie . . . Il y a l'histoire de la corruption politique, celle du crime organisé, de la mafia, celle, incroyable, de l'arrivée de la drogue.'[7] Another indication of the central place in French culture occupied by this genre is the fact that its iconic male actors who have succeeded in establishing an international reputation have found success playing criminals and gangsters in French films: Jean Gabin, Jean-Paul Belmondo, Alain Delon, Gérard Depardieu.[8] The portrayal of the marginal does not itself occupy a marginal position, culturally. But its hybrid cultural status is echoed in other complexities without which it would not exist at all.

The *roman policier* and *le roman noir* grew out of the nineteenth-century mystery and horror story, owing much to Balzac, Hugo, Sue, and Edgar Allen Poe (translated by Baudelaire), and the hard-boiled school of American fiction from 1920 onwards. The structures of mystery, the criminal underworld, and the psychology of murder ensured an overlap between the two. The English puzzle writers (Conan Doyle, Agatha Christie) reconstituting the causes of some complex murder or other mystery, and the American thriller writers tackling political and institutional corruption (Raymond Chandler, Dashiel Hammett) were extremely popular, and in spite of some important French authors, in general Anglo-Saxon writing dominated the genre in France; French writers were something of a rarity in the famous *Série noire* collection, founded in 1945 for Gallimard

[6] J. Forbes, *The Cinema in France* (Macmillan, 1992), 60. See also Adrian Rifkin, 'French Popular Song: Changing Myths', in Brian Rigby and Nicholas Hewitt, *France and the Mass Media* (Macmillan, 1991), 215–16 for a discussion of the importance of crime fiction in the formation and reformation of Parisian popular (and therefore national) identity.

[7] 'They will find the history of the whole century there. There is everything: the consequences of the First World War, of the Second World War, of the Vietnam War, of Korea, of Algeria. . . . There is the history of political corruption, of organized crime, of the Mafia, and the incredible history of drugs.' 'Le Roman noir est l'avenir de la fiction', *Temps Modernes, Roman Noir. Pas d'orchidées pour les TM*, 595 (Aug.–Sept. 1997), 94. Patrick Raynal was director of the *Série noire*.

[8] This point is made by Robin Buss in *French Film Noir* (Marion Boyars, 1994). See also Forbes, *Cinema*, 53–5.

by Maurice Duhamel.[9] Criminality and violence were to be found across the different traditions. But if American texts were the very embodiment of the modernity of *roman noir*, focused on urban living, on contemporary politics and society, and on the figure of the lonely hero pursuing as best he might the path of truth, they were not doing this through writing alone, for Hollywood was producing major and highly popular films of these texts, often with the writers employed as scriptwriters.

After the invisibility of all things American during the war, from 1945 onwards there was an immense excitement in the discovery and rediscovery of American writing and film. While Kuisel's views on modernity and the processes of modernization being articulated through the French/American relationship, and therefore through the boundaries between French and un-French, are more than pertinent here, this relationship is never a simple one. As Marc Vernet puts in at the outset of his fascinating reflection upon the *film noir*: 'The Americans made it, and then the French invented it.'[10] *Film noir* is an American phenomenon, yet baptized by the French, by Nino Frank in an article in *Écran français* in 1946, with reference to established French writing. Duhamel's *Série noire* is also a French cultural event which it has been argued created the modern *roman noir* by the way it brought together different kinds of writing, all of it in translation, under that label.[11] Most of the directors of *film noir* in Hollywood were European; in later American films such as *The Godfather* and *The French Connection*, 'European' stood for networks of illegality.[12] Many of the *romans noirs* and *films noirs* in France are simultaneously and inseparably American and French: the computer in *Alphaville* quoting Pascal to Eddie Constantine is a *mise en abyme* of the whole cultural phenomenon. The reader/spectator is always positioned as knowledgeable in both cultures.

If 'l'amer-ricanement'[13] is one dimension of the explicit textualization of the genre, the other is the symbiotic relationship of novel and film *noirs*. Alexandre Lous is right, that it is impossible to talk about one without

---

[9]   Serge Arcouet and Jean Meckert were the first French writers to write for the collection, under the Americanized pseudonyms of Terry Stewart (no. 18, 1948) and John Amila (no. 53, 1950) respectively (Jean-Paul Schweighaeuser, *Le Roman noir français* (PUF/Que Sais-je?, 1984), 19–23). Léo Malet published his first Nestor Burma novel, *120, rue de la Gare* in 1943, and was saluted as 'le père du roman noir français' (ibid. 31).

[10] '*Film Noir* on the Edge of Doom' in Copjec, *Shades of Noir*, 1.

[11] Francis Lacassin, *Mythologie du roman policier* (Christian Bourgois, 1993), 17. He argues that neither critics nor publishers in either country had previously put these writers together as a genre. Forbes ('Série noire' in Hewitt and Rigby) stresses the importance of the translations, drawing on Céline and Queneau to render the 'hard-boiled' style, in creating it as a French genre.

[12] Forbes, *Cinema*, 58.

[13] 'Amer-ricanisation/Bitter-unpleasant sniggering laugh'. Deleuze, *Pas d'orchidées pour les TM*, 61.

the other: 'Leur histoire se confond, leur esthétique est similaire, et (. . .) les auteurs des romans et des films noirs ont régulièrement travaillé ensemble. (. . .) Ils ont pu, au fil des années, tracer *clairement* les contours de leur univers commun.'[14] The notion of *cinécriture* which was so important to the Nouvelle Vague equally well describes the *film/roman noirs*, and again the process is part of the surface material of the genre: Truffaut's *Tirez sur le pianiste* was based on a novel by David Goodis whose name crops up time and again, including in *Tout va bien*: the project Jacques refuses as being one recuperative step too far is an adaptation of a novel by Goodis. Manchette himself had worked as a scriptwriter, and translated American thrillers. His cinematic written style is often commented on.

French and American, filmic and written: the *noir* is haunted by *doppelgängers*. It is also haunted by history. '*Film noir* consists, from the beginning, in being installed in repetition (. . .) (*film noir* is a cinephilic ready-made).'[15] The same is true of *roman noir*, due to the weight of tradition and genre, but also to the specific structures of *noir* story-telling. It all makes for a unique configuration.

In his interesting introduction to *Autopsies du roman policier*, Eisenzweig argues that the generic status of detective fiction both reveals and recreates the configurations of high and low culture. The genre is created by its critical discourse: 'Ce qui, d'une masse de textes plus ou moins proches sur la plan thématique (crimes, détectives etc) était d'abord devenu, sous la plume du critique, une categorie homogène sur le plan *moral*, se voit désormais investi d'une unité *générique* et esthétique.'[16] Yet this very constitution of the genre as the antithesis of literature is what is also going to be its abiding attraction:

> **Le récit policier, pour [Borges], est précisément une forme narrative privilégiée en ce qu'elle rompt, ou semble rompre, avec une certaine tradition romanesque, tout en s'inscrivant en une autre. C'est que le 'problème' et sa 'solution', dans un récit policier, se présentent comme 'nouveaux', 'originaux'; c'est-à-dire ils renvoient nécessairement, par contrecoup, à des problèmes et des solutions déjà imaginés dans des récits antérieurs.[17]**

[14] 'Their history merges, their aesthetics is similar, and the authors of *noir* novels and films have regularly worked together. They have been able, through the years, to draw *clearly* the contours of their common world.' 'Roman noir et cinéma', *Magazine littéraire*, 174 (June 1981), 83.
[15] Vernet, '*Film Noir* on the Edge of Doom', 2.
[16] 'From a mass of texts which were fairly close thematically (crimes, detectives, etc.) first a single *moral* category emerged in critical writings, later invested with a generic, aesthetic unity.' (Union générale d'éditions, 10/18, 1983),15.
[17] 'The detective story, for Borges, is precisely a privileged narrative form because it breaks, or seems to break, with a certain fictional tradition, while at the same time inscribing itself in another. The "problem" and its "solution", in a detective story, present themselves as "new", "original"; that is to say that there is a rebound, and they refer necessarily to problems and solutions already imagined in previous stories.' Ibid. 287–8.

Intertextuality is at the heart of the genre, as is the interplay of truth and fiction, of real and invented discourse, inevitably no doubt in a genre which proliferates paper identities for its authors, so many of whom have multiple pseudonyms. And sometimes even this game goes beyond the purely textual: when one knows that A.D.G.'s real name is Alain Fournier, it comes as no surprise to learn he has written a novel called *Le Grand Môme*.[18] 'Amilanar' was Jean Meckert's first choice of pseudonym (adapted to John Amila by Duhamel), meaning 'épouvante' (horror) in Spanish, and also decomposable into 'ami l'anar' (friend the anarchist).[19] It is a neat encapsulation of the subversive intentions which have underpinned the genre so often.

Roman noir and *roman policier* were in the doldrums in the early 1960s, dominated by English and American writers, with the French offering weak imitations. May 68 was the catalyst of renewal, bringing in new political and social themes and attitudes. Pierre Siniac's *Les Morfalous*, set during the Second World War, appeared at the end of that year, and by 1971 there had been a spate of novels which were recognized as ideological from A.D.G., Jean-Patrick Manchette, and Siniac himself, and summed up in the term 'néo-polar', coined by Manchette.[20] A.D.G. and Manchette are often compared, because of their politicized writing, and because the former was on the right, a contributor to *Minute*, the latter on the left. As well as a renewed emphasis on politics, and a political vision of social marginality and exclusion, 68 also produced new kinds of characters, such as Jean Amila's hippy policeman in *Contest-flic*, or Manchette's Eugène Tarpon, a former policeman turned private detective in *Morgue pleine*, trying to come to terms with having killed a protestor during a violent confrontation.

Manchette described his fiction as 'le polar d'intervention sociale très violent'. A. Viard wrote, quoting Manchette: 'Ainsi, Manchette développe-t-il, juste après les événements de 1968, la notion d'un roman policier ancré tout autant dans le genre que dans le temps et l'histoire, autrement dit ce: "monde où les salopards et la Contre-Révolution sont au pouvoir".'[21] Manchette's writings are an interplay of genre and style, of reality and fiction, of reference and self-reference, drawing its inspiration in part

---

[18] A virtual homonym of Alain-Fournier's famous novel *Le Grand Meaulnes*, whose story it also rewrites.

[19] Schweighaeuser, 'Du roman de voyou au roman engagé', *Pas d'orchidées pour les TM*, 110.

[20] *Pas d'orchidées pour les TM*, 72. Schweighaeuser, *Le Roman noir français*, 62 ff., 'Les retombées de mai 68'.

[21] 'Thus, Manchette develops, just after the 1968 events, the notion of a detective novel rooted equally in the genre and in its time and history, in other words this "world where the bastards of the Counter-Revolution are in power."' A. Viard, 'Manchette: Morgue Pleine' (obituary), *Libération* (5 June 1995), 31.

from the work of the situationists, and with a clear political project: 'opérer derrière les lignes ennemies avec des romans noirs'.[22]

It can be no accident that it is *le roman noir*, so intimately connected to *film noir*, which is transformed after 1968, for this is also the case with film. As Forbes says, for French cinema, May 68 was a watershed.[23] It gave a great impetus to political cinema, and to political themes in commercial cinema.[24] Manchette's *Nada* is a perfect vehicle for film adaptation, especially in the light of Chabrol's own preferences for subjects which place contemporary society under very critical scrutiny. He explores the weakness of the bourgeoisie,[25] through what has been termed the 'social thriller', namely: 'a suspense format to comment on the deviousness and duplicity of French society'.[26] Where he overlaps with *film noir* is in his obsession with 'the very fine line dividing good and evil, morality and madness, stupidity and frustration, and the way that social/bourgeois hypocrisy papers over that crack'.[27]

Une mise à mort impeccable[28]

Nada is the story of a group of *gauchistes* who kidnap the American Ambassador in order to provoke insurrection and revolution, threatening that unless their manifesto is read on national media they will execute him. Some of them are said to have been directly involved in 1968 protests, and indeed, after the kidnapping itself during which they happen to be filmed, they are identified from photographs taken during May's street battles. This is a plot that figured strongly in the real world. The political trajectory of those who formed armed terrorist groups in the 1970s is well documented: frustrated by the failure of the 1968 protests across the Western capitalist countries, convinced that the bourgeois state was a corrupt and violent force which could only be challenged by violence, the Red Brigades in Italy and the Red Army Faction in Germany kidnapped and executed leading industrialists and politicians.

There are six members of the group: Epaulard, Treuffais, Cash, Meyer, Diaz, and d'Arcy. The novel opens with Treuffais, a 30-year-old philosophy

---

[22] Manchette, quoted by Viard, ibid.: 'operating behind enemy lines with *romans noirs*'.

[23] *Cinema*, 13.

[24] See Sylvia Harvey, *May 68 and Film Culture* (BFI publishing, 1980); Philippe Maarek, *De Mai 68 ... aux films x* (Ed. Dujarric, 1979); CinémAction, *Le Documentaire français*, 41 and 25, *20 années d'utopie*.

[25] Susan Hayward, *French National Cinema* (London, Routledge, 1993), 260.

[26] Reader, 'French Film', in Malcolm Cook (ed.), *French Culture since 1945* (London, Longman, 1993), 86.

[27] Hayward, *French National Cinema*, 260.   [28] 'A perfect kill.'

teacher in a private secondary school, who has been involved with various political groups since 1962, including an Étudiants-Ouvriers group in 1968. D'Arcy is the alcoholic driver of the get-away car. We meet Véronique Cash at the farmhouse which belongs to the man who is keeping her. Epaulard and Diaz know each other from involvement in pro-FLN support work up to 1962. Epaulard is 50, frequently referred to as 'le cinquagénaire' (allowing him to occupy the Gabin/Ventura role[29]). We learn something of his past. He was involved in the Resistance, and after the disaster of the Vercors[30] from which he managed to escape, became a dedicated anti-Gaullist.[31] He joined the Communist Party after the war, but then left it. He worked as a contract killer, and as a conviction killer. After the FLN episode he helped trotskyist groups in Algiers for a time. As the novel opens, he is in Paris and it appears, with no particular project. He is contacted by d'Arcy, on the basis of his reputation as a hit-man; his initial refusal to join them reflects his low opinion of the idea. Their plan is to kidnap the ambassador on his weekly visit to a brothel (Epaulard being the worldly wise character who is knowledgeable enough to recognize the address of this, the one immoveable feast in the ambassador's weekly diary of engagements), and take him to the farmhouse where he is to be held until their demands are met. However, they are filmed by a surveillance camera, Diaz is identified, the address book found in his room gives the name of Treuffais, who is arrested (he had earlier decided not to take part in the kidnapping) and tortured, and of Meyer and Cash. A visit to the latter's flat yields the information about the farmhouse which is surrounded. All are killed except Diaz. The senior policeman involved, Commissaire Goémond, gives out the false information that Treuffais was a police spy in an attempt to lure Diaz to Paris for revenge. Diaz does return, takes his revenge on the lying policeman, and himself dies in the gun battle. The novel ends with Treuffais on the phone to a (foreign) news agency with the 'true story of the Nada group'.

It may depend on one's view of *le polar*, whether the group seems farcical or not. In one sense their political views are treated as clichés,[32] with no connection with popular sentiments. The film suggests this more clearly than the novel, as the voice-over reads the group's manifesto, the text of

[29] Gabin in late 1930s *films noirs*; Lino Ventura in the 1950s and 1960s; world-weary gangsters expressing a metaphysical criminality.
[30] Large numbers of *Resistants* were killed in a battle here when Allied arms failed to reach them.
[31] The Occupation is not infrequently invoked in contemporary *roman noir* to signal the continuity of the repressive, bourgeois state. Manchette, *Morgue pleine* or Japrisot's First World War novel *Un long dimanche de fiançailles*, which concludes with a very strong attack on Pétain's record.
[32] Cf. the manner in which Véronique Cash explains her political views, clearly marking them as 'off-the-peg' clichés. *Nada*, 51.

which is not given in the novel, over shots of police road-blocks being set up in empty streets. There is a singular absence of any sense of a crowd in either text. The world of the gangster and the criminal is by definition a closed world whose only relation with 'normality' is one of secrecy and trangression on the one hand, and violence on the other. *Nada* conforms to the model of *film noir*, in its portrayal of men living outside the law according to their own codes of honour and legality. Epaulard is on a kind of suicide mission: having refused to join the group, he stands alone in his bathroom holding a gun to his head: 'Il éprouve l'impression pénible et familière d'avoir raté sa vie.'[33] ' "Autant se flinguer tout de suite" déclara-t-il à son miroir. Il soupira et ne se flingua pas.'[34] He has moved into a mode of virtual death. It is made clear more than once that he does not believe in the 'cause', yet it is he who asks all the professional questions about their organization, who gets hold of weapons, and who refuses when offered the chance to move on, once the ambassador is delivered to the farmhouse. This is pure action, with no motivation other than its own. 'Epaulard est ici avec nous parce qu'il ne croit plus à la révolution, tandis que nous sommes ici avec lui parce que nous y croyons. Epaulard agit par désespoir.' Diaz explains to Treuffais, making Epaulard giggle, which turns it from explanation to rather empty cliché.[35] The title also points to the studied nihilism of the group. The law of the *polar* is that none will survive. Death is the inevitable end of the adherence to the codes of the night.

Film noir and *roman noir* rely, structurally, on the interchangeability of good and bad, the figures of the policeman and the criminal, in order to realize in action the questions of moral ambiguity, the otherness of transgression, which is so central to them. Society peers into the abyss and sees itself. In his statement to camera, the video he makes which will denounce the police, Diaz admits that his own political position had been naïve, and that *gauchiste* terrorism and state terrorism are mirror images of each other. The narrative has long prefigured this as a political reality. The terrorist group is a small group, there is no question of giving it a representative value. The option of direct action is not one of the masses or a mass movement, and such a representation would have foundered on the rock of referential reality. But the state too is a morass of factions, of internal divisions and aggressions. Different agencies of the state are

---

[33] *Nada*, 28: 'He has the painful and familiar impression of having ruined his life.' The scene is also a reprise of a famous scene from Louis Malle's *Le Feu follet*.

[34] Ibid. 30: ' "Might as well kill myself straightaway" he told his mirror. He sighed and did not kill himself.'

[35] Ibid. 38: 'Epaulard is here with us because he no longer believes in revolution, while we are here with him because we believe in it. Epaulard is motivated by despair.'

infiltrating each other, the action of the minister is as much directed at the destruction of his internal enemies as at the terrorists. Goémond is catapulted into his final madness when he is betrayed by the minister. In marked contrast to the agents of the state, ministers and high-ranking policemen, the Nada group do not betray each other, they believe each other on their word alone, and they are right to do so.[36] In a corrupt world, they represent justice.

Manchette's previous novel dealt with the Ben Barka affair, the kidnapping in Paris and disappearance of the Moroccan leader, with strong implications of French involvement. State terrorism is a vital part of the subject of *Nada* too, fitting easily into the bleak moral landscape of this violent genre. Having previously explained the necessity of putting an end to public sympathy for these desperadoes by demonstrating their willingness to kill in cold blood, the 'chef de cabinet du Ministre de l'Intérieur' suggests to Goémond that no one, neither the minister nor the Americans, would be surprised if the terrorists murdered their hostage, a coded instruction which Goémond carries out meticulously, including killing Cash and Epaulard himself. The violent demonstrations which follow the massacre ('Goémond salaud, le peuple aura ta peau'; 'Goémond, sale con, on en fera du saucisson'[37]) turn him into the perfect sacrificial victim; Chabrol's film uses footage of the well-organized maoist demonstrations, with demonstrators wearing helmets, running with linked arms, and operating as commandos in their running battles with the police.

The violent fate awaiting the group is explained in the opening pages, in the letter written by one of the *gendarmes* present, Georges Poustacrouille, to his 'chère Maman'. His ridiculous name (possibly a mocking recall of Joseph Rouletabille, the superintelligent hero of Gaston Leroux's detective novels in the 1920s), matched by his naïve style, poor spelling, and multiple crossings out, is a good example of the interlinked 'dérision de l'écriture' 'écriture de la dérision' singled out by Jean-Paul Demure as typical of the *polar*.[38] Poustacrouille's message to Mother is that the killing of the anarchists was essential: 'Tendre la joue c'est bien joli, mais que veux-tu faire quand tu as en face de toi des gens qui veulent tout détruire, je te le demande.'[39] Citing the support of the local priest for his views, he insists that only the police force prevents anarchy:

---

[36] Diaz guarantees Treuffais would never betray them; Epaulard accepts that.
[37] *Nada*, 166: 'Bastard Goémond, the people will have your hide'; 'Goémond, dirty bastard, we will make sausagemeat of you.'
[38] 'Écriture et dérision', *Pas d'orchidées pour les TM*, 157–63.
[39] *Nada*, 9: 'Turning the other cheek is all very well; what should you do when in front of you you have people who want to destroy everything, I ask you.'

> Sérieusement, petite Maman, tu voudrais d'un pays sans police? Tu voudrais que le fils Barquignat (je le prends juste comme un exemple) soit libre d'assaillir de ses mains lubriques ta fille qui est aussi ma sœur? Tu voudrais que sur notre bien péniblement amassé se ruent niveleurs et partageux dans une orgie de destruction? Je ne dis pas qu'il n'y a pas une majorité de bonnes gens au bourg mais toutefois, rien que dans notre paisible communauté rurale, s'il n'était pas su qu'il y a une police et prête à tirer au besoin, j'en vois déjà qui n'hésiteraient pas, sans parler des romanichels.[40]

Police, Church, Law, Order: all sustain and are sustained by violence. The letter not only places the group from the outset under sentence of death so that the laws of narrative finality and fate are adhered to, it also rewrites into the narrative the two quotations of the epigraph which combine ethico-metaphysical and technological structures of killing. The first, from Hegel, concludes: 'la conscience projette hors de soi la perversion qu'elle est elle-même'. The second from *Le Chasseur français* involves advice on the avoidance of messy fallout when shooting: 'Le faire proprement . . . en effet, une mise à mort impeccable doit être le souci majeur du bon chasseur: c'est l'essentiel du thème que nous développons.'[41] When the television news shows the 'fermette tragique' (p. 152), it takes a second to realize that it is referring to the death of the ambassador, and not sympathizing, as the reader inevitably has to, with the massacre of the group.

A-t-on entendu dans les rues de Paris le terrible 'Viva la muerte'?

It has been suggested that *Nada* is grotesquely recuperative, reducing political action to individual dramas,[42] a view which underplays the extent to which the police and the state are confirmed as acting in accordance with *gauchiste* views of them. Manchette espoused situationism after abandoning the extreme left,[43] and the whole problematic of contestation versus recuperation will have been a very familiar one to him, one that

[40] *Nada*, 10: 'Seriously, little Mother, would you like a country without police? Would you like Barquignat's son (I am just taking him as an example) to be free to assault your daughter who is also my sister with his lascivious hands? Would you like people bent on bringing everything down to their level, on grabbing a share of everything, to throw themselves in an orgy of destruction on our assets which have been so painstakingly amassed? I am not saying that there is not a majority of decent people in the town but all the same, even in our peaceful rural community, if it was not known that there was the police, prepared to shoot when necessary, I can see from here the ones who would not hesitate, not to mention the gypsies.'

[41] Ibid. 7: 'Consciousness projects beyond itself the perversion it itself is.' 'Do it cleanly . . . indeed, a perfect kill should be the prime concern of the good hunter; this is the central theme we shall develop.'

[42] CinémAction, *Vingt ans d'utopie* 25 (1982), 40.   [43] Obituary, *Libération* (5 June 1995), 31.

informs the political theses of the novel, that *gauchiste* terrorism and state terrorism are mirror images of one another, as well as the view, expressed by d'Arcy and repeating *gauchiste* doxa, that their deviance is itself the product of a rotten society: 'L'Histoire moderne nous a créés et ça prouve que la civilisation court à sa perte, d'une façon ou d'une autre, et croyez-moi, j'aime mieux finir dans le sang que dans le caca.'[44] *De la misère en milieu étudiant* will say no different: 'Les "Blousons noirs" sont produits par tous les côtés de *l'ordre* actuel: l'urbanisme des grands ensembles, la décomposition des valeurs, l'extension des loisirs consommables de plus en plus ennuyeux, le contrôle humaniste-policier de plus en plus étendu à toute la vie quotidienne, la survivance économique de la cellule familiale privée de toute signification.'[45]

The situationists made a virtue of marginality and delinquency. The black looters of America were celebrated as emblematic of the diktats of consumerism.[46] Students too were 'des délinquants en sursis. (. . .) Ils se trouvent plus proches des poubelles de la société que des sommets de son ancienne hiérarchie. (. . .) Ils ont beaucoup à apprendre, certes pas auprès des professeurs, mais auprès des "voyous des cités" qui ont plus de lucidité.'[47] Jean-Marie Domenach also noted important new links being forged. He compares 'Nous sommes tous des Juifs allemands', which he describes as an admirable slogan of fraternity, with 'la pègre, c'est nous',[48] rooted in a solidarity of a rather different kind: 'En lançant le slogan "la pègre c'est nous", (. . .) ils assumaient ces victimes de la société technique et rationalisée.'[49] Domenach places Marcuse at the centre of this analysis: 'Selon lui, ceux qui sont sans espoir, les parias, les chômeurs, les habitants des ghettos, expriment un besoin immédiat de bouleverser la

---

[44] 'Modern History has created us and that proves that civilization is rushing to its ruin, in one way or another, and believe me, I'd rather end up in blood than in poo.' *Nada*, III.

[45] 'The "Rockers" are produced on all sides by today's *order*: the urbanism of tower block estates, the decomposition of values, the extension of ever more boring consumerist leisure, ever greater humanist-police control over everyday living, the economic survival of the totally meaningless family unit.' *De la misère*, 30 (1976 edn.).

[46] Guy Debord, 'Le Déclin et la chute de l'Économie spectaculaire-marchande'. *Internationale situationniste*, 10 (Mar. 1966): republ. Pauvert, 1993. Cf. also *La Société du spectacle* (Gallimard, 1992), 115: 'une nouvelle lutte spontanée qui commence sous l'aspect *criminel*', discussed in S. Plant, *The Most Radical Gesture* (Routledge, 1992), 16.

[47] '. . . delinquents on suspended sentences. They are closer to the dustbins of society than to the summits of its former hierarchy. They have much to learn, certainly not from their teachers, but from the "hooligans of the estates" who see things more clearly.' 'Avant-propos' to *De la misère en milieu étudiant* (1995 edn.), 4–5.

[48] 'We are the criminal underworld'. A politician having dismissed the protestors as 'la pègre', the expression was instantly used in the classic *détournement*.

[49] 'In creating the slogan "we are the criminal underworld", they took on board the victims of the technical, rationalized society.' Domenach, 'L'Idéologie du mouvement', *Esprit* (Aug.–Sept. 1968), 48–9.

société: "Leur opposition est révolutionnaire même si leur conscience ne l'est pas." '[50] May 68 forged a collective 'nous' uniting all those excluded and marginalized by bourgeois society and the capitalist state, students, criminals, the young, the Third World, all actual or potential victims. This is also the favourite terrain of *le néo-polar*, a fusion of various kinds of exclusion, as well as a revalorization of the deviant and criminal, promoted to icons of suffering:

> Paumés, marginaux, marginalisés, chômeurs, laissés pour compte de la société, révoltés, etc., tout les désigne à la fonction de bouc émissaire et à celle de victime propitiatoire de la société qui les exclut. Leur mort étant le signe et la garantie de sa permanence. C'est au meurtre rituel de l'individu de la collect-ivité que nous convie le polar moderne, en posant plus que jamais un regard d'ethnologue sur notre société.[51]

There is unlikely to be agreement on the value to accord to this ethnolo-gist's gaze, across the very disparate authors of *noir* texts, but one crucially constant element is the city. If it is true that the Revolution is 'the primal factor in the constitution of Paris as an object of philosophical and cul-tural as well as economic and political speculation',[52] then one might say that in May 68 too, the politicization of the city is inseparable from its coding as a privileged bearer of philosophical and cultural meaning. For Debord and the situationists, liberation has to include liberation of the city, of the space of the everyday through 'un urbanisme libérateur':[53] Paris is a space to be appropriated and rewritten through the use of graffiti, ' "depuis l'insinuation psychogéographique jusqu'à la sub-version la plus simple", tel le splendide "vous dormez pour un patron" autour des Usines Renault et dans certains quartiers ouvriers'.[54] Urban and modern are synonymous terms, and from Baudelaire on Poe, from Sue's *Mystères de Paris* to Malet's *Nouveaux mystères de Paris*, from

---

[50] 'According to him, those who are without hope, the pariahs, the unemployed, the inhabitants of the ghettos, are expressing a direct need to overthrow society: "Their opposition is revolutionary even if their consciousness is not." ' Ibid. 49.

[51] 'Losers, marginals, the marginalized, unemployed, and abandoned of society, protesters etc., everything fits them for the function of scapegoat and of sacrificial victim of the society which excludes them. Their death being the sign and guarantee of its permanency. It is to the ritual murder of the individual of the collectivity that the modern *polar* summons us, as more than ever it turns an ethnologist's gaze on our society.' Deloux, 'Le Noir new-look', *Magazine littéraire*, 194 (Apr. 1983), 21.

[52] P. P. Ferguson, *Paris as Revolution* (Berkeley, University of Calif. Press, 1994), 231.

[53] Jean-François Martos, *Histoire de l'Internationale situationniste* (Editions Gérard Lebovici, 1989), 15.

[54] Ibid. 55: 'from a psycho-geographical suggestion to the simplest subversion, such as the splendid "you are sleeping for a boss" around the Renault factory and in some working-class districts'. Cf. 'A transformation of its environment, graffiti was as powerful a form of subversion and engagement as the larger *détournement* of the city it inspired and reported.' (Plant, *Most Radical Gesture*, 104.)

Alphaville to *Diva*, from Hitchcock to Orson Welles,[55] *le noir* in film and fiction is the literature of urban modernity.

Henri Lefebvre reflected on the relationship between contestation, violence, and spontaneity in *Nanterre: De l'irruption au sommet*, on the new politics consequent upon the spontaneous mass protests in the streets, and the emergence of the street as a site of power.[56] The street becomes a political site: 'l'espace social changeait de sens'.[57] This context may well be the one which gives the new impulse to the *néo-polar* to develop as narrative on the new political spaces of the city, but not everyone will consider it to be a positive development. Jean-Louis Blanc raises many questions about the way the *néo-polar* concentrates upon the modern city: 'Le paysage privilégié du néo-polar, c'est la nouvelle ville des années 60: la banlieue, le béton, les HLM, la tristesse et la mouise des habitants déportés dans des périphéries dépourvues d'urbanité.'[58] This new landscape, combined with the traditional sacred sites of the genre—'terrain vague, bâtiments vides, pâles lumières, désolation, saleté, boue, zones désertes'[59]—is informed by a new sensibility, as the *néo-polar* takes a stand against inequality and rejection. 'Du roman noir américain, il a retenu une certaine virulence dans la critique des pouvoirs urbains, et, du polar à la française, un sentiment aigu des inégalités sociales et des injustices. Il a donc toutes les allures d'une littérature très politique.'[60] Blanc describes the result as the creation of the 'polar-Molotov' (p. 195), which attacks the economic system, political corruption, police corruption, the contrast between the wretched poverty in popular districts and the riches of the powerful.

The novelists he discusses in this context are A.D.G., Vautrin, Vallet, Siniac and others who do indeed concentrate upon the miseries of the inhuman life in the *banlieues*, *cités* and *zones*. The use of Céline, thematically and stylistically, is often noted in the *néo-polar*, and A.D.G.'s *Cradoque's Band* is a deliberate reference to his *Guignol's Band*. Blanc pays great attention to the vocabulary used to describe these urban wastelands

---

[55] Mentioned by Jean-Jacques Beineix (director of *Diva*—a Delacorta novel—and *La Lune dans le caniveau*—a David Goodis novel) in relation to the literary and filmic inheritance of 'le polar', *Magazine littéraire*, 194, 53.

[56] In *Homme et la société*, 8 (1968), 74.   [57] Ibid. 71: 'Social space was changing meaning.'

[58] 'The special landscape of the *néo-polar* is the new city of the 1960s: suburb, concrete, council housing, gloom and the dismal poverty of the inhabitants deported to the town's edges which are devoid of urbanity.' Jean-Noel Blanc, *Polarville: Images de la ville dans le roman policier* (Lyons, Presses Universitaires de Lyon, 1991), 191.

[59] Ibid.: 'waste ground, empty buildings, dim lights, desolation, dirt, mud, deserted zones.'

[60] 'From the American *roman noir*, it retained a certain virulence in its criticism of the city authorities, and, from the French *polar*, an acute sense of social inequalities and injustices. It therefore has all the hallmarks of a very political literature.' Ibid. 193.

and the populace condemned to live in them, finding a great deal of stereotypical writing of degradation, drunkenness, unbridled sexuality, stupidity, and filth, with a defeatist narrative overview in relation to any possibility of change. The *néo-polar*, he concludes, says the very opposite from what it appears to say. Far from championing the cause of the victims of social and political inequality, it tends to write of them with scorn and arrogance. 'C'est bien cela, le propos du néo-polar. Que la ville en soi, toute la ville et toute ville, n'est qu'une sorte de magma insensé qui n'a pas de sens. Ni dessus ni dessous. Pas de secrets. Tout est donné, là, en surface, dans la grisaille et le non-sens. Rien à expliquer. Tout à refuser.'[61] He makes a strong case, although the energy of the protagonists of the Achélèmes (HLM) in *Cradoque's Band* is not taken into account, and in general, abstracting description from the overall economy of the narrative tends to distort the value one may or may not place upon it.

It does however throw an interesting light, by its very contrast, upon *Nada*, where the *banlieues* and *zones* do not figure at all. Like Lefebvre, Manchette places the city itself at the centre of the novel. While there is reference to street protests, the closed spaces of rooms in Paris (brothel, police headquarters, Ministry, Treuffais's room), and in the farmhouse combine primarily with roads as connecting links (in Paris, and in the intricate itinerary through the suburbs to go between Paris and farmhouse undetected).

The romanticism of pure violence which Lefebvre points to in relation to spontaneous contestation is carried here by the nihilism of the aptly named group. Lefebvre's description of anarchist violence suggests a very real convergence between the political activists and the more general anarchism typical of the heroes of *le polar*:

> **A-t-on entendu dans les rues de Paris le terrible: 'Viva la muerte!'? Non, sans doute. L'honneur des hommes qui suivent le drapeau noir, c'est qu'ils n'ont jamais engagé la vie des autres, amis ou ennemis, sans risquer la leur et sans réserves. Dans cet honneur, dans cette volonté, réside un grand danger pour un 'monde' sans honneur qui n'a d'autre volonté que de durer.**[62]

---

[61] *Polarville: Images de la ville dans le roman policier*, 206: 'That's what the *neo-polar* is about. That the town as such, the whole town and every town, is nothing but a great insane amalgam which makes no sense. No above and no below. No secrets. Everything is overt, there, on the surface, in the greyness and the absurdity. Nothing to explain. Everything to be rejected.' This is a remarkable anticipation of the kind of language which will be used, without the accusatory tone, once critical discourse has invented its contemporary descendants, such as *Diva*, as a postmodernist *cinéma du look*.

[62] 'Has anyone heard the terrible: "Viva la muerte!" in the streets of Paris? No, probably not. It is to the honour of the men who follow the black flag, that they have never put at risk the lives of others, friends or enemies, without risking their own, unreservedly. In that honour, in that wish, resides a great danger for a "world" without honour which has no other wish than to last.' 'L'Irruption', *Homme et société*, 8 (1968), 71.

Having realized the police has come to massacre, not to arrest, Diaz shoots the ambassador, watches Cash descend the stairs to certain death, and acknowledges that he too is now under the sign of death: 'Eh merde, grogna-t-il. Et vive la mort.'[63] Twice more he will utter 'vive la mort', the second time when he enters Treuffais's room to blow Goémond's head off. Yet his political understanding of the sterile, apocalyptic violence of state and terrorist allows the reader to place the diegetic development within a different critical frame.

Lefebvre establishes a distinction between latent and overt violence, arguing that the state ('le pouvoir') prefers the former to the latter. Indiscrimate use of military or police repression is not a strength; absolute power depends on using force only to eliminate totally the adversary, but that is to say that threats or partial repression are not possible, since they would only confer status on the adversary as a force to deal with, rather than crush. But there is a logic in the relationship between latent and overt: 'la violence latente fait surgir la contre-violence qui la révèle, qui peut la gêner et l'obliger à se déployer en frappant le grand coup. Il peut même arriver que la force s'use et que la contre-violence la casse. Dans ces conditions, le romantisme de la pure violence peut surgir.'[64] Diaz's commentary on the plot also suggests the apocalyptic violence of the showdown is a political degradation, yet interweaves it with situationist notions of spectacular control:

> Le terrorisme gauchiste et le terrorisme étatique, quoique leurs mobiles soient incomparables, sont les deux mâchoires du . . . (. . .) même piège à cons. (. . .) Le régime se défend évidemment contre le terrorisme. Mais le système ne s'en défend pas, il l'encourage, il en fait la publicité. Le desperado est une marchandise, une valeur d'échange, un modèle de comportement comme le flic ou la sainte. L'État rêve d'une fin horrible et triomphale dans la mort, dans la guerre civile absolument généralisée entre les cohortes de flics et de mercenaires et les commandos du nihilisme. C'est le piège qui est tendu aux révoltés et je suis tombé dedans. Et je ne serai pas le seul. Et ça m'emmerde bien.[65]

---

[63] *Nada*, 145: ' "Oh shit", he muttered "And long live death." ' He thus echoes Epaulard's own acknowledgement of action under the sign of death as he decides not to kill himself and to go to the Nada group meeting (p. 30): 'Eh merde, quoi! dit-il à son miroir.'

[64] 'L'Irruption', 71: 'Latent violence provokes the counter-violence which reveals it, which can frustrate it and force it to become overt by hitting it very hard. It can even happen that force weakens and the counter-violence breaks it. In those conditions, the romanticism of pure violence can appear.'

[65] *Nada*, 164: '*Gauchiste* terrorism and state terrorism are two sides of the same stupid trap, although their motivation cannot be compared. The government defends itself of course against terrorism. But the system does not defend itself, it encourages it, it advertises it. The desperado is a merchandise, an exchange value, a model of behaviour like the cop or the saint. The state dreams of a horrible, triumphant end in death, in a general civil war between gangs of police and of mercenaires and the commandos of nihilism. It's the trap which is held out to protestors and I fell into it. I will not be the only one. And it pisses me off.'

The angry aggression on the streets which Treuffais both meets and provokes as he drives home in his *deux chevaux*, and his violence to the charity seller at his door, in the first chapter; Meyer's violent (and suicidal) wife in the second chapter; these serve to generalize French society as a violent phenomenon, whose latent violence is ever ready to break the thin surfaces of convention and order, contextualizing the actions of the group as more than gratuitous provocation. Before going to his own apocalypse, Diaz records his story and his conclusions, and Treuffais's call to a news agency which closes the novel suggests the fight is to be taken to the true battleground of the spectacular system, namely the mass media.

The exuberance of Manchette's writing is another terrain bringing together the self-referential tradition of the *polar* and the political awareness of spectacle and meaning associated with the situationist *détournement*. Irony, pastiche, quotation, proliferate as Manchette plays with the codes of the genre. The description of the American Ambassador makes him sound like Lord Peter Wimsey.[66] Other literary jokes include a policeman finding an anarchist pamphlet 'Noir et rouge' which Goémond confidently informs him is a novel by Stendhal. He quickly admits he is wrong: 'Je confondais avec *La Chartreuse de Parme.*' (For some reason the film changes this to *Salammbô*. Perhaps someone thought it funnier to get the author wrong as well.) The filmic equivalent has Diaz looking as if he has stepped out of a spaghetti western: tall, in his black clothes and broad-rimmed hat, he is a mixture of Clint Eastwood, Lee Van Cleef, and Antonio das Mortes. He even has his own theme music. Another sustained set of references is to Roger Vailland and his Resistance novel *Drôle de jeu*. Epaulard has the *Écrits intimes* on his desk, and Véronique presents herself as the young middle-class woman Annie in *Drôle de jeu*, as well as remarking on Epaulard's resemblance to Vailland (a resemblance the film sustains). Annie and Marat meet at a farmhouse, where the derailment of a train is being prepared, and walk around the countryside while a Resistance group of activists carry out the work. It is an interesting choice of intertext, suggesting a thematic continuity between the solitude and the metaphysical and sexual crises of the 'man of action' (in a neat reversal of image, when Epaulard does go to bed with Véronique, he is impotent), as well as reinforcing the political continuity between the terrorists and the Resistance already put in place through Epaulard's own history. The countryside may seem a strange battleground for a *polar*, even with the Resistance historicization, but in fact May (or rather

---

[66] *Nada*, 56–7: Blue eyes, expressions of surprise and amusement giving way to interest.

June) did see running battles across fields between protestors, strikers, and CRS.[67]

Nada also includes graphic reproduction of newspaper front pages; repetition of various kinds of journalism on the story of the kidnapping, which in *Le Monde* appears under the heading 'Une page noire'; reproduction of a variety of left political discourses in the reaction to the farmhouse massacre, and a series of knowing 68 references: Boulevard Lefebvre, vallée du Morin. The novel also writes familiar elements of contemporary history into its plot: film of the terrorists is obtained from the relevant faction in the police, the out-of-control SAC, by releasing its leader from prison, echoing the OAS amnesty in 1968.[68] In short, we are never allowed to forget the ideological and cultural intertexts. The film is able to exploit the scene where the terrorists are filmed from the building opposite as they stand on the doorstep of the brothel, in order to accentuate the generic text: the very large camera is in a dark room, the face of the agent doing the filming is in part shadow, the shot to the street is a crane shot typical of Hitchcock, and the cinematic process and the conventions of *noir* and suspense are most deliberately highlighted in this game of light and darkness.

Engagé ou enragé?

In literary culture the post-68 years see the installation of the empire of the sign, as the Nouveau Roman and *Tel Quel*, together with structuralist criticism and philosophy, impose themselves on the public at large, proclaiming an impeccable *mise à mort* of existentialism and committed literature. In cinema and popular literature, political commitment enjoys a new lease of life.[69] In the case of *Nada*, it is not easy to determine whether Manchette's impressive rewriting of *le polar* allows any real political conclusion to be drawn, whether it is in the final analysis more *enragé* than *engagé*, more dramatization of subversion and writing than effective

---

[67] Cf. the photographs 'La chasse dans les Yvelines', Delale and Ragache, 149, and also in Rioux and Backmann, between p. 224 and p. 225: 'Ce fut parfois dans d'étranges décors champêtres, comme à Flins et Sochaux, que les heurts se produisirent et que les gaz lacrymogènes étendirent leur faux brouillard.' The police piling off the coaches in the village is one of the more incongruous sights in the film. It is also worth noting that in 1969 demonstrating farmers held a government minister prisoner for three hours in a farm near Nantes.

[68] SAC is also the acronym of the Service d'Action Civique, the Gaullist 'heavies' who kept order at rallies, etc.

[69] Cf. the articles by Schweighaeuser, Vautrin, Reboux, and Delteil, in *Pas d'orchidées pour les TM*, and P. Maarek, *De Mai 68 ... aux films X: Cinéma politique et société* (Editions Duijarric, 1979).

subversion. It has been argued that the *le roman policier* is the ultimate consumerist genre: 'A peine [le coupable] dénoncé, c'est-à-dire *énoncé*, il est renvoyé au vide par une machine à narrer qui s'interrompt et coupe. Au suivant. Car la machine repart, mettant en train une autre unité de la série, de même principe. Tout cela, on le voit, est très adapté à une certaine conception moderne de la production-consommation.'[70] But Dubois goes on to remind us that this transience is also the very condition of modernity as defined by Baudelaire. We have seen the importance of genre in the genre's creation as self-referential writing; it is as if the index of its modernity lay in this intersection of the referential and the self-referential: 'C'est un peu comme si l'histoire de crime-détection était devenue la dernière histoire racontable. Un peu comme si toutes les autres avaient perdu leur crédibilité et que celle-ci seule, avec sa conjonction de l'énigme ludique et de l'enquête dramatique, gardait tout son pouvoir d'attraction.'[71]

The situationists were not political defeatists. However powerful the spectacular machines, the aim was to destroy them: 'Just as everything which appears in opposition to the spectacle can be brought within it, so everything which appears within the spectacular society can be reclaimed by the consciousness which seeks to subvert it.'[72] Buenaventura Diaz remembers his father, killed in 1937 on the barricades of Barcelona. The Commune of Barcelona will be crushed, then buried 'sous la calomnie' (p. 165). Treuffais will tell the real story of the Nada group to the media, and perhaps the other story, the story of state and bourgeoisie already repeated to his mother by Poustacrouille, will itself be contested and subverted.

Jill Forbes has described the relationship between French and American cinema in the 1950s and 1960s as one of 'tension perceptible in an elaborate intertextuality', on the grounds that the American domination of the film industry is such as to condemn French cinema to purely local subjects, to invest French film-making with a structural nostalgia for what it can no longer aspire to, a tension felt all the more in the French *film noir*. It is an eloquent résumé of a most complex set of relationships. Yet the incompatibility she traces between American cinema and the realist attention to the everyday in French cinema of the 1960s, and expressed

[70] 'Hardly has the guilty one been denounced, that is to say, his name uttered, than he is returned to nothingness by the narrating machine which stops and cuts. Next. For the machine starts up again, setting off another unit in the series, on the same principle. All of which is, as one can see, perfectly suited to a modern conception of production-consumption.' Jacques Dubois, *Le Roman policier ou la modernité* (Nathan, 1992), 47.

[71] 'It is rather as if the story of crime detection had become the final story which could be told. Rather as if all other stories had lost their credibility and this one alone, with its combination of ludic enigma and dramatic enquiry, retained all its powers of attraction.' Ibid. 51.

[72] Plant, *Most Radical Gesture*, 104.

in narrative discontinuities and fragmentations, is less evident in the post-68 world of the *néo-polar* in novel and film. Many currents feed into the post-68 *polar*: situationism and its related texts, the events of 68, the politicization of the imaginary, the rewriting of the historiography of post-war France, and the complex inheritance of *roman noir*, *roman policier*, and *film noir*. The *néo-polar* demonstrates how far the fragmentations of narrative and textuality converge with sociological and philosophical discourse on 'the modern' to produce political narratives of contestation and protest.

In the 1960s any discussion taking place of textuality and the issues of representation or the materiality of language would indubitably have passed through the journal *Tel Quel* and the authors associated with it: Sollers, Kristeva, Thibaudeau, Barthes, Ricardou, etc. Sollers and Thibaudeau were the post-Nouveau Roman generation, the 'nouveaux nouveaux romanciers', whose works continued the trajectory of their predecessors in their intense concentration on the formal properties of textuality. Psychology and plot were even more rigorously eliminated, in an artistic exploration which also saw itself as offering a politics of the text, on the basis that the conventions of realism, with their naturalizing reflection of 'what is' stifling all critical awareness of the cultural and ideological work involved, were the vehicle *par excellence* of bourgeois ideology. They also adopted the *nouveau romancier*'s rejection of committed literature which Robbe-Grillet had defined as yet another variant on the attempt to impose non-literary ends on literature. For the *Tel Quel* group, committed literature was seeking to change the world, and literature was an unproblematized instrument in this project: 'La construction (. . .) d'une théorie tirée de la pratique textuelle que nous avons à développer nous semble susceptible d'éviter les impassses répétitives du discours "engagé"—modèles d'une mystification téléologico-transcendentale humaniste et psychologique, complice de l'obscurantisme définitif de l'état bourgeois.'[1] In line with Kristeva's influential analysis of avant-garde writing, *Tel Quel* knew that revolution was inseparable from cultural revolution, from the poetic revolution inherent in writing differently, in the politics of *écriture*.

However much *Tel Quel* diverged in practice from much of the cultural and political work of May, it converged very importantly around certain key themes which were part of the new sensibility: cultural revolution, contestatory art and writing. Even though it will have been prepared

---

[1] 'The construction of a theory drawn from the textual practice we have to develop seems to us likely to avoid the repetitive dead-ends of "committed" discourse—models of a humanist and psychological teleologico-transcendental mystification, an ally to the definitive obscurantism of the bourgeois state.' 'La Révolution ici et maintenant', *Tel Quel*, 34 (Summer 1968), 4. 'Mystification téléologico-transcendentale' is another way of saying that it presents literature falsely as being governed by ends beyond the text.

before the events, and even though *Tel Quel* is close to the PCF rather than the *gauchistes*, it does seem particularly apt that the author interviewed in the May 68 issue of the *Magazine littéraire* is Philippe Sollers, talking about his 'volonté de destruction de la littérature'.[2] The most extraordinary paradox is that, while the stress on the production of meaning, the attack on realism, the combination with cultural revolution and subjectivity as sites of political action, mean that *Tel Quel* and Sollers are close to the ideological and cultural sensibilities of May, politically they are not, as they champion the cause of the Parti Communiste and the communist union the CGT. Although there were elements within the PCF trying to move the cultural debate forward, they did not have an easy time in a party still dominated by those who tended to think of literature in terms of the debates around socialist realism. But however much it preached class struggle and the dictatorship of the proletariat, the formal response of *Tel Quel* to May was to set up 'Groupes d'Analyse théorique'.[3]

Sollers's introduction to Thibaudeau's *Mai 68 en France*, a text written for radio performance, is a cogent statement of the textual, cultural, and political revolution which Sollers is calling for. It starts with the statement—'*Mai 68 en France* est un texte réaliste'—which would have been gratuitous provocation and insult from his pen, if he had not just quoted Brecht's definition of realism: revealing the power relations within society, taking the viewpoint of the working class, seen as the class which will provide solutions to society's problems, and combining concrete realities with abstract conclusions.[4] Like the other authorities cited in the preface, namely Benjamin, Eisenstein, and Althusser, Brecht was a respected master of anti-realism, his work aiming for a critical awareness, within the production of the text, of both textual and political realities.

There is a definite authoritarianism in Sollers's prescriptive political discourse: Brecht says there is one point of view to write from; progressive writing means revealing the contradictions; the major contradiction is the contradiction between imperialism and socialism; future victory is 'inevitable'. In other words, the political text is univocal, and failure to read it correctly leads to an incoherent chaos of fragments.[5] Sollers makes extensive use of psychoanalytical concepts to situate progressive writing in the 'non-dit' of the primary contradiction, which is, he says, as inaccessible to the forces of reaction as the 'non-dit' is to the neurotic.

[2] *Magazine littéraire* (May 1968), 38.
[3] *Tel Quel*, 34 (Summer 1968), 4. Kristeva discusses the 'Groupes théoriques' in 'The Samurais "tel quels"', in Patrick ffrench (ed.), *From 'Tel quel' to 'L'Infini'*, *Parallax*, 6 (Jan.–Mar. 1998), 9–10.
[4] *Mai 68 en France*, preceded by Philippe Sollers *Printemps rouge* (Seuil, 1970), 7.
[5] Ibid. 11. Fragments which Sollers argues are often taken for the reality, in what sounds like a critique of political theses on consumerism.

Wittily describing the 30 May demonstration as 'le retour du refoulant',[6] he presents the terrain of revolutionary writing as being that of political and ideological repressions, for it serves to reveal the 'gaps' in political discourse. Because realist representation is culturally repressive, techniques of non-realism are politically charged: 'Le rôle d'une écriture "progressiste" est donc maintenant (. . .) [d]'être une machine complexe à représenter et dérepresenter l'histoire (à produire les conditions logiques d'une représentation non-figurative ou plutôt post-figurative qui défigure celle de l'ennemi ou sa prétention à se situer dans une non-représentation *pure et simple*), ses réserves inconscientes, son procès de transformation.'[7]

Thibaudeau's text does not really live up to this. Its challenge to representation lies primarily in its declamatory technique, divided between the fourteen voices who enunciate sections of varying lengths. It is in three parts, and the first two (I: 'Les Étudiants du 1er mai au 13'; II: 'La Lutte des Classes du 14 mai au 28') do not do much more than give a suitably heroic account of events. The third section, 'Le Pouvoir (29, 30, 31 mai)' is the more varied and interesting, mixing subjective accounts, judgements, evocations of earlier revolutions, incidents, a narrative of events at the Arc de Triomphe, and solemn homages to those who died in June, with references to strikes and student actions. The constant praise of the CGT and dismissal of *gauchisme* at Nanterre and elsewhere are its least typical sentiments, but the prominence given to the Communist Party does sit quite easily with the prescriptive literary discourse of political rectitude; in general, the discrepancy between the promotion of open signifying practices over bourgeois narrative closure and the ex-cathedra directives in the political sphere is an example of the kind of discourse which will not survive the corrosive attention to self-valorizing discourses, in post-structuralism and since. In other words, there is no slippage here between *énonciation* or *énoncé*, no unsettling disruption of *énoncé*, as far as the subject of the *political* text is concerned, and, as different texts are substituted in *Tel Quel*'s pages for the communist one,[8] the suspicion must remain that this always was a revolution for art's sake.

At one point Thibaudeau points succinctly to one of the central paradoxes of May: 'Le dimanche 5 mai tout est écrit déjà de ce qui va se

---

[6] 'The return of the represser': 'le retour du refoulé' or the 'return of the repressed' is the psychoanalytical concept being adapted.

[7] Ibid. 13. 'The role of "progressive" writing is therefore now to be a complex machine for representing and derepresenting history (producing the logical conditions of a non-figurative or rather post-figurative representation which disfigures that of the enemy or his pretention to situate himself in *pure and simple* non-representation), its unconscious reserves, its process of transformation.'

[8] *Tel Quel* notoriously switched attention from China to the United States, and then to religion and mysticism.

produire en France—et ailleurs—dans les semaines qui suivront: et rien n'est écrit,—car toute l'Histoire, comme elle se fera, reste à écrire.'⁹ The conundrum of the relations between event, language, and writing is endlessly reworked and never played out, because writing is always preceded by writing, can never be originary, can never found the event, or be founded by it. Be it in history, feminism, the *détournement de sens* of slogans, graffiti, and situationist writing, or of derision and *l'esprit de Nanterre*, an awareness of textuality is an ever-present dimension. It is therefore perhaps not surprising that May 68 also provoked pastiche and parody.

*La Chine m'inquiète*¹⁰ is a collection of pastiches published by Jean-Louis Curtis, who had already demonstrated his virtuosity as a stylist with *Haute École*. Curtis reiterates the relationship between multiplicity and collectivity characteristic of the imaginary of May by describing the essays as 'un petit roman unanimiste'.¹¹ The authors whose style and themes Curtis imitates are a varied bunch: de Gaulle, Proust, Céline, Bernanos, Léautaud, Valéry, Claudel, Giraudoux, Giono, Breton, Chardonne, Malraux, Green, Aragon, Beauvoir, and Sarraute. Even in 1968, Jacques Chardonne and Paul Léautaud are fairly marginal figures from a previous generation, but who may well have survived for the young in textbooks and anthologies. All the rest will have been familiar through at least one or two key works, to young and old alike, as part of the mainstream literary canon. Each chapter takes a feature of the writer's thematics and resituates it in May. Bernanos makes an 'Appel aux jeunes Français', Céline gives graphic descriptions of the street battles: 'Un pavé fracasse la vitrine, vrim, krasch! . . . Pluie de verre . . . ondée coupante! giclée de pizzicati! . . .'.¹² Proust registers surprise at Roberte Swann's support for the *gauchistes* and her virulent anti-Zionism. Curtis also has fun with Proustian subheadings which include: 'A l'ombre des émeutiers en fleurs.—M. de Charlus ravitaille les Katangais.'¹³ Natalie Sarraute stages a confrontation between 'art for art's sake' and 'committed literature', Beauvoir's characters conduct philosophical investigations on their selves and on society: ' "Je suis flouée", se dit Lucile en se dirigeant vers la salle de bains. L'attentat

⁹ 'On Sunday 5 May everything is already written about what is going to happen in France—and elsewhere—in the weeks to come: and nothing is written, for all History, as it will happen, is always to be written.' *Mai 68 en France*, 40.
¹⁰ Grasset, 1972.
¹¹ 'A unanimist little novel'—on the cover of the book, original edn. 'L'unanimisme', a literary doctrine associated with Jules Romains, strives to render the collective sensibility.
¹² Ibid. 62: 'A paving stone shatters the window, vrim, krasch! . . . Rain of glass . . . cutting wave . . . spurt of pizzicati! . . .'
¹³ Ibid. 29: 'In the shadow of rioters in full bloom, M. de Charlus gets provisions to the Katangais.'

n'aurait pas lieu. Elle ne changerait pas sa vie en destin. Mais, pendant quelques secondes, elle s'était enfin assumée.'[14] De Gaulle shifts between third and first person, hits the populist note to laud the people of Paris and their empathy for the students, and to attack politicians, notes that the Communist Party does not want revolution any more than he does,[15] and views the whole thing as History wrapped around his person.

The genre does allow Curtis to make some serious points. The possibility that Bernanos would have seen the students as descendants of the 'children in revolt' with whom he peopled his works (St Theresa of Lisieux, Mouchette, the terminally ill 'curé', the young soldiers of the Great War) is for example an intriguing one. As an author associated with the Hussards group in the 1950s,[16] Curtis could be expected to be hostile to May and what it represented. It hardly seems a coincidence that the final pieces are both by women, one of whom, Simone de Beauvoir, is a leading exponent of committed literature, the other, Natalie Sarraute, publicly associated with the writers' organization in support of the May protesters. The final words of the text show where the author's sympathies lie, as the rather precious and elusive central character of the Sarraute piece gets rid of some unwanted guests: 'dans un petit rire de jeune fille:—Et ne vous faites pas de soucis pour moi! La Chine ne m'inquiète pas, je vous assure. La Chine ne m'inquiète pas le moins du monde,'[17] elucidating the title *La Chine m'inquiète*. Sarraute thus baptizes the text in a countering move: the text is inscribed against May, as being truly worrying, in literature and in life.

The cumulative effect of *La Chine m'inquiète* is not so much the creation of a single novel as the imposition of the fictional at the expense of its referent. To read one novel is to maintain a balance between the writing and 'what it's about'; even for those with knowledge of the arbitrariness of the sign, the materiality of the signifier, discursive formations, and the death of the author reincarnated as rewriter and ghost, on a first reading at least the plot and conventions of illusion will suffice to generate a strong sense of subject-matter and purpose. To read Curtis's sixteen short narratives, in their totally contrasting styles, is to be drawn gradually into the

---

[14] *La Chine M'inquiète*, 242: ' "I have been duped", Lucile told herself on her way to the bathroom. The attack would not take place. She would not change her life into destiny. But, for a few seconds, she had assumed responsibility for herself.'

[15] This was certainly the view of many thousands of *gauchistes*, but not apparently, in real life, of de Gaulle whose anxiety at the communist-called demonstration on 29 May precipitated his departure for Baden-Baden.

[16] A group of young, right-wing, vehemently anti-existentialist writers who celebrated style over politics in literature.

[17] Ibid. 265: 'With a little girl's laugh. "And don't worry about me! China does not worry me, I assure you. China does not worry me at all." '

awareness that the only reality here is the reality of the text. The text of 'Céline' is no more true or false than that of 'de Gaulle', or 'Beauvoir'. It also forces reflection on the relationship between pastiche, parody, and irony, and the more explicit textual experimentation. Both pastiche and parody involve imitation of a discourse, and the former is often, although not necessarily, written with parodic intent. Each involves a theatricality of discourse, where a primary discourse is repeated, but differently; it is on display in the same way that the exponent of the materiality of language places discourses on display to counter ideological readings which natur-alize the processes of representation. Irony too involves difference and duality, from the coupling of negative and positive in the classic example of an utterance which actually means its opposite,[18] to the gap or dis-crepancy in discourse which can affect any part of it. The doubling of a discourse and its shadow is therefore another variant on the structural positioning of all discourse, that it always has to negotiate a position with the already written.

Bernard Poirot-Delpech's novel, *Les Grands de ce monde*,[19] is built around the rather good idea that when de Gaulle disappeared on 29 May, he did not go to Baden as generally supposed, but took to the streets, and met a 'garde républicain' called Manuelli Antonio in the Métro Balard. The recreation of the historical, combined with the fictional, allows Poirot-Delpech to make points about May and Gaullism, particularly in the con-text of Algeria and of the Occupation.[20] Poirot-Delpech has fun inscribing historical figures in the fictional reality. The novel also works at times like a pastiche of historical discourse, rather in the way that the film *Forrest Gump* famously does, distorting the familiar representations as they are intertwined with the narrative, as Manuelli and his friends lean against the Arc de Triomphe watching Malraux and Debré on 30 May (pp. 225–9). These narrative variations on the fictional and the historical are further complicated when we learn at the end that the account is ghosted by a journalist. The interplay between written and spoken is therefore at the centre of this novel, and the author plays with different kinds of discourse and authenticity: Manuelli insists for example that his girlfriend Josiane be identified, in the section devoted to their love-making, only as J., as this is more poetic, and more in accord with the way love should be written about (p. 274). Here too, the writer is the rewriter of discourse, of the

---

[18] One classic example being 'Behold this financial genius!' to designate a bankrupt.

[19] Gallimard, 1976. References to Folio edition.

[20] Manuelli meets Pétain as a child, for example; after May, the three friends go to Vichy on the day the death of Abel Bonnard (a collaborator) is announced.

historical, of the fictional, condemned to the interminable treadmill of repetition, although with the possibility of repeating it fictitiously rather than historically.

Frédéric Bon and Michel-Antoine Burnier wrote many political and socio-logical works together. *Si Mai avait gagné*[21] is rather different. Described as a 'facétie politique' on the title-page, it is an amusing pamphlet which has no great literary pretensions, and which uses science fiction as a vehicle to satirize some of the May 68 protagonists, especially the Communist Party. It is illustrated with cartoons by Wolinski. Its main invention is to make the protestors of May win: the May revolution becomes the prelude to the revolutionary forces taking power in 1969. It is set in the year 2156, and discusses the results of the recent archeological find under the Montagne Sainte-Geneviève in Paris, a journalist's diary of the events of the May revolution. This is the main text, which is glossed with copious footnotes. The format allows for many side-swipes at a range of targets, including André Malraux: 'On sait le bouleversement qu'introduisit dans la guerre moderne la découverte d'armes anti-mémoire (A.A.M), due au macabre génie d'un colonel des Brigades nationales d'Espagne.'[22] (We are told these weapons were banned in 1975.) There is regret at the fire which destroyed the holdings of the depot of the 887 works (ten copies of each) on May 68, 'dont 16 rédigés par Philippe Labro' (p. 11). One running joke throughout the little volume is whether it is true that the Communist Party had formed part of the official government after May 68, as in the cartoon with Pompidou and Séguy (General Secretary of the CGT) at the same table, uttering the same thought, 'On est dans la merde', with the caption: 'Langage commun'.[23] On balance, it is thought that their actions sug-gest they did. The satire ends with the fictional scenario reversed to fall back into history, but in the hypothetical mode: the journalist notes a *Nouvel Observateur* article is about to appear entitled 'Si de Gaulle était resté'. 'Supposons un instant (. . .) que les masses n'aient pu résister au chantage à la guerre civile, que les élections aient eu lieu, que l'U.D.R. les ait gagnées.' 'Tout cela n'est qu'un mauvais rêve', they conclude with relief.[24]

---

[21] Collection enragée, Jean-Jacques Pauvert, 1969.

[22] 'One knows the upheavals that the discovery of anti-memory weapons introduced into modern warfare, due to the sinister genius of a colonel of the national Brigades of Spain.' (Malraux's *Anti-mémoires* was published in 1968.)

[23] Ibid. 21: 'We are in the shit', 'Common language'.

[24] Ibid. 124: 'If de Gaulle had stayed'. 'Suppose for a moment that the masses could not resist the blackmail of the threat of civil war, that there had been elections, that the UDR won them.' ' That's just a bad dream'.

La vieille taupe de l'histoire/l'histoire de la vieille taupe

The ironies of utopian dream/bad dream intertwined with history/
imagination are also important in *L'Imprécateur*, by René-Victor Pilhes,[25]
a text to set beside Semprun's *La Deuxième Mort de Ramón Mercader* as a
political novel with a vertiginous exploitation of narrative structures, and
also beside Camus's *La Peste*, for its systematic 'literalization' of a central
metaphor through the full length of the novel. René Mouriaux wrote: 'Le
roman de Pilhes *L'Imprécateur* me semble inséparable de la "secousse" de
Mai chez les cadres, l'image même autour de laquelle s'organise le récit, la
fissure que menace des assises du siège social de la filiale française de
Rosserys and Mitchell importante firme internationale, renvoyant à un
vécu spécifique des cadres en grève.'[26] While it is pleasing to see Pilhes's
novel recognized in the context of May, it is my view that the novel gives
itself a much wider remit than the experiences of management, and that
the questions of society, of capitalism and neo-colonialism, of metaphysics
in the modern world, are equally important. Its structural complexity spins
a narrative of multiple levels, where the problematic of speech and writing
is the central conduit for disaster.

The novel is set in the (fictitious) impressive headquarters of the Paris
branch of an international firm. The building of Rosserys & Mitchell is
situated on the angle of the rue Oberkampf and the Boulevard de la
République, and we learn that it dominates all the surrounding Paris
squares: Place de la Bastille, Place de la Nation, Place de la République,
Place Voltaire. The narrator comments at one point that those listening to
him had difficulty with deciding how much of his story was true. 'Devant
mon obstination à désigner des endroits précis, ils doutent parfois
d'eux-mêmes. En revanche, d'apparentes inexactitudes renforcent leur
incrédulité.'[27] He thus knowingly points to the drama of verisimilitude and
reality-indexing in a novel which mingles so deliberately the fictitious, the
fictional, and the historical. All these squares are within walking distance
of each other, and the references to streets and métro stations are quite
authentic, but there has never been a skyscraper tall enough to overlook
them all. This fictitious centre or gap draws the description onto another

---

[25] Seuil, 1972.
[26] 'Pilhes's novel *L'Imprécateur* seems to me to be inseparable from the "shockwave" of May for managers.
The image around which the story is organized, the crack which is threatening the headquarters
of the French subsidiary of the important multinational firm Rosserys and Mitchell, refers to the very
specific experience of the striking managers.' R. Mouriaux, *Le Peuple*, special issue *May 68* (1978), 35.
[27] *L'Imprécateur*, 56: 'Faced with my insistence on naming precise places, they sometimes doubt
themselves. On the other hand, apparent inaccuracies reinforce their lack of belief.'

plane: the coherence of the siting becomes metaphorical, and one can only admire the perfection of this symbolic geography, as the monuments of the French State and Nation are combined in this way. Rosserys & Mitchell is an American-based multinational, and several of the leading American executives are involved in trying to cope with the disaster. This novel therefore uses the classic distinction of American versus French to articulate its critique of the modern world, in part no doubt because of the role the economics of consumerism plays.

The fact that the Cimetière de l'Est, the Père Lachaise, is nearby is also important both to the plot and to the symbolic geography. Paris is well known to be riddled with tunnels—it seems unlikely that one could go from the Oberkampf/République junction to the cemetery by tunnels alone, but it is in this warren of a dark rotten underworld that the dramatic dénouement takes place. Furthermore, it is not hard to read certain descriptions which are using this upper/lower, firm/weak opposition, in terms of other kinds of symbolism as well: 'Certes, il existait de nombreuses galeries, d'insondables souterrains, d'énormes et humides cavités au-dessous de l'avenue de la République.'[28] At whatever point one approaches the text, meanings proliferate and multiply.

The story is summed up at the outset as the tale of the collapse of the beautiful Rosserys & Mitchell tower in steel and glass and the unleashing of hysteria. The narrator is their director of personnel, who one day finds himself dealing with three strange occurrences. Arangrude, 'sous-directeur du *marketing* pour le Benelux', has been killed in a car accident the night before on the boulevard périphérique when returning home; a crack has appeared in the foundations of the building; a rolled-up document has been distributed to every employee in the building, and its contents are such as to sow doubt and unease. In fact all three events render the narrator uncomfortable. The first because it is unclear what kind of procedures should be followed, and who should deal with it, and the second because there seems no reason, given the extensive geological work which has preceded the construction of the building, for this to happen. As in any good horror story, the first indications of the disasters to come are minor and just strange. The major part of the narrative consists of the reactions and chain of events unleashed by the documents, four in all, and the ever-widening crack in the foundations. The group of managers finally descend into the gloom and the rottenness of the basement and the tunnels it gives access to, in order to try and solve the mystery of what is happening, and why.

---

[28] *L'Imprécateur*, 6: 'Certainly, there existed numerous galeries, unfathomably deep underground passages, enormous damp hollows beneath the avenue de la République.'

All this is related retrospectively. It becomes quickly clear that the narrator is in some kind of medical care, is gradually returning to health, and seems to be writing the narrative as part of his process of recovery. The short passages which interrupt the story therefore offer commentary on the commentary, but it is indicative of the undecidability of the text that it remains unclear whether the narrator is cured or not, and indeed, whether the building is really destroyed or not. In the final chapter, the narrator (finally identified with a name, Pilhes) is astounded to be visited by all his colleagues, whom he had thought dead under the collapsed building, and Arangrude too. None of it has actually happened; the narrator is informed he has been suffering from a bad blow on the head. But on the day that he returns to work after more than a month's absence, on the final page of the text, he is shocked indeed to learn that Arangrude had been killed that night on the boulevard périphérique . . . The whole plot might therefore have been some kind of 'crise de prémonition', to repeat Christiane Rochefort's term, with the implication that it was all about to start taking place. This circularity is a familiar literary device.[29] But in *L'Imprécateur*, however, we learn in the introductory section that this is going to be a story of destruction and moral corruption, and the narrator is preparing his story of the collapse of the building to bear witness to 'la nouvelle justice': 'l'ère des procès s'annonce' (the era of trials is upon us, p. 6). It is impossible to say whether this has been written before or after the conclusion, before or after the bang on the head. If before, the story has not actually happened; if afterwards, it has happened twice. The *énonciation* defies chronology,[30] and indeed, classification, given the problematic status of the narrator. First he might just be ill. In the slippage between the psychological and the socio-philosophical, *L'Imprécateur* recalls Sartre's *La Nausée*, where one has to decide whether the reaction of nausea is the product of a disordered mind or an objective reality underpinned by the philosophical reading of society and the human condition which reveals it. Is the human condition making Roquentin sick or is he just sick? The possibility of confusion is reinforced here when the narrator states that it is the hysteria that has led to the collapse of the walls. However much this is a narrative truth (teleologically, the novel is written to point to the moral corruption and disorder of the economics

[29] In *La Peste*, Rieux, being finally identified as the narrator, looks over the scenes of liberation and decides to write the chronicle we have just read. Both Proust and Joyce send their readers back to the beginning.

[30] The scenario is further complicated by the fact that the narrator faints at the sight of Arangrude's body ceremoniously laid out in the hall of the building, falls down the stairs and bangs his temple. An incident at the level of the *énoncé* is therefore anticipating/recalling the uncertainties of the *énonciation* and blurring the boundaries between them.

of consumerism, and the embodiment of that corruption could thus be said to be subordinate to it in the time of the *énonciation*), it is not a chronological one, and therefore at the level of the *énoncé* could again be pointing to a still poorly narrator.

At its most immediate level, the novel is an unkind parody of the science of management, and of the wit and wisdom of corporate executives. Biographies of every corporate character include their qualifications from the Massachusetts Institute, Boll Foundation, Harvard Business School; and their previous entrepreneurial experience. Discussion of the accident which killed Arangrude offers a typical exchange:

> —De quoi est-il mort au juste? questionna Portal
> —Tempe droite enfoncée . . . collision avec un camion Sotanel.
> —Sotanel? dit Brignon, bonne boîte, j'y ai un copain de promotion . . . 6 000 F par mois . . .
> —C'est le quatrième fabriquant français de poids lourds.
> —Implanté au Benelux, précisa Portal
> —Il appartenait à Amel Frères.
> —Amel? Bonne boîte aussi . . . le deuxième transporteur routier . . . , circule aussi beaucoup au Benelux.
> —Pauvre Arangrude, soupira Brignon.[31]

Arangrude, 'cadre d'élite qui disparut prématurément de l'organigramme de la société Rosserys & Mitchell-France',[32] is buried with great pomp. As is normal in France, his death is formally announced by his family, by Rosserys & Mitchell, and by his previous firm, Korvex: 'La Société Korvex, deuxième en Europe pour les charcuteries sous cellophane et première en Afrique, apprend avec un regret profond et une grande tristesse le décès subit de Roger Arangrude, ancien élève de l'École des hautes études commerciales, ancien et brillant chef de produit de la société (jambon Korvébon).'[33] The narrator can only reflect: 'Combien de jambons Korvébon avait-il dû se vendre partout en Europe, en Afrique et en Océanie, pour que le souvenir d'Arangrude fût resté si vivace au sein d'une entreprise désertée

[31] *L'Imprécateur*, 29: ' "What did he die of, exactly?" asked Portal. "Right temple bashed in . . . collision with a Sotanel lorry." "Sotanel?" said Brignon, "Good firm, I was a student with someone who works there . . . 6000 francs a month . . ." "It's the fourth French producer of lorries." "Established in the Benelux countries." "It belongs to Amel Brothers." "Amel? Another good firm . . . the second largest road transport haulier . . . also does a lot a business in the Benelux countries." "Poor Arangrude", sighed Brignon.'

[32] Ibid. 95: 'high-flying manager who disappeared prematurely from the organization chart of Rosserys and Mitchell-France'.

[33] Ibid. 96: 'Korvex Company, second in Europe for sellophane-wrapped pork products and first in Africa, has learnt with profound regret and great sadness of the sudden death of Roger Arangrude, former pupil of the École des hautes études commerciales, former and brilliant product manager of the company (Korvébon ham).'

par lui depuis si longtemps!'[34] Their values and yardsticks of judgement consist of the material proof of entrepreneurial quality and success, for which all characters have unmitigated, uncritical enthusiasm, until, that is, the events start to suggest that there is something seriously wrong.

The mixture of the formality of the style and the relentless optimism is not untypical of the writings of the business world. Through the espousal of entrepreneurial values and practice, all is always presented as being for the best in the best of all possible worlds. Each of the unsettling 'rouleaux' written by the anonymous and subversive *imprécateur* ends with the same words: 'Prions Dieu que notre société gagne la guerre économique pour le plus grand bonheur de tous les hommes, et supplions-Le de garder en bonne santé les chefs qui veillent sur notre croissance et notre expansion. En dévoilant un peu de ce qu'ils savent et de ce qu'ils supportent, j'aurai contribué à les faire mieux respecter.'[35] The mimicry of business-speak is accurate: the statement of the CNPF (Conseil National du Patronat Français) on the events of May belongs to the same discursive world:

> **Les structures actuelles de l'entreprise permettent le développement de la participation. (. . .) Des bouleversements de son statut juridique la feraient éclater en morceaux, y ruineraient les fondements de l'autorité, (. . .) briseraient les hiérarchies ou détruiraient l'efficacité du travail. (. . .)**
> **Notre système économique, fondé sur l'exercice des libertés, doit être non pas détruit, mais rendu plus fort et plus humain par une participation de plus en plus active de tous.**[36]

Challenging authority, hierarchy, and efficiency: some of the May protestors at least were hopeful that this would indeed sweep away the economic order, and certainly saw the destructive potential in attacking 'les fondements de l'autorité'. In other words, it is difficult not to see *L'Imprécateur* as an extended metaphor for the events of May.

In his introduction to *La Révolte étudiante*, one of the major early texts on May,[37] Hervé Bourges offers a typical *gauchiste* view of the events and

---

[34] *L'Imprécateur*, 97: 'How many Korvébon hams must he have sold throughout Europe, Africa, and Oceania, for the memory of Arangrude to have remained so alive in a firm he had left behind so long ago.'

[35] Ibid. 16: 'Let us pray to God that our company wins the economic war for the greater happiness of all mankind, and let us beg Him to keep in good health the directors who watch over our growth and our expansion. In revealing a little of what they know and what they bear, I will have contributed to making them better respected.'

[36] 'The current structures of business permit the development of participation. (. . .) Drastic changes to its legal status would make it explode into pieces, would ruin the foundations of authority, would break hierarchies or destroy efficient working. (. . .) Our economic system, founded on the exercise of freedom, must be not destroyed, but made stronger and more human by more and more participation by all.' *Revue politique, parlementaire, économique*, special issue on May, 98.

[37] *La Révolte étudiante: Les Animateurs parlent* (Seuil, 1968).

their aftermath, with the revolutionary movement being recuperated by the establishment, by 'l'immense tartuferie sociale', which had been for one moment 'prise au piège de la vérité nue'.[38] The deviousness of routine and social convention is disrupted by unmediated truth. 'L'ordre établi s'effondra dans les barricades. La révolte déferla sur les usines. L'État semblait se dissoudre. La société craquait.' But the film was wound back again: 'la vie reprit. Tout rentra dans l'ordre.'[39] One has the plot of *L'Imprécateur* in a nutshell. There are the first rumblings of things not going quite right, and which quickly escalate out of any real control. The narrator keeps trying to decide whether there were any pointers in the past to the state of things they were going through, and at the time and later, in his reflections on his narrative, he keeps trying to decide what the true significance of it all is. But when the building and the social order it contained had cracked, dissolved, fallen down, it proved to have been a nasty dream and it all went back up again. The nasty dream had kept him off work for just over one month.

As well as the structural similarity, there are many oblique comments which serve to suggest May as the 'historical real' of the text. The first rouleau, entitled like the others 'Que savent-ils, ceux qui dirigent Rosserys & Mitchell?', is bemusing since it is full of praise for their skills and knowledge, yet all its examples are rather simple ones, such as the elementary equations underlying the law of supply and demand. Some of its readers see the praise, others see a worrying irony. The narrator compares it straightaway to 'avis syndicaux, des textes politiques, et même des tracts révolutionnaires'.[40] When asked about it by his colleagues, he refers to it as 'cette espèce de tract' (p. 42). And there are later references to contestation movements: as the American executive explains: 'nos ennemis ont des noms et des visages, ils s'appellent les ouvriers, les artistes, les intellectuels, les jeunes dépravés aux longs cheveux, les gouvernants dirigistes et nationalistes, les peuples qui nous jalousent'.[41] The oil crisis is gloomily evaluated by the narrator as an event which will put a smile on the face of the technocratic tiger, making it forget 'le mauvais quart d'heure' it has had to go through because of 'le courroux des jeunes et des intellectuels'.[42]

---

[38] *Révolte étudiante*, 7: 'Enormous social hypocrisy', 'caught in the trap of naked truth'.

[39] Ibid.: 'The established order collapsed in the barricades. Revolt spread to the factories. The state seemed to dissolve. Society was cracking apart.' Cf. Sollers in *Délivrance*, the text of his radio discussions with Maurice Clavel: 'La fissure ouverte par Mai 68 va devenir fission.' and 'le premier craquement du 3 mai 1968.' (p. 152). 'The fissure opened up by May 68 would become a split.' 'the first creaks heard on 3 May.'

[40] *L'Imprécateur*, 17: 'Union notices, political texts, and even revolutionary tracts.'

[41] Ibid. 185: 'our enemies have names and faces, they are called workers, artists, intellectuals, depraved youth with long hair, interventionist and nationalist political leaders, peoples who envy us.'

[42] Ibid. 208: 'the uncomfortable moment', 'the anger of youth and intellectuals'.

The frequent references within the story to 'les événements', coupled with the inability of anyone to decide what precisely was happening and what major significance it may have, offer a repetition of the discourses on May. The constraints and structures of Party, Government, and Business cannot contain that which by definition they cannot include: the unstructured, unreason and imagination, the force of direct truth. Within the rhetoric of order opposed to disorder, their disorderliness is disruptive.

Thematically too, therefore, in its underlying argument for social change and identification of contemporary society and its economic order as dehumanising, *L'Imprécateur* is a text enunciating the themes of May, targeting the abundance, consumerism, dehumanization, and bureaucracy of contemporary society and its institutions, as well as the deliberate impoverishment and exploitation of the Third World, and the continuing attempts at colonial domination in the waging of the Vietnamese War.

> Si les habitants des pays industrialisés avaient connu une amélioration spectaculaire de leur niveau de vie, ce n'était donc pas seulement dû à leur intelligence, à leur travail, à leur habilité, mais aussi pour une bonne part en raison du faible prix qu'ils avaient payé leurs matières premières. Voilà qui expliquait l'affamation quasi générale d'une immense partie du monde et la prospérité, le gâchis, de l'autre partie.[43]

The imperialism of the American multinationals is constantly underlined, at times satirically: 'Les Américains avaient assisté à cette scène sans y rien comprendre, car leur libéralisme international n'allait pas jusqu'à apprendre la langue des pays où ils gagnaient de l'argent.'[44] As often as not, the tone is that of hatred and anger: 'Imaginez le spectacle des ces hordes terrifiantes (. . .) dévastant NOS champs de café au Brésil, NOS mines au Chili, NOS plantations en Afrique, NOTRE gaz en URSS, NOS poissons en mer de Chine, NOS têtards dans les étangs en France, NOS moutons en Australie, NOS porcs en Nouvelle-Zélande!'[45]

The analysis of a society of total control, eliminating all possibility of imaginative negation, underpinned by an economic order based on exploitation, where desires are alienated and reified in commodities,

[43] *L'Imprécateur*, 194: 'If the inhabitants of the industrialized countries had seen a spectacular improvement in their standard of living, this was not only due to their intelligence, their work, their cleverness, but also because of the low price they had paid for their primary materials. This is what explained the almost general starvation of the majority of the globe and the prosperity and waste of the rest.'

[44] Ibid. 55: 'The Americans had been present at this scene without having understood anything, since their international liberalism did not extend to learning the language of those countries where they made money.'

[45] Ibid. 98–9: 'Imagine the spectacle of those terrifying hordes (...) devastating OUR coffee fields in Brazil, OUR mines in Chile, OUR African plantations, OUR gas in the Soviet Union, OUR fish in China's seas, OUR tadpoles in French lakes, OUR sheep in Australia, OUR pigs in New-Zealand.'

probably owes much to Marcuse and Baudrillard.[46] The recuperative power of capitalism is displayed in the totally incongruous details of the social and political allegiances of the managers: Le Rantec is a member of the socialist revolutionary party, Abéraud is an anarchist. The critique of the institutional bureaucracy is also very much of its time, and the description of the Parisian multinational in Crozier's *Le Phénomène bureaucratique* is very recognizable. Jean-Charles of *Les Belles Images* would be at home here, with the professed optimism that material and moral well-being were advancing together. But as the above quotations show, the cracks in the façade are unleashing very sinister forces, infernal forces, associated also with the imagination. The narrator comments early in the novel on the 'poètes inhumés' in the Père Lachaise cemetery, a significant pointer to the network of disorder, of imagination, poetry, unreason, hysteria, madness, which will engulf the firm. And this too partakes of the thematics of May. Edgar Morin frequently used the metaphor of a building to communicate his thesis of social change. For him, the real changes are those going on in the 'sous-sols', basements, cellars, of society, the long-term changes which are less immediately noticeable but fundamental. With its sudden outpourings opening the way to new ideas and modalities, May was a revelation of changes which had been taking place. It also, he argued, had the effect of destroying the confidence and optimism of the bourgeoisie that the modern social and economic order had effectively re-engineered the human condition. 'La société est construite sur de la nuit' is his compelling phrase.[47] Uncertainty was once again part of the social order, as the ambition to eliminate it was always an impossible one.

Underlying the literal plot of the bright building brought down into the dark chasm beneath is the symbolic plot, of the death of the bourgeoisie by the forces of darkness within it. Marx comments very famously on Hegel's metaphor, borrowed from Hamlet, of the 'grubbed mole', the 'vieille taupe', representing history. But, as Macherey points out, Marx does so in ironic terms: 'For Marx (. . .) the mole of history constantly grubs deeper and deeper so as to lay bare the hidden mechanisms of the revolution: the revolution will take place not in spirit's sunshine, but in the dark subterranean passages through which the proletariat is trying to make its way in the dark.'[48] This metaphor was quite familiar to the May protestors. *Tel Quel* published Georges Bataille's 'La "vieille taupe" et le

[46] Baudrillard's comment that consumerism and the denunciation of consumerism can be mapped onto the opposition between God and Devil in the Middle Ages is also close to the metaphors governing the novel's structure: *La Société de consommation* (Seuil, 1970), 316.

[47] 'Society is built on night'. Morin, 'Mai 68: Complexité et ambiguïté', *Pouvoirs* (1986), 39, 77.

[48] Pierre Macherey, *The Object of Literature*, trans. David Macey (Cambridge: Cambridge University Press, 1995), 103.

préfixe *sur* dans les mots: *sur*homme et *sur*réaliste' in its Summer 1968 issue. Bataille writes: 'C'est en creusant la fosse puante de la culture bourgeoise qu'on verra peut-être s'ouvrir dans les profondeurs du sous-sol les caves immenses et mêmes sinistres où la force et la liberté humaine s'établiront.'[49] Or as one graffiti writer put it: 'La vieille taupe de l'histoire semble bel et bien ronger la Sorbonne. (Télegramme de Marx, 13 Mai 1968).'[50]

L'Imprécateur too attacks the discourses of moral and social confidence, demonstrating that the discourse of plenty contains within it its own destruction, setting out on a journey into the heart of darkness of the modern bourgeois order. This society secretes its own rottenness, sows its own seeds of destruction. Most chillingly of all, the senior executives, American and French, are led, in the name of the defence of their order, to torture and murder the man they believe to be the *imprécateur*, in what the narrator describes as a travesty of justice. This is the 'Justice d'Entreprise' (p. 244). For many of a certain generation, torture and murder in basements and cellars in Paris would inevitably recall the fate of Algerians during the Algerian War. This would be close to Sartre's arguments, that the ideology of humanism enlisted to the colonialist cause led logically to the torture of Algerians, were it not for the fact that the forces here are those of an entrepreneurial totalitarianism which is attempting to turn the world into one business and substitute itself both for humanism and for religion.

The metaphysical project embodied in the ideology of the consumer society is well recognized, and is crucial to the plot. Management-speak is the mouthpiece of triumphant capitalism, of the economic order of abundance which will spread happiness and well-being. As *l'imprécateur* explains in his first *rouleau*, there is now no difference between material goods and a non-material, intangible good. Everything is a commodity which can be measured and paid for. Souls become part of the profit motive. The novel is also a novel of the human condition, pointing to the metaphysical angst which no amount of good marketing skills can banish. The attempt to reinvent the world in terms of the logic and rationality of marketing are the ravings of the mad scientists, from alchemists to Frankenstein, who present a diabolical mirror image of good spirituality, creation, and riches. Its challenge to the state, to religion, to philosophy, its pretention to rule the human soul, is in part what unleashes the irrational and uncontrollable disorder. The use of Gothic horror is the vehicle

---

[49] 'It is in digging the stinking grave of bourgeois culture that one might see opening up in the depths of the soil the immense and even sinister caves where force and human freedom will establish themselves.' *Tel quel* (1968), 34, 17.

[50] 'The grubbed mole of history seems to be well and truly gnawing the Sorbonne (Telegram from Marx, 13 May 1968)'. Marc Rohan, *Paris 68* (Impact Books, 1988), 116.

for the metaphysical battle between the forces of good and evil, with the evil ones uttering what is a sinister appropriation of the moral discourse of *bien-être*, usurping what is not rightfully theirs. 'Ils avaient perdu de vue qu'ils étaient de simples hommes.'[51] Betty (Beatrice?) Saint-Ramé, the daughter of the managing director, has a fit at the dinner organized for the senior executives, assisted by their director of personnel, to sort out the implications and meaning of the first *rouleau*. As she rolls on the floor she utters a few phrases: 'Dante, le paradis, le démon' (p. 54), and the final section is certainly a 'descent into hell': 'Oh mes chefs! Oh, mes collègues du *staff*! Où êtes-vous? Dormez-vous d'un sommeil paisible, ou continuez-vous d'errer en blasphémant dans les dédales?'[52] Or in the words of the American executive, 'Hell, where are we?' (p. 79).

What becomes immensely problematical in the new order is the whole question of good and evil, since it is irrelevant and alien to the discourse of profit and loss. Much of the crisis of the novel is the spiritual crisis of dehumanization which the triumphant imposition of the values of wealth and material success imposes. There is no possibility of judgement in ethical terms when any good has been turned into goods in order to be measured, and this is the only measurement of value: 'Qui pourrait en vouloir aujourd'hui à un riche planteur du Missouri d'avoir, sa vie durant, violé les négresses et enterré vivants leurs esclaves de maris? Le planteur est-il en enfer? Et où est l'enfer?'[53] This aporia of judgement recalls no one as much as Camus, and particularly *La Chute*; the fall is a moral fall and literal fall, and *l'imprécateur* is the one who, like Clamence, is drawing people into the hell of doubt, of uncertainty, from which there is no salvation in the modern world. 'Que devient alors l'homme juste?' asks the narrator.[54] Clamence's confession is at one and the same time a denunciation of his interlocuteur; the narrator here is an equally duplicitious figure of reason and insanity, now hounding his colleagues on behalf of the firm, now criticizing the firm in the name of humanity, but the real counterpart to Clamence is *l'imprécateur*, who uses flattery to accuse.

Much of the text is delivered in actual or imagined speeches. 'Imprécation' is the opposite of 'bénédiction', and means uttering words to bring misfortune, the uttering of ill wishes and curses rather than good wishes and blessings. The first ironic text of the *imprécateur*, the purpose

---

[51] *L'Imprécateur*, 254: 'They had lost sight of the fact they were just men.' The story of the Golem, the monster created from clay, is also referred to, and they dine at the tavern called Le Goulim (p. 186).

[52] Ibid. 284: 'Oh my bosses! Oh, my colleagues of the staff. Where are you? Are you sleeping a peaceful sleep, or are you still wandering and blaspheming in the maze of tunnels?'

[53] Ibid. 222: 'Who could blame today a rich Missouri plantation owner for having, all his life, raped the negresses and buried their slave husbands alive? Is the plantation owner in hell? And where is hell?'

[54] Ibid. 210: 'What then becomes of the just man?'

of which is so obscure and troubling, engages the metaphysical battle with its invocation of God and benediction as a disguised attack. The imitation of discourse is paralleled by a wilful imitation of the senior executive's voice. In the course of the novel, there are many formal speeches, impassioned outpourings, and written texts: the mantle of the *imprécateur* passes to each of the managers in turn. Fournier's moment of delirium is typical of the intensifying disaffection:

> Et toi aussi, McGanter, vieux porc, assassin, fasciste, tu crèveras enterré vivant, et ce sera bien fait pour toi qui as fait massacrer tant de nègres et tant de pauvres types partout dans le monde! Et vous, pauvres cons de cadres à plat ventre dans la boue du boyau, vous avez l'air fin, maintenant! Je vous en foutrai, moi, des salaires de salopards, des HEC, des ENA, des Harvard, des Business mon cul![55]

With typical irony the narrative combines this with memories of dinner-party conversations about 'the good life' where Fournier groans that he only ever wanted to live in the country and raise sheep (pp. 261–2). It is the managing director, Saint-Ramé, who denounces himself as author of the final three *imprécations* during another lengthy oration (he had discovered the first one was written by an anarchist student on a holiday job).

L'Imprécateur is a polyphonic text, a production of rhetoric and discourse with no clear boundaries of true and false, believable or unbelievable. All the characters join the narrator as 'chasseurs de sens', and one of the central ambiguities of fiction, the relationship between story and interpretative commentary, fiction and metafiction, is systematically exploited. Similarly with the interplay of literal and figural: the metaphor of a rotten society is literally realized within the narrative to carry the historical and metaphysical symbols of soulless modernity. In this and in many ways the novel can be productively compared to *La Peste*. The commentary upon the human condition, the ambiguous status of the narrative and systematic blurring of narrative levels, the proliferation of socio-political and metaphysical discourses in a wide variety of registers and languages, held together by a masterly assumption of a tone of formality and detachment, create a text which can be considered an excellent example of May as enunciating subject, if May is taken for the disruptive locus of disorder and misrule. Like Clamence, the narrator is troubled by a loud laugh he can neither trace nor explain. One ignores that which falls outside the bourgeois moral façade of order at one's peril:

---

[55] *L'Imprécateur*, 261: 'And you too, McGanter, old pig, assassin, fascist, you will die buried alive, and you will deserve it, for you had so many negroes and so many unlucky people massacred throughout the world! And you, stupid managers flat on your stomachs in the mud of the tunnel, you do look fine! You can stuff your bloody salaries of HEC, ENA, Harvard, Business, up your arse!'

Les acteurs [des péripéties qui vont suivre] furent les puissants *managers* et leurs *staffistes*. Ceux qui se moquaient des prêtres et des poètes. Ils disaient au Ciel: 'Aide-toi et nous t'aiderons.' Ils auraient poussé l'orgueil jusqu'à prêter leur âme à Dieu au taux rentable de 14.5%.

Place! Les *managers* ont soif! Place! Les maréchaux et leurs laquais vont maintenant descendre dans les entrailles de la terre et s'abreuver dans le noir! Laissez-les boire![56]

[56] 'The actors [of the dramas to come] were powerful managers and their staff. Who mocked priests and poets. They said to Heaven: "Help yourself and we will help you." They would have been arrogant enough to lend their souls to God at the profitable rate of 14.5%. Make way! The managers are thirsty! Make way! The generals and their lackeys are now going to descend into the entrails of the earth and quench their thirst in the darkness. Let them drink!'

Conclusion **From modernity to postmodernity**

Given the current dominance of theories of postmodernity, and the frequency with which its paradigms (the arguments that philosophical and scientific discourses on the human condition, particularly those of progress and rationality, can no longer be seen as absolute, true, and factual, but rather as themes underpinning self-validating narratives) are used to investigate a wide historical range of material, it is not surprising that May too has been discussed with reference to them. In one of the best works on May, Gilles Bousquet points out that for some the failure of the revolutionary project of May, implicitly drawing on the Enlightenment discourse of change and progress towards ever greater equality and justice, is in fact a step on the road to postmodern individualism.[1] 'Dans un tel contexte, Mai ne peut qu'appartenir à un univers de pensée et d'action dont le post-moderne entend signifier la disparition. (. . .) Dans l'aporie du temps ouverte par la postmodernité, c'est tout le réenchantement de l'histoire mis en scène par Mai 68 qui s'annule.'[2] The conclusion seems to be that May is rebarbative to a postmodern reading. The thematics of subjectivity and autobiography, with its concomitant values of authenticity and immediacy, is also at the polar opposite of the postmodern: 'Mai 68 exalte-t-il, pour la dernière fois, l'historicité, le vécu du sens dans et par l'histoire, dans la présence d'un sujet, dans la puissance du faire et du dire?'[3]

Roger Martelli has also presented May as a threshold to a new era as a possible reading: '1968 marque l'entrée résolue dans la "postmodernité". Nous vivrions la fin des utopies, qu'elles soient libérales ou révolutionnaires. La fin des ambitions totales, à l'échelle de la société tout entière. Nous serions irrémédiablement projetés dans l'ère de la complexité, de l'imprévisible, du modeste, de l'ambition

---

[1] Bousquet, *Apogée et déclin de la modernité* (L'Harmattan, 1993), 252, discussing Lipovetsky's *Ère du vide* (Gallimard, 1983).

[2] 'In such a context, May can only belong to a world of thought and action of which postmodernism intends to signal the end. In the aporia of time opened by postmodernity, the whole re-enchantment of history enacted by May 68 is abolished.' Ibid. 253.

[3] 'Does May celebrate for the last time historicity, the lived experience of meaning in and through history, in the presence of a subject, in the real power of action and speech?' Ibid. 254.

limitée.'[4] This is an interpretation he would not wish to endorse. But one has to note that many of the multiple, fragmented writings such as the texts of Godard, which converge perfectly with the cultural dynamic of May, also converge perfectly with the ironic, ludic, unstable dynamic of postmodernist texts.

It is true that May is inescapably situated in relation to history and modernity. These extremely powerful events, whose complexity continues to baffle and fascinate, have always demanded a rethinking of society in relation to them, in the conflicting claims that May changed everything, that 'rien ne sera jamais plus comme avant', and that nothing changed, that the recuperative powers of ideology, culture, and class embraced and neutralized May. Modernization and modernity were central to this positioning of May in relation to history, in that the dynamic forces of modernization, with their related expression of new attitudes, their new emphasis on individual desire as opposed to other, more traditional hierarchies, were seen to be behind May's demands; it can therefore be argued that May is crucial to ushering France forward into the modern world. On the other hand, the near collapse of order, the suddenness and unexpectedness of it, were unsettling enough for Edgar Morin to argue that May introduced France to the anxieties of modernity: 'Tout était euphorique jusqu'en 68.'[5]

This notion of May as a disruptive force, completely opposed to the logics of rationality and order, is found in texts such as *Détruire dit-elle*, by Marguerite Duras, or *Vous les entendez*? by Natalie Sarraute, where the surface of the narrative is elliptical and fragmented, and the oblique references to May make it clear that the apparent disorder is that of the new order, the different order, which cannot be accommodated or assimilated without disturbance. For Lynn Higgins too, the disruptive text of May is one where May is to be found not at the level of the *énoncé*, but as subject of the *énonciation*, again provoking disturbance at the level of language, representation, and order.[6]

It seems to me that it is difficult to say that May is 'this', or 'that', to read it in terms of one single definition, given the wide range of political and cultural strands brought together, converging and conflicting, the interplay of real and imaginary as events unfurl, and the ways in which

[4] 'Que ferons-nous de mai 68?', *Société française*, 30, *1968 aujourd'hui* (Jan.–Mar. 1989): '1968 is the moment when we resolutely entered "post-modernity". According to this view, we are living the end of utopias, be they liberal or revolutionary. The end of total ambitions, at the level of society as a whole. According to this view, we have now been irremediably projected into the era of complexity, of the unexpected, the era of the small scale, and of limited ambition.'
[5] E. Morin, 'May 68: Complexité et ambiguïté', *Pouvoirs*, 77.
[6] *New Novel, New Wave, New Politics* (Lincoln, Neb.: University of Nebraska Press, 1996).

'l'après-mai' also defines the nature of May. For history moved on very fast after May, with the mediatized domination of structuralism, the rise of the *nouveaux philosophes* proclaiming the death of Marx and seeking post-marxist explanations of society, the cultural importance of *Tel Quel* and its revolutionary claims for writing, and for decentring the subject, echoed also in the development of 'l'écriture féminine'. Moreover, what May proper still represented was itself subjected to severe critique from the new political forms it had helped produce, the best example being feminism, which angrily pointed to the traditionalism which had persisted within the forces of contestation.

Michel de Certeau and Pascal Ory have both seen the changes wrought by May as operating at the level of representation of politics and society, rather than directly at the level of the social order itself. And it is true that the palimpsests of history and memory to which May so powerfully contributes its rewriting, are themselves operating here. May is a palimpsest, a complex metanarrative on the nature of society and the modern world as well as an evolving part of that modern world, intertwining archaic and modern, modern and postmodern. There is nothing morally reprehensible about pulling any one strand and labelling it 68, be it collectivism, individualism, or structuralism, as long as this is seen as part of the dynamic of intellectual exchange about the history of ideas rather than historical fact.

In its awareness of the political nature and political effects of meaning, May is a dazzling source of reflection on modernity and its metanarratives, including postmodernity, on the relations of the everyday and of history, of contestation and recuperation. The conundrum of interpretation is a central political gesture in May; the political vision of contestatory art and the disruption of textuality continues to reverberate:

> L'artiste véritablement 'témoin de son temps' (. . .) est celui qui voit *comment le sol de la culture présente s'effrite et s'effondre, qui désire cet effondrement et l'exprime*. Les mythes de l'Occident imitent ces buildings qui (. . .) se gondolent et vacillent. (. . .) Plus qu'à tout autre moment de notre histoire, l'art désigne aujourd'hui l'abîme qui se creuse. Il instaure un vertige.[7]

---

[7] 'The artist who is genuinely "a witness of his time" is the one who sees *how* the ground of our present culture is fragmenting and collapsing, who desires this collapse and can express it. More than in any other moment of our history, art today points to the abyss which is being hollowed out. It installs a vertigo.' G. Lascault in Jean Cassou *et al.*, *Art et contestation* (Brussels, La Connaissance, 1968), 63.

Chronology: May–July 1968

Nous avons des problèmes à résoudre: seuls les morts n'en ont pas.

De Gaulle in Bucharest, May 68

L'année dernière, nous étions au bord du gouffre. Cette année, nous avons fait 1 pas en avant.[1]

Handwritten cartoon of de Gaulle, May 68; reproduced in Miroir de l'histoire, 7

1 May   The traditional 1 May march is held in Paris for the first time since the Algerian War. Union officials refuse to allow students from Nanterre to participate.

2 May   The university campus at Nanterre is closed after several weeks of upheaval, temporary closures, occupations, sit-ins, and violence between left and right.
   The Prime Minister Georges Pompidou leaves France on a visit to Iran and Afganistan.

3 May   Protest meetings about the Nanterre closure are held in the Sorbonne. The police move in to clear the buildings, and lectures are suspended.
   Official negotiations between the United States and the Vietnamese open in Paris.

4 May   The next few days are dominated by seven students from Nanterre, including Daniel Cohn-Bendit, going through disciplinary proceedings, and four student demonstrators are given prison sentences.

6 May   The first barricades appear on the streets of Paris. Meetings and demonstrations are held in many other cities.

7 May   In protest against the prison sentences, a demonstration of 30,000 students goes from Denfert-Rochereau to the Arc de Triomphe, demanding the withdrawal of the police from the Quartier Latin, an amnesty for all students, and the reopening of the university. They sing the *Internationale* before the tomb of the Unkonwn Warrior. *Lycées* and provincial universities start joining the protest.

8 May   Letter from French Nobel Prize winners (including François Mauriac) to de Gaulle seeking an amnesty for the students.

9 May   The Rector of the Sorbonne announces an end to the suspension of lectures for Friday.

---

1 'We have problems to solve, everyone does, except the dead.' 'Last year we were on the edge of a precipice. This year we've taken one step forward.'

10 May   The first 'night of the barricades', the very violent confrontations in the rue Gay Lussac and neighbouring streets, takes place on the night of 10–11 May. Violent demonstrations in cities throughout France.

11 May   The major unions call for a demonstration on Monday 13 May to protest against police brutality. Pompidou returns from Afghanistan.

12 May   The arrested students are freed.

13 May   Between 500,000 and 800,000 participate in the march from the Gare de l'Est to Denfert-Rochereau. The Sorbonne reopens. There is a twenty-four-hour official general strike.

14 May   De Gaulle leaves France on an official visit to Romania. Sud-Aviation, Nantes, goes on unofficial strike.

15 May   The Odéon is occupied. Renault at Cléon is occupied.

18 May   De Gaulle returns from Romania. First signs of unrest on the railways, the Post Office, and the state television network ORTF.

19 May   At the Conseil des Ministres, de Gaulle pronounces his famous: 'la réforme oui! la chienlit non!' (pronounced 'chie-en-lit', *chienlit* is a vulgar term for chaos).

20 May   Cohn-Bendit is banned from France, and 'nous sommes tous des indésirables' becomes yet another of the slogans generated from government statements. Nearly 10 million workers in the public and private sectors are on strike.

21 May   Censure vote fails in the National Assembly.

22 May   Confrontations in the Quartier Latin.

24 May   De Gaulle broadcasts to the nation on television and announces a referendum. A night of violence throughout Paris. A fire is started at the Paris Bourse. There are many injuries and 795 arrests. A *commissaire de police* is killed in Lyons.

25 May   Staff at the ORTF go on strike. Negotiations between the government, the unions, and the employers over working conditions and pay open at the Ministère des Affaires Sociales, in the rue de Grenelle. The outcome (known as the accords de Grenelle) will be made public on 27 May, and rejected at Renault and elsewhere the same day.

27 May   Massive meeting at the Charléty stadium attended by Pierre Mendès France. The meeting was later seen as a first sign of the end of the student protest as the political establishment began to place itself again at centre stage.

28 May   Mitterrand holds a press conference to announce that he will stand for the presidency if necessary, and calls for the formation of a provisional government led by Pierre Mendès France.

29 May   De Gaulle 'disappears', is rumoured to be at Colombey-les-deux-églises, his personal residence, but has in fact gone to Baden-Baden in Germany to have talks with Général Massu, commander of the French Army in Germany. Turnout of between 300,000 and 400,000 at the CGT's demonstration.

30 May   De Gaulle returns. In his radio broadcast to the nation at 4.30 p.m. he dissolves the Naitonal Assembly and announces a general election for the end of June. There is

a huge turn-out for the Gaullist demonstration from Concorde to the Arc de Triomphe that evening.

31 May   Petrol is suddenly available again.

1 June   Over the weekend of the Feast of Pentecost there are massive traffic jams to the coast, and 70 die on the roads. May seems to be over as suddenly as it began.

4 June   The return to work starts, and grows over the next few days.

6 June   Violent incidents and confrontations between strikers and students from Paris outside the occupied Renault factory at Flins.

10 June   The *lycée* student Gilles Tautin drowns during one such incident. The election campaign starts.

11 June   Another night of the barricades in Paris. 400 injured, 1,500 arrested. A demonstrator is shot dead at Montbéliard.

12 June   *Gauchiste* organizations are banned.

13 June   The 'Katangais', the underworld characters who joined the occupation at the Sorbonne and became legendary figures whose notorious power was symptomatic for many of the romantic naivety of left-wing student politics, are expelled from the Sorbonne by students.

14 June   The police clear the Odéon.

15 June   An amnesty is announced for Général Salan and ten others, imprisoned or exiled for subversion during the Algerian War. Others who had been judged *in absentia* return to France.

16 June   The police clear the Sorbonne.

23 June   First round of the general elections. Strong showing by the Gaullist UDR (Union pour la Défense de la République).

30 June   Second round of the general elections. Landslide victory for the ruling coalition which wins 358 of the 485 seats. The UDR wins 291 seats (as opposed 197 in the 1967 elections).

10 July   Pompidou replaced as prime minister by Maurice Couve de Murville.

13 July   Confrontations between demonstrators and police in the Quartier Latin, continuing over the next few days.

14 July   Amnesty for the May militants, affecting 3,471 who have been sentenced or held.

24 July   Vote on proposed amnesty before National Assembly particularly concerning the events in Algeria.

SOURCES: Joffrin, *Mai 68*, Viansson-Ponté, *Histoire de la République gaullienne 2*.

Select Bibliography

Books and Articles

Unless otherwise stated, the place of publication for French texts is Paris, for English texts is London.

A.D.G., *Cradoque's Band* (Gallimard, 1972).

Amila, Jean, *Contest-flic* (Gallimard, 1972).

Arguments, facsimile reproduction, 2 vols. (Toulouse: Éditions Privat, 1983).

Aron, Raymond, *L'Opium des intellectuels* (Gallimard, 1955; new edn. with 'Note pour la réédition', 1968).

—— *La Révolution introuvable: Réflexions sur la révolution de mai* (Fayard, 1968).

Artous, Antoine (ed.), *Retours sur mai* (Montreuil: La Brèche-PEC, 1988).

Atack, Margaret, 'Posing the Limits of Modernity: The Aesthetics of Commitment in the 1960s', *Journal of the Institute of Romance Studies*, 4 (1996), 229–39.

—— 'Edgar Morin and the Sociology of May 68', *French Cultural Studies*, 8/4, special issue on Edgar Morin, ed. Michael Kelly (1997), 295–307.

—— 'The Silence of the Mandarins: Writing the Intellectual and May 68 in *Les Samouraïs*', *Paragraph*, 20/3, special issue ed. Anne-Marie Smith, 'Powers of Transgression/Julia Kristeva' (1997), 240–57.

—— '*L'Armée des ombres* and *Le Chagrin et la pitié*: Reconfigurations of Law, Legalities and the State in post-68 France', in Helmut Peitsch, Charles Burden, and Claire Gorrara (eds.), *European Memories of World War II* (New York: Berghahn, 1999).

Autrement 68–78: dix années sacrilèges, 12 (Feb. 1978).

Baudrillard, J., *La Société de consommation* (Seuil, 1970).

Beauvoir, Simone de, *La Force des choses* (Gallimard, 1963).

—— *Les Belles Images* (Gallimard, 1966).

—— *Tout compte fait* (Gallimard, 1972).

Bédarida, François, and Michael Pollak, *Cahiers de l'I.H.T.P.*, 11, *Mai 68 et les sciences sociales* (Apr. 1989).

Bénéton, Philippe, and Jean Touchard, 'Les Interprétations de la crise de mai-juin 1968', *Revue française de science politique*, 20/3 (June 1970), 503–43.

Benoist, Jean-Marie, *La Révolution structurale* (Grasset, 1975).

Bensaïd, Daniel, and Henri Weber, *Mai 68: Une répétition générale* (Maspero, 1968).

Bergmann, Uwe, Rudi Dutschke, Wolfgang Lefèvre, and Bernd Rabehl, *La Révolte des étudiants allemands* (Gallimard, Idées, 1968).

Berstein, Serge, *La France de l'expansion*, i. *La République gaullienne 1958–1969* (Nouvelle histoire de la France contemporaine, 16; Seuil, 1989).

Bertolino, Jean, *Les Trublions: Reportage photographique Bertolino-Sipaliogo* (Stock, 1968).

Besançon, Julien (ed.), *Les Murs ont la parole mai 68: Journal mural, Sorbonne, Odéon, Nanterre etc . . .* (Claude Tchou, 1968).

Bibliothèque Nationale, *Les Affiches de mai 68 ou l'imagination graphique* (Bibliothèque nationale, 1978).

Bizot, J. F., *Les Déclassés* (Sagittaire, 1976).

Bon, Frédéric, and M. A. Burnier, *Si Mai avait gagné* (Pauvert, 1968).

—— *Les Nouveaux Intellectuels* (Seuil, 1971).

Bourdieu, Pierre, *Homo academicus* (Minuit, 1984).

—— and Jean-Claude Passeron, *Les Héritiers: Les Étudiants et la culture* (Minuit, 1964).

Bousquet, Gilles, *Apogée et déclin de la modernité* (L'Harmattan, 1993).

Braudeau, Michel, *Esprit de mai* (Gallimard, 1995).

Brossat, Alain, *Libération fête folle* (Autrement, 1994).

Cahiers du cinéma (1966–70).

Capdevielle, Jacques, and René Mouriaux, *Mai 68: L'Entre-deux de la modernité, histoire de 30 ans* (Presses de la Fondation nationale des sciences politiques, 1988).

Cardinal, Marie, *Les Mots pour le dire* (Grasset et Fasquelle, 1975).

Caron, Gilles, *et al.*, *Sous les pavés la plage: mai 68 vu par G. Caron (textes), J. F. Bizot, D. Cohn-Bendit, J. Daniel et al.* (La Sirène, 1993).

Cassou, Jean, *et al.*, *Art et contestation* (Brussels, La Connaissance, s.a., 1968).

Cayrol, Jean, *Poésie-Journal* (Seuil, 1968).

Certeau, Michel de, *La Prise de la parole et autres écrits politiques* (Seuil, 1994).

Charles Posner (ed.), *Reflections on the Revolution in France: 1968* (Pelican, 1970).

Chebel d'Appolonia, Antonia, *Histoire politique des intellectuels en France 1944–1954*, 2 vols. (Ed. Complexe, 1991).

CinémAction, Vingt ans d'utopie 60–80, 25 (1982).

—— *Le Documentaire français*, dossier collected by René Prédal, preface by J.-E. Jeannesson (Cerf, 1987).

Clavel, Maurice, *Combats de franc-tireur pour une libération* (Jean-Jacques Pauvert, 1968).

—— *Combat de la résistance à la révolution juillet 68* (Flammarion, 1972).

Clément, Catherine, *La Putain du diable* (Flammarion, 1996).

Cohn-Bendit, Daniel, *Le Grand Bazar* (Belfond, 1975).

—— *Nous l'avons tant aimée, la révolution* (Seuil, 1986).

—— and Gabriel Cohn-Bendit, *Le Gauchisme: Remède à la maladie sénile du communisme* (Seuil, 1968).

Collectif Cléon, *Notre arme, c'est la grève* (Maspero, 1968).

Combes, Patrick, *La Littérature et le mouvement de mai 68* (Seghers, 1984).

Communications, 12. *La Prise de parole* (1968).

Crozier, Michel, *La Société bloquée* (Seuil, 1974).

Curtis, Jean-Louis, *La Chine m'inquiète* (Grasset, 1975).

Debord, Guy, *La Société du spectacle* (Gallimard, Folio, 1992; 1st edn. 1967).

Debord, Guy, *œuvres cinématographiques complètes 1952–1978* (Gallimard, 1994).

Debray, Régis, *Modeste contribution aux discours et cérémonies officielles du dixième anniversaire* (Maspero, 1978).

Dejacques, Claude, *A toi l'angoisse à moi la rage: Mai 68 les fresques de Nanterre* (Ed. Edmond Nalis, 1968).

Delale, Alain, and Gilles Ragache, *La France de 68* (Seuil, 1978).

De la misère en milieu étudiant considérée sous ses aspects économique, politique, psychologique, sexuel et notamment intellectuel et de quelques moyens pour y remédier, supplement to *L'Internationale situationniste*, 11 (1968).

Delannoi, Gil, *Les Années utopiques 1968–1978* (Ed. La Découverte, 1990).

Delvaille, Bernard (ed.), *La Nouvelle Poésie française* (Seghers, 1974).

Demonet, Michel, *et al.*, *Des tracts en mai 68: Mesures de vocabulaire et de contenu* (Fondation nationale des sciences politiques/Armand Colin, 1975).

Domenach, Jean-Marie, *Enquête sur les idées contemporaines* (Seuil, 1981).

Dosse, François, *Histoire du structuralisme*, 2 vols. (Seuil, 1992).

Drake, David, 'Sartre and May 1968: The Intellectual in Crisis', *Sartre Studies International*, 3/1 (1997), 43–65.

Dreyfus-Armand, Geneviève et Laurent Gervereau (eds.), *Mai 68: Les Mouvements étudiants en France et dans le monde* (BDIC, 1988).

Du rôle de l'intellectuel dans le mouvement révolutionnaire selon J.-P. Sartre, B. Pingaud, D. Mascolo (Eric Losfeld, 1971).

Duchen, Claire, *French Connections: Writings from the Women's Liberation Movement in France* (Hutchinson, 1986).

——— *Women's Rights and Women's Lives in France 1944–1968* (Routledge, 1994).

Dumontier, Pascal, *Les Situationnistes et mai 68: Théorie et pratique de la révolution 1968–1972* (Lebovici, 1990).

Duneton, Claude, *Je suis comme une truie qui doute* (Seuil, Points Actuels, 1976).

Duras, Marguerite, *Détruire, dit-elle* (Minuit, 1969).

Duteuil, Jean-Pierre, *Nanterre 1965–66–67–68: Vers le mouvment du 22 mars*, preface by Daniel Cohn-Bendit (Mauléon, Association Acratie, 1988).

Epistémon (pseud. of Didier Anzieu), *Ces idées qui ont ébranlé la France: Nanterre novembre 1967–juin 1968* (Fayard, 1968).

Esprit, Structuralismes: Idéologie et méthode (May 1967).

Esprit, 36 (1968).

Etcherelli, Claire, *L'Arbre voyageur* (Gallimard, 1978).

Fernandez, Dominique, *L'Étoile rose* (Grasset et Fasquelle, 1974).

Ferry, Luc, and Alain Renaut, *La Pensée 68: Essai sur l'anti-humanisme contemporain* (Gallimard, 1985).

Gary, Romain, *Chien blanc* (Gallimard, 1970).

Gavi, Philippe, Jean-Paul Sartre, and Pierre Victor, *On a raison de se révolter* (Gallimard, 1974).

Gildea, Robert, *The Past in French History* (New Haven and London, Yale University Press, 1994).

Girard, Jacques, *Le Mouvement homosexuel en France 1945–1980* (Ed. Syros, 1981).

Glucksmann, André, *La Stratégie de la révolution* (Christian Bourgois, 1968).

Gombin, Richard, *Projet révolutionnaire* (Mouton & cie, 1969).

—— *Les Origines du gauchisme* (Seuil, 1971).

Goustine, Luc de, *10 mai 1968: Manifestation théâtrale en trois points et un schéma* (Seuil, 1968).

Guillebaud, Jean-Claude, *Les Années orphelines* (Le Seuil, 1978).

Hamon, H., and P. Rotman, *Les Intellocrates: Expédition en haute intelligentsia* (Ed. Ramsay, 1981; Brussels, Ed. Complexe, 1985).

—— and —— *Générations*, i. *Les Années de rêve*; ii. *Les Années de poudre* (Seuil, 1988).

Hanley, D. L., and A. P. Kerr, *May 68: Coming of Age* (Macmillan, 1989).

Harvey, Sylvia, *May 68 and Film Culture* (BFI Publishing, 1980).

Hazareesingh, Sughir, *Intellectuals and the French Communist Party: Disillusion and Decline* (Oxford, Clarendon Press, 1991).

Higgins, Lynn, *New Novel, New Wave, New Politics* (Lincoln, Neb.: University of Nebraska Press, 1996).

Hocquenhem, Guy, *L'Après-mai des faunes*, preface by Gilles Deleuze (Grasset, 1974).

Hoffmann, Stanley, *Decline or Renewal: France since the 1930s* (New York, The Viking Press, 1974).

—— *Sur la France* (Seuil, 1976).

Hollifield, James F., and George Ross, *Searching for the New France* (New York and London: Routledge, 1991).

Ikor, Roger, *Le Tourniquet des innocents* (Albin Michel, 1972).

Jean, Raymond, *Les Deux Printemps* (Seuil, 1969).

Jennings, Jeremy, *French Intellectuals in the Twentieth Century: Mandarins and Samurais* (Macmillan, 1993).

Joffrin, Laurent, *Mai 68: Histoire des événements* (Seuil, 1987).

Judt, Tony, *Marxism and the French Left: Studies on Labour and Politics in France 1830–1981* (Oxford, Clarendon Press, 1986).

July, Serge, Alain Geismar, and Erlyn Morane, *Vers la guerre civile* (Editions Premières, 1969).

Kergoat, Danièle, *Bulledor ou l'histoire d'une mobilisation ouvrière* (Seuil, 1973).

Kessel, Patrick, *Le Mouvement 'maoiste' en France*, i. *Textes et documents 1963–1968*; ii. *1968–69* (Union générale d'éditions 10/18, 1972).

Khilnani, Sunil, *Arguing Revolution: The Intellectual Left in Postwar France* (New Haven and London, Yale University Press, 1993).

Kidd, William, 'Liberation in Novels of 68', in R. Kedward and N. Wood (eds.), *The Liberation of France: Image and Event* (Berg, 1995).

Kristeva, Julia, *Les Samouraïs* (Fayard, 1990).

Kuisel, Richard, *Seducing the French: The Dilemma of Americanization* (Berkeley, University of California Press, 1996).

Labro, Philippe, *Les Barricades de mai* (Solar, 1968).

—— Michèle Manceaux, and the 'Édition spéciale' team, *Ce n'est qu'un début* (Éditions et publications premières, no. 2, 1968).

Lainé, Pascal, *L'Irrévolution* (Gallimard, 1971).

L'Arc, *Jean-Paul Sartre* (1966).

—— *Simone de Beauvoir et la lutte des femmes* (1975).

Leclerc, Annie, *Parole de femme* (Grasset et Fasquelle, 1974).

Le Dantec, Jean-Paul, *Les Dangers du soleil* (Les Presses d'aujourd'hui, 1978).

Le Débat, 50, *Matériaux pour servir à l'histoire intellectuelle de la France 1953–1987* (May–Aug. 1988); *Le Mystère 68 (suite)*, 51 (Sept.–Oct. 1988).

Lefebvre, Henri, 'L'Irruption: De Nanterre au sommet', *L'Homme et la société*, 8 (1968; Ed. Anthropos, 1968; Syllepse, 1998).

—— *Au-delà du structuralisme* (Editions Anthropos, 1971).

L'Enragé: Collection complète des 12 numéros introuvables mai–novembre 1968 (J.-J. Pauvert, 1968).

Les Révoltes logiques, special issue, *Les Lauriers de mai ou les chemins du pouvoir (1968–1978)* (Christian Bourgois 10/18, 1978).

L'Événement, Première histoire de la Révolution de mai, 29 (June 1968).

Lévi-Strauss, Claude, *La Pensée sauvage* (Plon, 1962).

Lévy, Bernard-Henri, *Les Aventures de la liberté: Une histoire subjective des intellectuels* (Grasset, 1991).

L'Homme et la société: Revue internationale de recherches et de synthèses sociologiques, 8. *Au dossier de la révolte étudiante* (April, May, June 1968).

Lilla, Mark (ed.), *New French Thought: Political Philosophy* (Princeton: Princeton University Press, 1994).

Lindenberg, Daniel, '1968 ou la brèche du situationnisme', *Esprit*, 'Mai 68 et l'idéologie révolutionnaire', 242 (May 1998), 127–40.

L'Internationale situationniste, facsimile reproduction (Fayard, 1997).

Lipovetsky, Gilles, *L'Ère du vide: Essais sur l'individualisme contemporain* (Gallimard, 1983).

Lyotard, Jean-François, *Dérive à partir de Marx et Freud* (Union Générale d'Editions, 10/18, 1973).

Maarek, Philippe J., *De Mai 68 . . . aux films X: Cinéma, politique, et société* (Ed. Dujarric, 1979).

Mallet, Serge, *La Nouvelle Classe ouvrière*, 2nd edn. (Seuil, 1969).

Manchette, Jean-Patrick, *Nada* (Gallimard, 1972).

—— *Morgue pleine* (Gallimard, 1973).

Marcuse, Herbert, *One-Dimensional Man* (Routledge, 1964).

Martel, Frédéric, *Le Rose et le noir: Les Homosexuels en France depuis 1968* (Seuil, 1996).

Merle, Robert, *Derrière la vitre* (Gallimard, 1970).

Minces, Juliette, *Un ouvrier parle: Enquête* (Seuil, 1969).

Miroir de l'histoire, T276, *Mai 68* (June–July 1973).

Monteil, Claudine, *Simone de Beauvoir, Le Mouvement des Femmes: Mémoires d'une jeune fille rebelle* (Montreal: Ed. Stanké, 1995).

Morin, Edgar, and Marek Halter, *Mai* (Oswald, 1978; Neo/Soco Invest, 1988).

Morin, Edgar, Claude Lefort, and J. M. Coudray, *Mai 68: La Brèche* (Fayard, 1968; Editions Complexe, 1988).

Mouriaux, René, Annick Percheron, Antoine Prost, and Danielle Tartakowsky, *1968: Exploration du mai français*, i. *Terrains*; ii. *Acteurs* (Ed. L'Harmattan, 1992).

Mouvement du 22 mars, *Ce n'est qu'un début continuons le combat*, ed. Emile Copfermann (François Maspero, 1968).

Notre arme c'est la guerre (Maspero, 1968).

Nous sommes en marche: manifeste du comité d'Action Censier (Seuil, 1968).

Nouveau Roman: Hier aujourd'hui, colloque de Cerisy, i. (10/18, 1972).

Opus International, 7, 'Violence/mai 68' (June 1968).

Ory, Pascal (ed.), *L'Entre-deux-mai: Histoire culturelle de la France mai 1968–mai 1981* (Seuil, 1983).

—— (ed.), *Nouvelle Histoire des idées politiques* (Hachette, 1987).

—— *L'Aventure culturelle française 1945–1989* (Flammarion, 1989).

—— and Jean-François Sirinelli, *Les Intellectuels en France de l'Affaire Dreyfus à nos jours* (Armand Colin, 1986).

Partisans, Ouvriers, étudiants: Un seul combat, 42 (May–June 1968).

—— *Le Mouvement des lycéens* (Sept.–Oct. 1969).

Pavel, Thomas, *The Feud of Language: A History of Structuralist Thought* (Oxford: Blackwell, 1989).

Perec, Georges, *Les Choses* (Julliard, 1966).

Perrot, Michelle, Madeleine Rebérioux, and Jean Maitron (eds.), *La Sorbonne par elle-même, Le Mouvement social*, 69 (1968).

Pfister, Thierry, *Tout savoir sur le gauchisme* (Ed. Filipacchi, 1972).

Pic, *Au cœur du Vietnam*, preface by Jean-Paul Sartre (François Maspero, 1968).

Pilhes, René-Victor, *L'Imprécateur* (Seuil, 1974).

Plant, Sadie, *The Most Radical Gesture: The Situationist International in a Post Modern Age* (Routledge, 1992).

Poèmes, chants, dessins: Mai 70 Mai 68 (Front culturel, 1970).

Poèmes de la révolution: Mai 1968, preface by Bruno Durocher (B. Durocher, 1969).

Posner, Charles (ed.), *Reflections on the Revolution in France: 1968* (Pelican, 1970).

Poster, Mark, *Existential Marxism in Postwar France* (Princeton: Princeton University Press, 1975).

Pouvoirs, 39, 'Mai 68' (1986).

Pouy, Jean-Bernard, *Spinoza encule Hegel* (Baleine, 1996; 1st publ. 1979).

Prédal, René, *Le Cinéma français depuis 1945* (Nathan, 1991).

Prévert, Jacques, *Choses et autres* (Gallimard, 1972).

Quelle université? Quelle société? (Seuil, 1968).

Quid: Dossiers de l'histoire, '1968' (1988).

Raspaud, Jean-Jacques, and Jean-Pierre Voyer, *L'Internationale situationniste: Protagonistes/chronologie/bibliographie (avec un index des noms insultés)* (Ed. Champlibre, 1972).

Reader, Keith, with Khursheed Wadia, *The May 1968 Events in France: Reproductions and Interpretations* (London, Macmillan, 1993).

Ricardou, Jean, *Les Révolutions minuscules* (Gallimard, 1971).

Rieffel, Rémy, *Les Intellectuels sous la Ve République*, 3 vols. (Calmann-Lévy/CNRS, 1993).

Rioux, J.-P., and J.-F. Sirinelli (eds.), *La Guerre d'Algérie et les intellectuels français* (Ed. Complexe, 1991).

Rioux, Lucien, and René Backmann, *L'Explosion de mai, 11 mai 1968: Histoire complète des 'événements'* (Robert Laffont, 1968).

Rochefort, Christiane, *Une rose pour Morrison* (Grasset, 1966).

—— *Printemps au parking* (Grasset, 1969).

Rohan, Marc, *Paris 68* (Impact Books, 1988).

Ross, Kristin, *Fast Cars, Clean Bodies: Decolonization and the Reordering of French Culture* (Cambridge, Mass.: The MIT Press, 1994).

Rousso, Henry, *Le Syndrome de Vichy* (Seuil, 1983).

Sabot, Jean-Yves, *Le Syndicalisme étudiante et la guerre d'Algérie* (L'Harmattan, 1995).

Salvaresi, Elizabeth, *Mai en héritage* (Syros-Alternatives, 1988).

Sarraute, Natalie, *Vous les entendez?* (Gallimard, 1972).

Sartre, Jean-Paul, *Plaidoyer pour les intellectuels* (Gallimard, 1972).

—— *Situations VIII: Autour de mai* (Gallimard, 1972).

Sauvageot, J., A. Geismar, D. Cohn-Bendit, and J.-P. Duteuil, *La Révolte étudiante: Les Animateurs parlent* (Seuil, 1968).

Sayad, Abelmalek, with Eliane Dupuy, *Un Nanterre algérien, terre de bidonvilles* (Autrement, 1995).

Schnapp, Alain, and Pierre Vidal-Naquet (eds.), *Journal de la Commune étudiante: Textes et documents novembre 1967–juin 1968*, edn. with a preface by Pierre Sorlin and a 'postface' by Pierre Vidal-Naquet written in 1970 (Seuil, 1988).

Simon, Jean-Pierre (ed.), *La Révolution par elle-même: Tracts révolutionnaires de la crise de mai à l'affaire tchécoslovaque* (Albin Michel, 1968).

Simonin, Anne, and Hélène Clastres (eds.), *Les Idées en France 1945–1988* (Gallimard, 1989).

Sirinelli, Jean-François (ed.), *Cahiers de l'I.H.T.P.*, 6, *Générations intellectuelles* (Nov. 1987).

Sociologie du travail, Le Mouvement ouvrier en France, special 12th year issue, 3 (July–Sept. 1970).

Sollers, Philippe, and Maurice Clavel, *Délivrance* (Gallimard, 1977).

Starr, Peter, *Logics of Failed Revolt: French Theory after May '68* (Stanford: Stanford University Press, 1995).

Stéphane, André, *L'Univers contestationnaire ou les nouveaux chrétiens: Étude psych-analytique* (Payot, 1969).

Talbo, J.-Ph. (ed.), *La Grève à Flins* (Maspero, 1968).

Tel Quel, 34 (Summer 1968).

Temps modernes, Problèmes du structuralisme (1966).

—— *Roman Noir: Pas d'orchidées pour les T.M.*, 595 (Aug.–Sept. 1997).

Thibaudeau, Jean, *Mai 68 en France* précédé de 'Printemps rouge' de Philippe Sollers, (Seuil, 1970).

Touraine, Alain, *Le Communisme utopique: Le Mouvement de mai* (Seuil, 1968, 1972).

Tristan, Anne, and Annie de Pisan, *Histoires du M.L.F.* (Calmann-Levy, 1977).

UNEF, *Le Livre noir* (Seuil, 1968).

—— *Ils accusent* (Seuil, 1969).

Vaneigem, Raoul, *Traité de savoir-vivre à l'usage des jeunes générations* (Gallimard, 1967, 1992).

Vedel, Georges (ed.), *La Dépolitisation: Mythe ou réalité* (Fondation nationale des sciences politiques, 1962).

Vercier, B., and J. Lecarme, *La Littérature en France depuis 1968* (Bordas, 1982).

Viansson-Ponté, Pierre, *Histoire de la république gaullienne*, ii. *Le Temps des orphelins* (Fayard, 1971).

Viénet, R., *Enragés et situationnistes dans le mouvement des occupations* (Gallimard, 1968).

Weber, Henri, *Vingt ans après: Que reste-t-il de 68?* (Seuil, 1988).

Willener, Alfred, *L'Image-action de la société* (Seuil, 1970).

Winock, Michel, *Chronique des années soixante* (Seuil, 1987).

Wylie, Laurence, Franklin D. Chu, and Mary Terrall, *A Critical Bibliography: France The Events of 1968* (Pittsburgh: Council for European Studies, 1973).

Zegel, Sylvain, *Les Idées de mai* (Gallimard, Idées, 1968).

Films

Cinétracts (1968).

J. L. Comolli and A. S. Labarthe *Les Deux Marseillaises* (1968).

Douillon, Jacques, *L'An 01* (1972).

Godard, Jean-Luc, *La Chinoise* (1967).

Godard, Jean-Luc, *Letter to Jane* (1972).

Godard, Jean-Luc, *Tout va bien* (1972).

Godard, Jean-Luc, *Weekend* (1967).

Goupil, Romain, *Mourir à trente ans* (1982).

Karmitz, Marin, *Coup pour coup* (1972).

Kurys, Diane, *Cocktail Molotov* (1979).

Lawaetz, Gudie, *Mai 68: Il y a 25 ans* (1993).

Malle, Louis, *Milou en mai* (1989).

Malle, Louis, *Lacombe Lucien* (1974).

Marker, Chris, *Le Fond de l'air est rouge*, 1. *Les Mains fragiles*; 2. *Les Mains coupées* (1977).

Mocky, Jean-Pierre, *Solo* (1969).

Ophuls, Marcel, *Le Chagrin et la pitié: Chronique d'une ville française sous l'occupation allemande* (1971).

Resnais, A., W. Klein, J. Ivens, A. Varda, C. Lelouch, J.-L. Godard, C. Marker, M. Ray, *Loin du Vietnam* (1967).

Tanner, Alain, *Le Pouvoir est dans la rue* (1968).

Techiné, André, *Souvenirs d'en France* (1975).

Index